THE GODLY MAN'S PICTURE

The Godly Man's Picture

Drawn with a Scripture Pencil,
or,
Some Characteristic Marks of a Man
who is Going to Heaven

THOMAS WATSON

THE BANNER OF TRUTH TRUST

THE BANNER OF TRUTH TRUST
3 Murrayfield Road, Edinburgh EH12 6EL, UK
P.O. Box 621, Carlisle, PA 17013, USA

*

First published 1666
First Banner of Truth edition 1992
Reprinted 1999
Reprinted 2003
Reprinted 2007
Reprinted 2009

ISBN: 978 0 85151 595 3

*

Printed in the USA by
Versa Press, Inc.
East Peoria, IL

CONTENTS

To the Reader

CHRISTIAN READER,

The soul being so precious, and salvation so glorious, it is the highest point of prudence to make preparations for another world. It is beyond all dispute that there is an inheritance in light, and it is most strenuously asserted in Holy Scripture that there must be a fitness and suitability for it (*Col. 1:12*). If anyone asks, 'Who shall ascend into the hill of the Lord?', the answer is, 'He that hath clean hands, and a pure heart' (*Psa. 24:4*). To describe such a person is the work of this ensuing treatise. Here you have the godly man's portrait, and see him portrayed in his full lineaments. What a rare thing godliness is! It is not airy and puffed up, but solid, and such as will take up the heart and spirits. Godliness consists in an exact harmony between holy principles and practices. Oh, that all into whose hands this book shall providentially come, may be so enamoured with piety as to embrace it heartily. So sublime is godliness that it cannot be delineated in its perfect radiance and lustre, though an angel should take the pencil. Godliness is our wisdom. 'The fear of the Lord, that is wisdom' (*Job 28:28*). Policy without piety is profound madness. Godliness is a spiritual queen, and whoever marries her is sure of a large dowry with her. Godliness has the promise of the present life and of that which is to come (*1 Tim. 4:8*). Godliness gives assurance, yes, holy triumph in God, and how sweet that is (*Isa. 32:17*). It was old Latimer who said, 'When sometimes I sit alone, and have a settled assurance of

[7]

the state of my soul, and know that God is my God, I can laugh at all troubles, and nothing can daunt me.' Godliness puts a man in heaven before his time. Christian, aspire after piety; it is a lawful ambition. Look at the saints' characteristics here, and never leave off till you have got them stamped upon your own soul. This is the grand business that should swallow up your time and thoughts. Other speculations and quaint notions are nothing to the soul. They are like wafers which have fine works printed upon them, and are curiously damasked to the eye, but are thin, and yield little nourishment. But I will not keep you longer in the porch. Should I have enlarged upon any one characteristic of the godly man, it would have required a volume, but designing to go over many, I have contracted my sails, and given you only a brief summary of things. If this piece (however undigested) conduces to the good of souls, I shall have my desire. That the God of grace will effectually accomplish this shall be the prayer of him who is

Yours in all Christian affection,

THOMAS WATSON

1: *For this shall every one that is godly pray unto thee' (Psa. 32:6)*

Holy David at the beginning of this psalm shows us wherein true happiness consists; not in beauty, honour, riches (the world's trinity), but in the forgiveness of sin. 'Blessed is he whose transgression is forgiven' (v.l). The Hebrew word 'to forgive' signifies 'to carry out of sight', which agrees well with the words of Jeremiah: 'In those days, saith the Lord, the sins of Judah shall be sought for, and they shall not be found' (*Jer. 50:20*). This is an incomprehensible blessing, and such as lays a foundation for all other mercies. I shall just glance at it, and lay down these five assertions about it:

1. Forgiveness of sin is an act of God's free grace
The Greek word for 'forgive' (*charizomai*) makes clear the source of pardon; pardon does not arise from anything inherent in us, but is the pure result of free grace (*charis*). 'I, even I, am he that blotteth out thy transgressions for mine own sake' (*Isa. 43:25*). When a creditor forgives a debtor, he does it freely. Pardon of sin is a fine thread, spun out of the heart of free grace. Paul cries out, 'I obtained mercy' (*1 Tim. 1:13*) – 'I was be-mercied'. He who is pardoned is all bestrewn with mercy. When the Lord pardons a sinner, he does not pay a debt, but gives a legacy.

2. God, in forgiving sin, remits the guilt and penalty
Guilt cries for justice. No sooner had Adam eaten the apple, than he saw the 'flaming sword' and heard the curse; but in

remission God indulges the sinner; he seems to say to him, 'Though you have fallen into the hands of my justice and deserve to die, yet I will absolve you, and whatever is charged against you shall be discharged.'

3. Forgiveness of sin is through the blood of Christ

Free grace is the impulsive cause; Christ's blood is the meritorious. 'Without shedding of blood is no remission' (*Heb. 9:22*). Justice would be revenged either on the sinner or on the surety. Every pardon is the price of blood.

4. Before sin is forgiven, it must be repented of

Therefore repentance and remission are linked together: 'that repentance and remission of sins should be preached in his name' (*Luke 24:47*). Not that repentance in a popish sense merits forgiveness. Christ's blood must wash our tears away, but repentance is a qualification, though not a cause. He who is humbled for sin will value pardoning mercy the more. When there is nothing in the soul but clouds of sorrow, and now God brings a pardon – which is a setting up of a rainbow in the cloud, to tell the sinner that the flood of wrath shall not overflow him – oh, what joy there is at the sight of this rainbow! The soul that before was steeped in tears now melts in love to God (*Luke 7:38,47*).

5. God having forgiven sin, he will no longer call it to remembrance (*Jer. 31:34*)

The Lord will make an act of indemnity. He will not upbraid us with former unkindness, nor sue us with a cancelled bond. 'He will cast all our sins into the depths of the sea' (*Mic. 7:19*). Sin shall not be cast in like cork which rises up again, but like lead which sinks to the bottom. How we should all labour for this covenant blessing!

(i) *How sad it is to lack it!* It must of necessity go badly with the malefactor who lacks his pardon. All the curses of God stand in full force against the unpardoned sinner; his very blessings are cursed (*Mal. 2:2*). Caesar wondered at one of his soldiers who was so merry when he was in debt. Can the sinner be merry who is heir to all God's curses, and does not know how soon he may take up his lodgings among the damned?

(ii) *How sweet it is to have it!* (a) The pardoned soul is out of the gunshot of hell (*Rom. 8:33*). Satan may accuse, but Christ will show a discharge. (b) The pardoned soul may go to God with boldness in prayer. Guilt clips the wings of prayer so that it cannot fly to the throne of grace, but forgiveness breeds confidence. He who has his pardon may look his prince in the face with comfort.

This great mercy of pardon David had obtained, as appears in verse 5: 'Thou forgavest me'. And because he had found God 'a God of pardons' (*Neh. 9:17*), he therefore encouraged others to seek God in the words of the text: 'For this cause shall every one that is godly pray unto thee'.

2: *Expounding the Nature of Godliness*

It will first be enquired, 'What is godliness?' I answer in general, 'Godliness is the sacred impression and workmanship of God in a man, whereby from being carnal he is made spiritual.' When godliness is wrought in a person, he does not receive a new soul, but he has 'another spirit' (*Numb. 14:24*). The faculties are not new, but the qualities are; the strings are the same, but the tune is corrected. Concerning godliness, I shall lay down these seven maxims or propositions:

1. Godliness is a real thing

It is not a fantasy but a fact. Godliness is not the feverish conceit of a sick brain; a Christian is no enthusiast, one whose religion is all made up of fancy. Godliness has truth for its foundation; it is called 'the way of truth' (*Psa. 119:30*). Godliness is a ray and beam that shines from God. If God is true, then godliness is true.

2. Godliness is an intrinsic thing

It lies chiefly in the heart: 'circumcision is that of the heart' (*Rom. 2:29*). The dew lies on the leaf, the sap is hidden in the root. The moralist's religion is all in the leaf; it consists only in externals, but godliness is a holy sap which is rooted in the soul: 'in the hidden part thou shalt make me to know wisdom' (*Psa. 51:6*). The Chaldean expounds it, 'in the close place of the heart'.

3. Godliness is a supernatural thing

By nature we inherit nothing but evil. 'When we were in the flesh, the motions of sins did work in our members' (*Rom. 7:5*). We sucked in sin as naturally as our mother's milk, but godliness is the 'wisdom from above' (*Jas. 3:17*). It is breathed in from heaven. God must light up the lamp of grace in the heart. Weeds grow of themselves; flowers are planted. Godliness is a celestial plant that comes from the New Jerusalem. Therefore it is called a 'fruit of the Spirit' (*Gal. 5:22*). A man has no more power to change himself than to create himself.

4. Godliness is an extensive thing

It is a sacred leaven that spreads itself into the whole soul: 'the very God of peace sanctify you wholly' (*1 Thess. 5:23*). There is light in the understanding, order in the affections, pliableness in the will, exemplariness in the life. We do not call a black man white because he has white teeth. He who is good only in some part is not godly. Grace is called 'the new man' (*Col. 3:10*), not a new eye, or tongue, but a new man. He who is godly is good all over; though he is regenerate only in part, yet it is in every part.

5. Godliness is an intense thing

It does not lie in a dead formality and indifference, but is vigorous and flaming: 'fervent in spirit' (*Rom. 12:11*). We call water hot when it is so in the third or fourth degree. He whose devotion is inflamed is godly and his heart boils over in holy affections.

6. Godliness is a glorious thing

As the jewel to the ring, so is piety to the soul, bespangling it in God's eyes. Reason makes us men; godliness makes us earthly angels; by it we 'partake of the divine nature' (*2 Pet. 1:4*). Godliness is near akin to glory: 'glory and virtue' (*2 Pet. 1:3*). Godliness is glory in the seed, and glory is godliness in the flower.

7. *Godliness is a permanent thing*

Aristotle says, 'Names are given from the habit'. We do not call the one who blushes sanguine, but the one who is of a ruddy complexion (*1 Sam. 17:42*). A blush of godliness is not enough to distinguish a Christian, but godliness must be the temper and complexion of the soul. Godliness is a fixed thing. There is a great deal of difference between a stake in the hedge and a tree in the garden. A stake rots and moulders, but a tree, having life in it, abides and flourishes. When godliness has taken root in the soul, it abides to eternity: 'his seed remaineth in him' (*1 John 3:9*). Godliness being engraved in the heart by the Holy Ghost, as with the point of a diamond, can never be erased.

3: *A Reproof to Such as are Only Pretenders to Godliness*

Here is a sharp rebuke to such as are 'glittering dross' Christians, who only make a show of godliness, like Michal, who put 'an image in the bed', and so deceived Saul's messengers (*1 Sam. 19:16*). These our Saviour calls 'whited sepulchres (*Matt. 23:27*) – their beauty is all paint! In ancient times a third part of the inhabitants of this island were called Picts, which signifies 'painted'. It is to be feared that they still retain their old name. How many are painted only with the vermilion of a profession, whose seeming lustre dazzles the eyes of beholders, but within there is nothing but putrefaction! Hypocrites are like the swan, which has white feathers, but a black skin; or like the lily, which has a fair colour, but a bad scent. 'Thou hast a name that thou livest, and art dead' (*Rev. 3:1*). These the apostle Jude compares to 'clouds without water' (*Jude 12*). They claim to be full of the Spirit, but they are empty clouds; their goodness is but a religious cheat.

Question: But why do persons content themselves with a show of godliness?

Answer: This helps to keep up their fame: 'honour me now before the people' (*1 Sam. 15:30*). Men are ambitious of credit, and wish to gain repute in the world, therefore they will dress themselves in the garb and mode of religion, so that others may write them down for saints. But alas, what is one the better for having others commend him, and his conscience condemn him? What good will it do a man when he is in hell that others think he has gone to heaven? Oh, beware of this! Counterfeit piety is double iniquity.

1. To have only a show of godliness is a God-enraging sin

The man who is a pretender to saintship, but whose heart tells him he has nothing but the name, carries Christ in his Bible but not in his heart. Some politic design spurs him on in the ways of God; he makes religion a lackey to his carnal interest. What is this but to abuse God to his face, and to serve the devil in Christ's livery? Hypocrisy makes the fury rise up in God's face; therefore he calls such persons 'the generation of his wrath' (*Isa. 10:6*). God will send them to hell to do penance for their hypocrisy.

2. To make only a show of godliness is self-delusion

Ajax in his frenzy took sheep for men, but it is a worse mistake to take a show of grace for grace. This is to cheat yourself: 'deceiving your own souls' (*Jas. 1:22*). He who has counterfeit gold instead of true, wrongs himself most. The hypocrite deceives others while he lives, but deceives himself when he dies.

3. To have only a name, and make a show of godliness, is odious to God and man

The hypocrite is born under a sad planet; he is abhorred by all. Wicked men hate him because he makes a show, and God hates him because he only makes a show. The wicked hate him because he has so much as a mask of godliness, and God hates him because he has no more. 'Thou hast almost persuaded me to be a Christian' (*Acts 26:28*). The wicked hate the hypocrite because he is almost a Christian, and God hates him because he is only almost one.

[16]

4. To be only comets and make a show of piety is a vain thing
Hypocrites lose all they have done. Their dissembling tears drop beside God's bottle; their prayers and fasts prove abortive. 'When ye fasted and mourned, did ye at all fast unto me, even to me?' (*Zech. 7:5*). As God will not recompense a slothful servant, neither will he recompense a treacherous one. All the hypocrites' reward is in this life: 'They have their reward' (*Matt. 6:5*). A poor reward, the empty breath of men. The hypocrite may make his receipt and write, 'Received in full payment'. Augustus Caesar had great triumphs granted him, but the senate would not allow him to be consul, or sit in the senate house. Hypocrites may have the praise of men, but though these triumphs are granted them, they shall never have the privilege of sitting in the senate house of heaven. What acceptance can he look for from God, whose heart tells him he is no better than a mountebank in divinity?

5. To have only a pretence of godliness will yield no comfort at death
Will painted gold enrich a man? Will painted wine refresh him who is thirsty? Will the paint of godliness stand you in any stead? How were the foolish virgins better for their 'blazing lamps', when they had no oil? What is the lamp of profession without the oil of grace? He who has only a painted holiness shall have a painted happiness.

6. You who have nothing but a specious pretext and mask of piety expose yourself to Satan's scorn
You shall be brought forth at the last day, as was Samson, to make the devil sport (*Judges 16:25*). He will say, 'What has become of your vows, tears, confessions? Has all your religion come to this? Did you so often defy the devil, and have you now come to dwell with me? Could you meet with no weapon to kill you, but what was made of gospel metal?

[17]

Could you not suck poison anywhere but out of ordinances? Could you find no way to hell, but by seeming godly?' What a vexation this will be, to have the devil thus reproach a man! It is sad to be crowed over in this life. Cleopatra, Queen of Egypt, when she saw she was reserved by the enemy for a triumph, put asps to her breasts, and died, so that she might avoid the infamy. What, then, will it be to have the devil triumph over a man at the last day!

Let us therefore take heed of this kind of pageantry or devout stage play. That which may make us fear our hearts the more is when we see tall cedars in the church worm-eaten with hypocrisy. Balaam a prophet, Jehu a king, Judas an apostle – all of them stand to this day on record as hypocrites.

It is true that there are the seeds of this sin in the best; but as it was with leprosy under the law, all who had swellings or spots in the skin of the flesh were not reputed unclean and put out of the camp (*Lev. 13:6*); so all who have the swellings of hypocrisy in them are not to be judged hypocrites, for these may be the spots of God's children (*Deut. 32:5*). But that which distinguishes a hypocrite is when hypocrisy is predominant and is like a spreading fluid in the body.

Question: When is a man under the dominion and power of hypocrisy?

Answer: There are two signs of its predominance: (i) A squint eye, when one serves God for sinister ends. (ii) A good eye, when there is some sin dear to a man, which he cannot part with. These two are as clear signs of a hypocrite as any I know.

Oh, let us take David's candle and lantern, and search for this leaven, and burn it before the Lord.

[18]

Christian, if you mourn for hypocrisy, yet find this sin so potent that you cannot get the mastery of it, go to Christ. Beg of him that he would exercise his kingly office in your soul, that he would subdue this sin, and put it under the yoke. Beg of Christ to exercise his spiritual surgery upon you. Desire him to lance your heart and cut out the rotten flesh, and that he would apply the medicine of his blood to heal you of your hypocrisy. Say that prayer of David often: 'Let my heart be sound in thy statutes' (*Psa. 119:80*). 'Lord, let me be anything rather than a hypocrite.' Two hearts will exclude from one heaven.

4: *Showing the Characteristics of a Godly Man*

It will be enquired in the next place, 'Who is the godly man?' For the full answer to this I shall lay down several specific signs and characteristics of a godly man.

SECTION I: THE FIRST FUNDAMENTAL SIGN IS THAT A GODLY MAN IS A MAN OF KNOWLEDGE

'The prudent are crowned with knowledge' (*Prov. 14:18*). The saints are called 'wise virgins' (*Matt. 25:4*). A natural man may have some discursive knowledge of God, but he 'knoweth nothing yet as he ought to know' (*1 Cor. 8:2*). He does not know God savingly. He may have the eye of reason open, but he does not discern the things of God in a spiritual manner. Waters cannot go beyond their spring-head. Vapours cannot rise higher than the sun draws them. A natural man cannot act above his sphere; he is no more able to judge sacred things aright than a blind man is to judge colours. (i) He does not see the evil of his heart. If a face be never so black and deformed, yet it is not seen under a veil; the heart of a sinner is so black that nothing but hell can pattern it, yet the veil of ignorance hides it. (ii) He does not see the beauties of a Saviour. Christ is a pearl, but a hidden pearl.

But a godly man is *theodidaktos*, taught by God: 'the anointing teacheth you of all things' (*1 John 2:27*), that is, all things essential to salvation. A godly man has 'the good knowledge of the Lord' (*2 Chron. 30:22*). He has 'sound wisdom' (*Prov. 3:21*). He knows God in Christ. To know God out of Christ is to know him as an enemy, but to know him in Christ is sweet and delicious. A gracious soul has 'the savour of his knowledge' (*2 Cor. 2:14*). There is a great difference between one who has read of a country, or viewed it on the map, and another who has lived in the country, and tasted its fruits and spices. The knowledge with which a godly man is adorned has these eight rare ingredients in it:

1. It is a grounded knowledge
'If ye continue in the faith grounded' (*Col. 1:23*). It is not a believing as the church believes, but this knowledge rests upon a double basis: the Word and Spirit. The one is a guide, the other a witness. Saving knowledge is not changeable or doubtful, but has a certainty in it. 'We believe and are sure that thou art that Christ' (*John 6:69*); 'being always confident' (*2 Cor. 5:6*). A godly man holds no more than he will die for. The martyrs were so confirmed in the knowledge of the truth that they would seal it with their blood.

2. It is an appreciative knowledge
The lapidary who has the skill to value a jewel is said to know it. He who esteems God above the glory of heaven and the comforts of the earth knows him (*Psa. 73:25*). To compare other things with God is to debase deity; as if you should compare the shining of a glow-worm with the sun.

3. It is an enlivening knowledge
'I will never forget thy precepts, for with them thou hast quickened me' (*Psa. 119:93*). Knowledge in a natural man's head is like a torch in a dead man's hand. True knowledge animates. A godly man is like John the Baptist,

'a burning and a shining lamp'. He not only shines by illumination, but he burns by affection. The spouse's knowledge made her 'sick of love' (*Song 2:5*). 'I am wounded with love.' I am like a deer that is struck with a dart; my soul lies bleeding, and nothing can cure me, but a sight of him whom my soul loves.

4. *It is an appropriating knowledge*

'I know that my redeemer liveth' (*Job 19:25*). A medicine is best when it is applied; this applicative knowledge is joyful. Christ is called a 'surety' (*Heb. 7:22*). Oh what joy, when I am drowned in debt, to know that Christ is my surety! Christ is called an 'advocate' (*1 John 2:1*). The Greek word for advocate, *parakletos*, signifies a comforter. Oh, what comfort it is when I have a bad cause, to know Christ is my advocate, who never lost any cause he pleaded!

Question: But how shall I know that I am making a right application of Christ? A hypocrite may think he applies when he does not. Balaam, though a sorcerer, still said, 'my God' (*Numb. 22:18*).

Answer:

(i) He who rightly applies Christ puts these two together, Jesus and Lord: 'Christ Jesus my Lord' (*Phil. 3:8*). Many take Christ as Jesus, but refuse him as Lord. Do you join 'Prince and Saviour' (*Acts 5:31*)? Would you as well be ruled by Christ's laws as saved by his blood? Christ is 'a priest upon his throne' (*Zech. 6:13*). He will never be a priest to intercede unless your heart is the throne where he sways his sceptre. A true applying of Christ is when we so take him as a husband that we give up ourselves to him as Lord.

(ii) He who rightly applies Christ derives virtue from him. The woman in the Gospel, having touched Christ, felt virtue coming from him and her fountain of blood was dried up (*Mark 5:29*). This is to apply Christ, when we feel a sin-mortifying virtue flow from him. Naturalists tell us there is an antipathy between the diamond and the lodestone, insomuch that if a piece of iron is laid by the diamond, the diamond will not allow it to be drawn away by the lodestone. So that knowledge which is applicatory has an antipathy against sin, and will not allow the heart to be drawn away from it.

5. It is a transforming knowledge

'We all, with open face beholding as in a glass the glory of the Lord, are changed into the same image' (*2 Cor. 3:18*). As a painter looking at a face draws a face like it in the picture, so looking at Christ in the mirror of the gospel, we are changed into his similitude. We may look at other objects that are glorious, yet not be made glorious by them. A deformed face may look at beauty, and yet not be made beautiful. A wounded man may look at a surgeon, and yet not be healed. But this is the excellence of divine knowledge, that it gives us such a sight of Christ as makes us partake of his nature – like Moses when he had seen God's back parts, his face shone; some of the rays and beams of God's glory fell on him.

6. It is a self-emptying knowledge

Carnal knowledge makes the head giddy with pride (*1 Cor. 8:1,2*). True knowledge brings a man out of love with himself. The more he knows, the more he blushes at his own ignorance. David, a bright star in God's church, still thought himself rather a cloud than a star (*Psa. 73:22*).

7. It is a growing knowledge

'Increasing in the knowledge of God' (*Col. 1:10*). True knowledge is like the light of the morning, which increases on the horizon till it comes to the full meridian. So sweet is

[23]

spiritual knowledge that the more a saint knows, the more thirsty he is for knowledge. It is called 'the riches of knowledge' (*1 Cor. 1:5*). The more riches a man has, the more still he desires. Though St Paul knew Christ, yet he wanted to know him more: 'That I may know him, and the power of his resurrection' (*Phil. 3:10*).

8. It is a practical knowledge

'The sheep follow him: for they know his voice' (*John 10:4*). Though God requires 'knowledge of God more than burnt offerings, (*Hos. 6:6*), yet it is a knowledge accompanied by obedience. True knowledge not only improves a Christian's sight, but improves his pace. It is a reproach to a Christian to live in a contradiction to his knowledge, to know he should be strict and holy, yet to live loosely. Not to obey is all one with not to know: 'the sons of Eli knew not the Lord' (*1 Sam. 2:12*). They could not but know, for they taught others the knowledge of the Lord; yet they are said not to know, because they did not obey. When knowledge and practice, like Castor and Pollux, appear together, then they herald much happiness.

Use 1: Let us test ourselves by this characteristic:

1. Are they godly, who are still in the region of darkness? 'That the soul be without knowledge, it is not good' (*Prov. 19:2*). Ignorant persons cannot give God 'a reasonable service' (*Rom. 12:1*). It is sad that after the Sun of righteousness has shone so long in our hemisphere, persons should still be under the power of ignorance. Perhaps in the things of the world they know enough, none shall outreach them, but in the things of God they have no knowledge. Nahash wanted to make a covenant with Israel, that he might 'put out their right eyes' (*1 Sam. 11:2*). The devil has left men their left eye – knowledge in secular matters – but he has put out their right eye – they do not understand the mystery of godliness. It may be said of them as of the Jews, 'to this day the veil is upon their heart' (*2 Cor. 3:15*). Many Christians are no better than baptized heathens. What a shame it is to be without knowledge! 'Some have not the knowledge of God: I speak this to your shame' (*1 Cor. 15:34*). Men think it a shame to be ignorant of their trade, but no shame to be ignorant of God. There is no going to heaven blindfold. 'It is a people of no understanding: therefore he that made them will not have mercy on them' (*Isa. 27:11*).

Surely ignorance in these days is affected. It is one thing not to know, another thing not to be willing to know: 'men loved darkness rather than light' (*John 3:19*). It is the owl that loves the dark. Sinners are like the Athlantes, a people in Ethiopia, who curse the sun. Wicked men shut their eyes wilfully (*Matt. 13:15*), and God shuts them judicially (*Isa. 6:10*).

2. Are they godly, who, though they have knowledge, yet do not know 'as they ought to know'. They do not know God experimentally. How many knowledgeable persons are ignorant? They have illumination, but not sanctification. Their knowledge has no powerful influence upon them to make them better. If you set up a hundred torches in a garden they will not make the flowers grow, but the sun is influential. Many are so far from being better for their knowledge, that they are worse: 'thy knowledge hath perverted thee' (*Isa. 47:10*). The knowledge of most people makes them more cunning in sin; these have little cause to glory in their knowledge. Absalom might boast of the hair of his head, but that hanged him; so these may boast of the knowledge of their head, but it will destroy them.

3. Are they godly, who, though they have some glimmering of knowledge, yet have no trustful application of Christ? Many in the old world knew there was an ark, but were drowned, because they did not get into it. Knowledge which is not applied will only light a man to hell. It would be better to live a savage than to die an infidel under the gospel. Christ not believed in is terrible. Moses' rod, when it was in his hand, did a great deal of good. It wrought miracles; but when it was out of his hand, it became a serpent. So Christ, when laid hold on by the hand of faith, is full of comfort, but not laid hold on, will prove a serpent to bite.

Use 2: As we would prove ourselves to be godly, let us labour for this good knowledge of the Lord. What pains men will take for the achievement of natural knowledge! I have read of one, Benchorat, who spent forty years in finding out the motion of the eighth sphere. What pains, then, should we take in finding out the knowledge of God in Christ! There must be digging and searching for it, as one would search for a vein of silver: 'If thou seekest her as silver' (*Prov. 2:4*).

This is the best knowledge. It as far surpasses all other as the diamond does the crystal. No jewel we wear so adorns us as this: 'She is more precious than rubies' (*Prov. 3:15*). 'Man knoweth not the price thereof; the depth saith, It is not in me; it cannot be valued with the gold of Ophir, with the precious onyx, or the sapphire' (*Job 28: 13–16*). The dark chaos was a fit emblem of an ignorant soul (*Gen. 1:2*), but when God lights up the lamp of knowledge in the mind, what a new creation is there! Here the soul sparkles like the sun in its glory.

This knowledge is encouraging. We may say of the knowledge of nature, as did Solomon, 'He that increaseth knowledge increaseth sorrow' (*Eccles. 1:18*). To know arts and science is to gather straw, but to know God in Christ is to gather pearl. This knowledge ushers in salvation (*1 Tim. 2:4*).

Question: But how shall we get this saving knowledge?

Answer: Not by the power of nature. Some speak of how far reason will go if put to good use; but, alas! the plumb-line of reason is too short to fathom the deep things of God. A man can no more reach the saving knowledge of God by the power of reason, than a pigmy can reach the pyramids. The light of nature will no more help us to see Christ, than the light of a candle will help us to understand. 'The natural man receiveth not the things of the Spirit of God: neither can he know them' (*1 Cor. 2:14*). What shall we do, then, to know God in a soul-saving manner? I answer, let us implore the help of God's Spirit. Paul never saw himself blind till a light shone from heaven (*Acts 9:3*). God must anoint our eyes before we can see. What need did Christ have to bid Laodicea to come to him for eyesalve, if she could see before (*Rev. 3:18*)? Oh, let us beg the Spirit, who is 'the Spirit of revelation' (*Eph. 1:17*). Saving knowledge is not by speculation, but by inspiration, 'the inspiration of the Almighty giveth them understanding' (*Job 32:8*).

We may have excellent notions in divinity, but the Holy Ghost must enable us to know them in a spiritual manner. A man may see the figures on a dial, but he cannot tell how the day goes unless the sun shines. We may read many truths in the Bible, but we cannot know them savingly till God's Spirit shines upon us: 'the Spirit searcheth all things, yea, the deep things of God' (*1 Cor. 2:10*). The Scripture reveals Christ *to* us, but the Spirit reveals Christ *in* us (*Gal. 1:16*). The Spirit makes known that which all the world cannot do, namely, the sense of God's love.

Use 3: You who have this saving, sanctifying knowledge flourishing in you, bless God for it; this is the heavenly anointing. The most excellent objects cannot be seen in the dark, but when the light appears, then every flower shines in its native beauty. So while men are in the midnight of a natural state, the beauty of holiness is hidden from them; but when the light of the Spirit comes in a saving manner, then those truths which they slighted before appear in that glorious lustre, and transport them with wonder and love.

Bless God, you saints, that he has removed your spiritual cataract, and has enabled you to discern those things which by nature's spectacles you could never see. How thankful Christ was to his Father for this! 'I thank thee, O Father, Lord of heaven and earth, because thou hast hid these things from the wise and prudent, and hast revealed them unto babes' (*Matt. 11:25*). How you should admire free grace, that God has not only brought the light to you, but given you eyes to see it; that he has enabled you to know the truth 'as it is in Jesus' (*Eph. 4:21*); that he has opened, not only the eye of your understanding, but the eye of your conscience! It is a mercy you can never be thankful enough for, that God has so enlightened you that you should not 'sleep the sleep of death'.

SECTION 2: A GODLY MAN IS A MAN MOVED BY FAITH

As gold is the most precious among the metals, so is faith among the graces. Faith cuts us off from the wild olive of nature, and grafts us into Christ. Faith is the vital artery of the soul: 'The just shall live by his faith' (*Hab. 2:4*). Such as are destitute of faith may breathe, but they lack life. Faith enlivens the graces; not a grace stirs till faith sets it working. Faith is to the soul what the animal spirits are to the body, exciting lively activity in it. Faith excites repentance; it is like the fire to the still which makes it drop. When I believe God's love to me, this makes me weep that I should sin against so good a God. Faith is the mother of hope; first we believe the promise, then we hope for it. Faith is the oil which feeds the lamp of hope. Faith and hope are two turtle-dove graces; take away one, and the other languishes. If the sinews are cut, the body is lame; if this sinew of faith is cut, hope is lame. Faith is the ground of patience; he who

believes that God is his God, and that all providences work
for his good, patiently yields himself to the will of God. Thus
faith is a living principle.

And the life of a saint is nothing but a life of faith. His
prayer is the breathing of faith (*Jas. 5:15*). His obedience is
the result of faith (*Rom. 16:26*). A godly man by faith lives in
Christ, as the beam lives in the sun: 'I live; yet not I, but
Christ liveth in me' (*Gal. 2:20*). A Christian by the power of
faith sees above reason, trades above the moon (*2 Cor. 4:18*).
By faith his heart is finely quietened; he trusts himself and all
his affairs to God (*Psa. 112:7*). As in a time of war, men get
into a garrison and trust themselves and their treasures
there, so 'the name of the Lord is a strong tower' (*Prov.
18:10*), and a believer trusts all that ever he is worth in this
garrison. 'I know whom I have believed, and am persuaded
that he is able to keep that which I have committed unto him
against that day' (*2 Tim. 1:12*). God trusted Paul with his
gospel, and Paul trusted God with his soul.

Faith is a catholicon – a remedy against all troubles. It is a
godly man's sheet-anchor that he casts out into the sea of
God's mercy, and is kept from sinking in despair. 'If only
faith is firm, no ruin harms.'

Use: Let us test ourselves by this characteristic. Alas, how
far from being godly are those who are destitute of faith!
Such are altogether drowned in sense. Most men are spiritually purblind; they can only see just before them (*2 Pet. 1:9*).
I have read of a people in India who are born with one eye.
Such are they who are born with the eye of reason, but lack
the eye of faith, who because they do not see God with bodily
eyes, do not believe in a god. They may as well not believe
they have souls, because being spirits they cannot be seen.

Oh, where is he who lives in the heights, who has gone into
the upper region and sees 'things not seen' (*Heb. 11:27*)? 'If
men lived by faith, would they use sinful means for a

[29]

livelihood?' (*Chrysostom*). If there were faith, would there be so much fraud? If theirs were living faith, would men, like dead fish, swim downstream? In this age there is scarcely so much faith to be found among men as there is among the devils, 'for they believe and tremble' (*Jas. 2:19*). It was a grave and serious comment of Mr Greenham, that he feared not papism, but atheism would be England's ruin. But I shall not expatiate, having written at greater length on this head in another discourse.

SECTION 3: A GODLY MAN IS FIRED WITH LOVE TO GOD (Psa. 116:1)

Faith and love are the two poles on which all religion turns. A true saint is carried in that chariot, 'the midst whereof is paved with love' (*Song 3:10*). As faith enlivens, so love sweetens every duty. The sun mellows the fruit, so love mellows the services of religion, and gives them a better relish. A godly man is sick of love: 'Lord, thou knowest that I love thee' (*John 21:16*). 'Though, dear Saviour, I denied thee, yet it was for lack of strength, not for lack of love.' God is the fountain and quintessence of goodness. His beauty and sweetness lay constraints of love upon a gracious heart. God is the saint's portion (*Psa. 119:57*). And what more loved than a portion? 'I would hate my own soul,' says Augustine, 'if I found it not loving God.' A godly man loves God and therefore delights to be in his presence; he loves God and therefore takes comfort in nothing without him. 'Saw ye him whom my soul loveth?' (*Song 3:3*).

The pious soul loves God and therefore thirsts for him. The more he has of God, the more still he desires. A sip of the wine of the Spirit whets the appetite for more. The soul loves God and therefore rejoices to think 'of his appearing' (*2 Tim. 4:8*). He loves him and therefore longs to be with him. Christ was in Paul's heart, and Paul would be in

Christ's bosom (*Phil. 1:23*). When the soul is once like God, it would gladly be with God. A gracious heart cries out, 'O that I had wings', that I might fly away, and be with my love, Christ. The bird desires to be out of the cage, though it is hung with pearl.

Such is the love a gracious soul has to God, that many waters cannot quench it. He loves a frowning God.

> Though I am out of sight, and clean forgot,
> Let me not love thee, if I love thee not.
>
> (George Herbert)

A godly man loves God, though he is reduced to straits. A mother and her nine-year-old child were about to die of hunger. The child looked at its mother and said, 'Mother, do you think God will starve us?' 'No, child,' said the mother, 'he will not.' The child replied, 'But if he does, we must love him, and serve him.'

Use: Let us test our godliness by this touch-stone: Do we love God? Is he our treasure and centre? Can we, with David, call God our 'joy', yes, our 'exceeding joy' (*Psa. 43:4*)? Do we delight in drawing near to him, and 'come before his presence with singing' (*Psa. 100:2*)? Do we love him for his beauty more than his jewels? Do we love him, when he seems not to love us?

If this be the sign of a godly man, how few will be found in the number! Where is the man whose heart is dilated in love to God? Many court him, but few love him. People are for the most part eaten up with self-love; they love their ease, their worldly profit, their lusts, but they do not have a drop of love to God. If they loved God, would they be so willing to be rid of him? 'They say unto God, Depart from us' (*Job 21:14*). If they loved God, would they tear his name by their oaths? Does he who shoots his father in the heart love him? Though they worship God, they do not love him;

they are like the soldiers who bowed the knee to Christ, and mocked him' (*Matt. 27:29*). He whose heart is a grave in which the love of God is buried, deserves to have that curse written upon his tombstone, 'Let him be Anathema Maranatha' (*1 Cor. 16:22*). A soul devoid of divine love is a temper that best suits damned spirits. But I shall waive this, and pass to the next.

SECTION 4: A GODLY MAN IS LIKE GOD

He has the same judgment as God; he thinks of things as God does; he has a Godlike disposition; he 'partakes of the divine nature' (*2 Pet. 1:4*). A godly man bears God's name and image; godliness is Godlikeness. It is one thing to profess God, another thing to resemble him.

A godly man is like God in holiness. Holiness is the most brilliant pearl in the King of Heaven's crown: 'glorious in holiness' (*Exod. 15:11*). God's power makes him mighty; his mercy makes him lovely; but his holiness makes him glorious. The holiness of God is the intrinsic purity of his nature and his abhorrence of sin. A godly man bears some kind of analogy with God in this. He has the holy oil of consecration upon him: 'Aaron the saint of the Lord' (*Psa. 106:16*). Holiness is the badge and livery of Christ's people: 'The people of thy holiness' (*Isa. 63:18*). The godly are a holy as well as a royal priesthood (*1 Pet. 2:9*). Nor have they only a frontispiece of holiness, like the Egyptian temples which were fair outside, but they are like Solomon's temple, which had gold inside. They have written upon their heart, 'Holiness to the Lord'. The holiness of the saints consists in their conformity to God's will, which is the rule and pattern of all holiness.

Holiness is a man's glory. Aaron put on garments 'for glory and for beauty' (*Exod. 28:2*). So when a person is invested with the embroidered garment of holiness, it is for glory and beauty.

The goodness of a Christian lies in his holiness, as the goodness of the air lies in its clarity, the worth of gold in its purity.

Question: In what do the godly reveal their holiness?

Answer:

1. In hating 'the garment spotted by the flesh' (Jude 23). The godly set themselves against evil, both in purpose and in practice. They are fearful of that which looks like sin (*1 Thess. 5:22*). The appearance of evil may prejudice a weak Christian. If it does not defile a man's own conscience, it may offend his brother's conscience; and to sin against him is to sin against Christ (*1 Cor. 8:12*). A godly man will not go as far as he may, lest he go further than he should; he will not swallow all that others (bribed with promotion) may plead for. It is easy to put a golden colour on rotten material.

2. In being advocates for holiness. 'I will speak of thy testimonies also before kings, and will not be ashamed' (*Psa. 119:46*). When piety is calumniated in the world, the saints will stand up in its defence; they will wipe the dust of a reproach off the face of religion. Holiness defends the godly, and they will defend holiness; it defends them from danger, and they will defend it from disgrace.

Use 1: How can those who are unlike God be reputed to be godly? They have nothing of God in them, not one shred of holiness. They call themselves Christians, but blot out the word holiness; you may as well call it day at midnight.

So impudent are some, that they boast they are none of the holy ones. Is it not the Spirit of holiness which marks off the sheep of Christ from the goats? 'Ye were sealed (or marked) with the holy Spirit' (*Eph. 1:13*). And is it a matter for men to boast of, that they have none of the Spirit's earmark upon them? Does not the apostle say that 'without holiness no man shall see the Lord' (*Heb. 12:14*)? Such as bless themselves in their unholiness had best go and ring the bells for joy that they shall never see God.

There are others who hate holiness. Sin and holiness never meet but they fight. Holiness discharges its fire of zeal against sin, and sin spits its venom of malice at holiness. Many pretend to love Christ as a Saviour but hate him as he is the Holy One (*Acts 3:14*).

Use 2: Let us strive to be like God in holiness.

1. This is God's great design he drives on in the world. It is the object of the Word preached. The silver drops of the sanctuary are to water the seed of grace, and make a crop of holiness spring up. What use is there in the promises if not to bribe us to holiness? What are all God's providential dispensations for, but to promote holiness? As the Lord makes use of all the seasons of the year, frost and heat, to produce the harvest, so all prosperous and adverse providences are for the promoting of the work of holiness in the soul. What is the object of the mission of the Spirit, but to make the heart holy? When the air is unwholesome by reason of fog and mist, the wind is a fan to winnow and purify the air. So the blowing of God's Spirit upon the heart is to purify it, and make it holy.

2. Holiness is that alone which God is delighted with. When Tamerlane was presented with a pot of gold, he asked whether the gold had his father's stamp upon it. But when he saw it had the Roman stamp, he rejected it. Holiness is God's stamp and impress; if he does not see this stamp upon us, he will not own us.

3. Holiness fits us for communion with God. Communion with God is a paradox to the men of the world. Not everyone who hangs about the court speaks with the king. We may approach God in duties, and as it were hang about the court of heaven, yet not have communion with God. That which keeps up the intercourse with God is holiness. The holy heart enjoys much of God's presence; he feels heart-warming and heart-comforting virtue in an ordinance. Where God sees his likeness, there he gives his love.

SECTION 5: A GODLY MAN IS VERY EXACT AND CAREFUL ABOUT THE WORSHIP OF GOD

The Greek word for 'godly' signifies a true worshipper of God. A godly man reverences divine institutions, and is more for the purity of worship than the pomp. Mixture in sacred things is like a dash in the wine, which though it gives it a colour, yet only adulterates it. The Lord wanted Moses to make the tabernacle 'according to the pattern shewed thee in the mount' (*Exod. 25:40*). If Moses had left out anything in the pattern, or added anything to it, it would have been very provocative. The Lord has always given testimonies of his displeasure against such as have corrupted his worship. Nadab and Abihu offered 'strange fire' (other than God had sanctified on the altar), 'and fire went out from the Lord, and devoured them' (*Lev. 10:1,2*). Whatever is not of God's own appointment in his worship he looks upon as 'strange fire'. And no wonder he is so highly incensed at it, for it is as if God were not wise enough to appoint the manner in which he will be served. Men will try to direct him, and as if the rules for his worship were defective, they will attempt to correct the copy, and superadd their inventions.

A godly man dare not vary from the pattern which God has shown him in the Scripture. This is probably not the least reason why David was called 'a man after God's own heart', because he kept the springs of God's worship pure, and in matters sacred did not superinduce anything of his own devising.

THE GODLY MAN'S PICTURE

Use: By this characteristic we may test ourselves, whether we are godly. Are we careful about the things of God? Do we observe that mode of worship which has the stamp of divine authority upon it? It has dangerous consequences to make a medley in religion.

1. Those who will add to one part of God's worship will be as ready to take away from another. 'Laying aside the commandment of God, ye hold the tradition of men' (*Mark 7:8*). They who will bring in a tradition, will in time lay aside a command. This the Papists are very guilty of; they bring in altars and crucifixes, and lay aside the second commandment. They bring in oil and cream in baptism, and leave out the cup in the Lord's Supper. They bring in praying for the dead, and lay aside reading the Scriptures intelligibly to the living. Those who will introduce into God's worship that which he has not commanded, will be as ready to blot out that which he has commanded.

2. Those who are for outward commixtures in God's worship are usually regardless of the vitals of religion: living by faith, leading a strict mortified life; these things are of less concern to them. Wasps have their combs, but no honey in them. The religion of many may be likened to those ears which all run to straw.

3. Superstition and profanity kiss each other. Has it not been known that those who have kneeled at a pillar have reeled against a post?

4. Such as are devoted to superstition are seldom or never converted: 'publicans and harlots go into the kingdom of God before you' (*Matt. 21:31*). This was spoken to the chief priests, who were great formalists, and the reason why such persons are seldom wrought upon savingly is because they have a secret antipathy to the power of godliness. The snake has a fine colour, but it has a sting. So outwardly men may look zealous and devout, but retain a sting of hatred in their hearts against goodness. Hence it is that they who have been most hot on superstition have been most hot on persecution. The Church of Rome wears white linen (an emblem of innocence), but the Spirit of God paints her out in scarlet (*Rev. 17:4*). Why is this? Not only because she puts on a scarlet robe, but because her body is of a scarlet dye, having imbrued her hands in the blood of the saints (*Rev. 17:6*).

Let us, then, as we would show ourselves to be godly, keep close to the rule of worship, and in the things of Jehovah go no further than we can say, 'It is written'.

SECTION 6: A GODLY MAN IS A SERVANT OF GOD, NOT A SERVANT OF MEN

This characteristic has two distinct branches. I shall speak of both in order.

A: A godly man is a servant of God
'We are the servants of the God of heaven' (*Ezra 5:11*); 'Epaphras, a servant of Christ' (*Col. 4:12*).

Question: In what sense is a godly man a servant of God?

Answer: In seven respects:

1. A servant leaves all others, and confines himself to one master. So a godly man leaves the service of sin, and betakes himself to the service of God (*Rom. 6:22*). Sin is a tyrannizing thing; a sinner is a slave when he sins with most freedom. The wages which sin gives may deter us from its service: 'the wages of sin is death' (*Rom. 6:23*). Here is damnable pay! A godly man enlists himself in God's family, and is one of his menial servants: 'O Lord, truly I am thy servant; I am thy servant' (*Psa. 116:16*). David repeats himself, as if he had said, 'Lord, I have given my pledge;

[37]

no-one else can lay claim to me; my ear is bored to thy service'.

2. A servant is not independent, at his own disposal, but at the disposal of his master. A servant must not do what he pleases, but be at the will of his master. Thus a godly man is God's servant. He is wholly at God's disposal. He has no will of his own: 'Thy will be done on earth'. Some will say to the godly, 'Why cannot you behave like others? Why will you not drink and swear and profane the Sabbath as others do?' The godly are God's servants; they must not do what they want, but be under the rules of the family; they must do nothing but what they can show their master's authority for.

3. A servant is bound. There are covenants and indentures sealed between him and his master. Thus there are indentures drawn in baptism, and in conversion the indentures are renewed and sealed. There we bind ourselves to God to be his sworn servants: 'I have sworn, and I will perform it, that I will keep thy righteous judgments' *(Psa. 119:106)*. A godly man has tied himself to the Lord by vow, and he makes conscience of his vow. He would rather die by persecution than live by perjury *(Psa. 56:12)*.

4. A servant not only wears his master's livery, but does his work. Thus a godly man works for God. St Paul 'spent and was spent for Christ' *(2 Cor. 12:15)*. He worked harder than all the other apostles *(1 Cor. 15:10)*. A godly man is active for God to his last breath, 'even unto the end' *(Psa. 119:112)*. Only 'the dead rest from their labours' *(Rev. 14:13)*.

5. A servant follows his master; thus a godly man is a servant of God. While others wonder after the beast, he follows after the Lamb (*Rev. 13:3; 14:4*). He wants to tread in the steps of Christ. If a master leaps over hedge and ditch, the servant will follow him. A godly man will follow Christ through afflictions: 'If any man will come after me, let him take up his cross daily, and follow me' (*Luke 9:23*). Peter wanted to follow Christ on the water. A godly man will follow Christ though it is death every step. He will keep his goodness when others are bad. As all the water in the salt sea cannot make the fish salt, but they still retain their freshness, so all the wickedness in the world cannot make a godly man wicked, but he still retains his piety. He will follow Christ in the worst times.

6. *A servant is satisfied with his master's allowance.* He does not say, 'I will have such provisions made ready'. If he has short commons, he does not find fault. He knows he is a servant, and accepts his master's carving. In this sense, a godly man is God's servant; he is willing to live on God's allowance; if he has only some left-overs, he does not grumble. Paul knew he was a servant, therefore whether more or less fell to his share, he was indifferent (*Phil. 4:11*). When Christians complain at their condition, they forget that they are servants, and must live on the allowance of their heavenly Master. You who have the least bit from God will die in his debt.

7. *A servant will stand up for the honour of his master.* He cannot hear his master reproached, but will vindicate his credit. Thus, every godly man will stand up for the honour of his Master, Christ. 'My zeal hath consumed me' (*Psa. 119:139*). A servant of God stands up for his truths. Some can hear God's name reproached, and his ways spoken against, yet remain silent. God will be ashamed of such servants, and reject them before men and angels.

Use: Let us declare ourselves godly by being servants of the most high God. Consider:

1. God is the best Master. He is punctilious in all his promises: 'There is no God like thee, in heaven above, or on earth beneath, who keepest covenant and mercy with thy servants . . . there hath not failed one word of all his good promise' (*1 Kings 8:23,56*). God is of a most sweet, gracious disposition. He has this quality that he is 'slow to anger' and 'ready to forgive' (*Psa. 103:8; 86:5*). In our wants, he relieves us; in our weakness, he pities us. He reveals his secrets to his servants (*Psa. 25:14; Prov. 3:32*). He waits on his servants. Was there ever such a Master? 'Blessed are those servants, whom the Lord when he cometh shall find watching: verily I say unto you, that he shall gird himself, and make them to sit down to meat, and will come forth and serve them' (*Luke 12:37*). When we are sick, he makes our bed: 'thou wilt make all his bed in his sickness' (*Psa. 41:3*). He holds our head when we are fainting. Other masters may forget their servants, and cast them off when they are old, but God will not: 'thou art my servant: O Israel, thou shalt not be forgotten of me' (*Isa. 44:21*). It is a slander to say, 'God is a hard Master'.

2. God's service is the best service. There are six privileges in God's service:

(i) *Freedom.* Though the saints are bound to God's service, yet they serve him freely. God's Spirit, who is called a 'free Spirit' (*Psa. 51:12*), makes them free and cheerful in obedience. The Spirit carries them on the wings of delight; he makes duty a privilege; he does not force, but draw. He enlarges the heart in love and fills it with joy. God's service is perfect freedom.

(ii) *Honour.* David the king professed himself one of God's pensioners: 'I am thy servant' (*Psa. 143:12*). St Paul, when he wants to blaze his coat of arms, and set forth his best heraldry, does not call himself 'Paul, a Hebrew of the Hebrews', or 'Paul, of the tribe of Benjamin', but 'Paul, a servant of Jesus Christ' (*Rom. 1:1*). Theodosius thought it a greater dignity to be God's servant, than to be an emperor. Christ himself, who is equal with his Father, is nevertheless not ashamed of the title 'servant' (*Isa. 53:11*). Every servant of God is a son, every subject a prince. It is more honour to serve God than to have kings serve us. The angels in heaven are servants of the saints on earth.

(iii) *Safety*. God takes care of his servants. He gives them protection: 'Thou art my servant; fear not; for I am with thee' (*Isa. 41:9,10*). God hides his servants: 'in the secret of his tabernacle shall he hide me' (*Psa. 27:5*). That is, he shall keep me safe, as in the most holy place of the sanctuary, where none but the priests might enter. Christ's wings are both for healing and for hiding, for curing and securing us (*Mal. 4:2*). The devil and his instruments would soon devour the servants of God, if he did not set an invisible guard about them, and cover them with the golden feathers of his protection (*Psa. 91:4*). 'I am with thee, and no man shall set on thee to hurt thee' (*Acts 18:10*). God's watchful eye is always on his people, and the enemies shall not do the mischief they intend; they shall not be destroyers, but physicians.

(iv) *Gain*. Atheists say, 'It is vain to serve God: and what profit is it that we have kept his ordinances?' (*Mal. 3:14*). Besides the advantages which God gives in this life (sweet peace of conscience), he reserves his best wine till last; he gives a glorious kingdom to his servants (*Heb. 12:28*). The servants of God may for a while be kept under and abused, but they shall have promotion at last: 'where I am, there shall also my servant be' (*John 12:26*).

(v) *Assistance*. Other masters cut out work for their servants, but do not help them in their work. But our Master in heaven gives us not only work, but strength:

'thou strengthenedst me with strength in my soul' (*Psa. 138:3*). God bids us serve him, and he will enable us to serve him: 'I will cause you to walk in my statutes' (*Ezek. 36:27*). The Lord not only fits work for us, but fits us for our work; with his command he gives power.

(vi) *Supplies*. A master will not let his servants be in want. God's servants shall be provided for: 'verily thou shalt be fed' (*Psa. 37:3*). Does God give us a Christ, and will he deny us a crust? 'The God which fed me all my life long' (*Gen. 48:15*). If God does not give us what we crave, he will give us what we need. The wicked, who are dogs, are fed (*Phil. 3:2*). If a man feeds his dog, surely he will feed his servant! Oh, then, who would not be in love with God's service?

3. *We are engaged to serve God.* We are 'bought with a price' (*1 Cor. 6:20*). This is a metaphor taken from such as ransom captives from prison by paying a sum of money for them. They are to be at the service of those who ransomed them. So when the devil had taken us prisoners, Christ ransomed us with a price, not of money, but of blood. Therefore we are to be only at his service. If any can lay a better claim to us than Christ, we may serve them; but Christ having the best right to us, we are to cleave to him and enrol ourselves for ever in his service.

B: A godly man is not the servant of men
'Be not ye the servants of men' (*1 Cor. 7:23*).

Question: But is there no service we owe to men?

Answer: There is a threefold serving of men:

1. *There is a civil service we owe to men*, as the inferior to the superior. The servant is a living tool, as Aristotle says. 'Servants, obey your masters' (*Eph. 6:5*).

[42]

2. There is a religious service we owe to men, when we are serviceable to their souls: 'your servants for Jesus' sake' (*2 Cor. 4:5*).

3. There is a sinful serving of men. This consists of three things:

(i) When we prefer men's injunctions before God's institutions. God commands one thing; man commands another. God says, 'Sanctify the Sabbath'; man says, 'Profane it.' When men's edicts have more force with us than God's precepts, this is to be the servants of men.

(ii) When we voluntarily prostitute ourselves to the impure lusts of men, we let them lord it over our consciences. When we are pliable and conformable to anything, either Arminian or atheist, for either the gospel or the Koran. When we will be what others will have us be, then we are just like Issachar, who is 'a strong ass couching down between two burdens' (*Gen. 49:14*). This is not humility, but sordidness, and it is men-serving.

(iii) When we are advocates in a bad cause, pleading for any impious, unjustifiable act; when we baptize sin with the name of religion, and with our oratory wash the devil's face, this is to be the servants of men. In these cases, a godly person will not so unman himself as to serve men. He says, like Paul, 'If I yet pleased men, I should not be the servant of Christ' (*Gal. 1:10*); and like Peter, 'We ought to obey God rather than men' (*Acts 5:29*).

Use: How many leagues distant from godliness are those who serve men, who either for fear of punishment, or from hope of promotion, comply with the sinful commands of men, who will put their conscience under any yoke, and sail with any wind that blows profit. These are the 'servants of men'; they have abjured their baptismal vow, and renounced the Lord who bought them.

To the one who is such a Proteus as to change into any form, and bow as low as hell to please men, I would say two things:

1. You who have learned all your postures, who can cringe and tack about, how will you look Christ in the face another day? When you say on your death bed, 'Lord, look on your servant', Christ shall disclaim you and say, 'My servant? No, you renounced my service, you were "a servant of men"; depart from me; I do not know you.' What a cold shoulder this will be at that day!

2. What does a man get by sinfully enslaving himself? He gets a blot on his name, a curse on his estate, a hell in his conscience; no, even those that he basely stoops to will scorn and despise him. How the high priests kicked off Judas! 'See thou to that' (*Matt. 27:4*).

That we may not be the servants of men, let us abandon fear and advance faith (*Esther 8:17*). Faith is a world-conquering grace (*1 John 5:4*). It overcomes the world's music and crucible; it steels a Christian with divine courage, and makes him stand immovable, like a rock in the midst of the sea.

SECTION 7: A GODLY MAN PRIZES CHRIST

To illustrate this, I shall show:
   A. That Jesus Christ is in himself precious.
   B. That a godly man esteems him precious.

A: Jesus Christ is in himself precious
'Behold, I lay in Sion a chief corner stone, elect, precious' (*1 Pet. 2:6*).

1. Christ is compared to 'a bundle of myrrh' (Song 1:13). Myrrh is very precious; it was one of the chief spices of which the holy anointing oil was made (*Exod. 30:25*).

(i) Myrrh is of a perfuming nature. So Christ perfumes our persons and services, so that they are a sweet odour to God. Why is the church, that heavenly bride, so perfumed with grace? Because Christ, that myrrh tree, has dropped his perfume upon her (*Song 3:6*).

(ii) Myrrh is of an exhilarating nature. Its smell comforts and refreshes the spirits. So Christ comforts the souls of his people, when they are fainting under their sins and suffering.

2. *Christ is compared to a pearl*: 'when he had found one pearl of great price' (*Matt. 13:46*). Christ, this pearl, was little with regard to his humility, but of infinite value. Jesus Christ is a pearl that God wears in his bosom (*John 1:18*); a pearl whose lustre drowns the world's glory (*Gal. 6:14*); a pearl that enriches the soul, the angelic part of man (*1 Cor. 1:5*); a pearl that enlightens heaven (*Rev. 21:23*); a pearl so precious that it makes us precious to God (*Eph. 1:6*); a pearl that is consoling and restorative (*Luke 2:25*); a pearl of more value than heaven (*Col. 1:16,17*). The preciousness of Christ is seen in three ways:

(i) He is precious in his person; he is the picture of his Father's glory (*Heb. 1:3*).

(ii) Christ is precious in his offices, which are several rays of the Sun of righteousness:

(a) Christ's prophetic office is precious (*Deut. 18:15*). He is the great oracle of heaven; he has a preciousness above all the prophets who went before him; he teaches not only the ear, but the heart. He who has 'the key of David' in his hand opened the heart of Lydia (*Acts 16:14*).

(b) Christ's priestly office is precious. This is the solid basis of our comfort. 'Now once hath he appeared to put away sin by the sacrifice of himself' (*Heb. 9:26*). By virtue of this sacrifice, the soul may go to God with boldness: 'Lord, give me heaven; Christ has purchased it for me; he hung upon the cross, that I might sit upon the throne.' Christ's blood and incense are the two hinges on which our salvation turns.

(c) Christ's regal office is precious: 'He hath on his vesture, and on his thigh a name written, King of kings, and Lord of lords' (*Rev. 19:16*). Christ has a pre-eminence above all other kings for majesty; he has the highest throne, the richest crown, the largest dominions, and the longest possession: 'Thy throne, O God, is for ever and ever' (*Heb. 1:8*). Though Christ has many assessors – those who sit with him (*Eph. 2:6*) – he has no successors. Christ sets up his sceptre where no other king does; he rules the will and affections; his power binds the conscience. The angels take the oath of allegiance to him (*Heb. 1:6*). Christ's kingship is seen in two royal acts:

(1) In ruling his people. He rules with clemency; his regal rod has honey at the end of it. Christ displays the ensign of mercy, which makes so many volunteers run to his standard (*Psa. 110:3*). Holiness without mercy, and justice without mercy, would be dreadful, but mercy encourages poor sinners to trust in him.

(2) In overruling his enemies. He pulls down their pride, befools their policy, restrains their malice: 'the remainder of wrath shalt thou restrain' (*Psa. 76:10*), or as it is in the Hebrew, 'thou shalt girdle up'. That stone 'cut out of the mountain without hands, which smote the image' (*Dan. 2:34*) was an emblem, says Augustine, of Christ's monarchical power, conquering and triumphing over his enemies.

(iii) Christ is precious in his benefits. By Christ all dangers are removed; through Christ all mercies are conveyed. In his blood flows justification (*Acts 13:39*); purgation (*Heb. 9:14*); fructification (*John 1:16*); pacification (*Rom. 5:1*); adoption (*Gal. 4:5*); perseverance (*Heb.*

[46]

12:2); glorification (*Heb. 9:12*). This will be a matter of sublimest joy to eternity. We read that those who had passed over the sea of glass stood with their harps and sang the song of Moses and the Lamb (*Rev. 15:2,3*). So when the saints of God have passed over the glassy sea of this world, they shall sing hallelujahs to the Lamb who has redeemed them from sin and hell, and has translated them into that glorious paradise, where they shall see God for ever and ever.

B: A godly man esteems Christ precious

'Unto you therefore which believe, he is precious' (*1 Pet. 2:7*). In the Greek it is 'an honour'. Believers have an honourable esteem of Christ. The psalmist speaks like one captivated with Christ's amazing beauty: 'there is none upon earth that I desire beside thee' (*Psa. 73:25*). He did not say he had nothing; he had many comforts on earth, but he desired none but God; as if a wife should say that there is no-one's company she prizes like her husband's. How did David prize Christ? 'Thou art fairer than the children of men' (*Psa. 45:2*). The spouse in the Song of Solomon looked upon Christ as the Coriphaeus, the most incomparable one, 'the chiefest among ten thousand' (*Song 5:10*). Christ outvies all others: 'As the apple tree among the trees of the wood, so is my beloved among the sons' (*Song 2:3*). Christ infinitely more excels all the beauties and glories of this visible world than the apple tree surpasses the trees of the wild forest. Paul so prized Christ that he made him his chief study: 'I determined not to know anything among you, save Jesus Christ' (*1 Cor. 2:2*). He judged nothing else of value. He knew Christ best: 'have I not seen Jesus Christ our Lord?' (*1 Cor. 9:1*). He saw him with his bodily eyes in a vision, when he was caught up into the third heaven (*2 Cor. 12:2*), and he saw him with the eye of his faith in the blessed supper. Therefore he knew him best. Consider how he slighted and despised other things in comparison with Christ: 'I count all things but loss for the excellency of the knowledge of Christ Jesus my Lord' (*Phil. 3:8*). Gain he esteemed loss, and gold dung for Christ. Indeed, a godly person cannot choose but set a high valuation upon Christ; he sees a fulness of value in him:

1. A fulness in regard to variety. 'In whom are hid all the treasures' (*Col. 2:3*). No country has all commodities of its own growth, but Christ has all kinds of fulness – fulness of merit, of spirit, of love. He has a treasure adequate for all our wants.

2. A fulness in regard to degree. Christ has not only a few drops, or rays, but is more full of goodness than the sun is of light; he has the fulness of the Godhead (*Col. 2:9*).

3. A fulness in regard to duration. The fulness in the creature, like the brooks of Arabia, is soon dried up, but Christ's fulness is inexhaustible; it is a fulness overflowing and ever-flowing.

And this fulness is for believers: Christ is a common thesaurus (as Luther says), a common treasury or store for the saints: 'of his fulness have all we received' (*John 1:16*). Put a glass under a still and it receives water out of the still, drop by drop. So those who are united to Christ have the dews and drops of his grace distilling on them. Well, then, may Christ be admired by all those who believe.

Use 1: Is a godly man a high prizer of Christ? Then what is to be thought of those who do not put a value upon Christ? Are they godly or not? There are four sorts of persons who do not prize Christ:

1. The Jews. They do not believe in Christ: 'unto this day, the veil is upon their heart' (*2 Cor. 3:15*). They expect their future age and a Messiah still to come, as their own Talmud reports. They blaspheme Christ; they slight righteousness imputed; they despise the virgin Mary, calling her in derision Marah, which signifies bitterness; they vilify the gospel; they deny the Christian Sabbath; they hold Christians in abomination; they regard it as not lawful for a Jew to take medicine from a Christian. Schecardus relates the story of one, Bendema, a Jew who was bitten by a snake. A Christian came to heal him, but he refused his help and chose rather to die than to be healed by a Christian. So do the Jews hate Christ and all that wear his livery.

2. *The Socinians*, who acknowledge only Christ's humanity. This is to set him below the angels, for human nature, simply considered, is inferior to the angelic (*Psa. 8:5*).

3. *Proud nominal Christians*, who do not lay the whole stress of their salvation upon Christ, but would mingle their dross with his gold, their duties with his merits. This is to steal a jewel from Christ's crown and implicitly to deny him to be a perfect Saviour.

4. *Airy theorists*, who prefer the study of the arts and sciences before Christ. Not that the knowledge of these is not commendable: 'Moses was learned in all the wisdom of the Egyptians' (*Acts 7:22*). Human learning is of good use to prepare for the study of better things, as a coarser dye prepares the cloth for a richer and a deeper dye. But the fault is when the study of Christ is neglected. The knowledge of Christ ought to have the pre-eminence. It was surely not without a mystery that God allowed all Solomon's writings about birds and plants to be lost, but what he wrote about spiritual wisdom to be miraculously preserved, as if God would teach us that to know Christ (the true Wisdom) is the crowning knowledge (*Prov. 8:12*). One leaf of this tree of life will give us more comfort on a death-bed than the whole idea and platform of human science. What is it to know all the motions of the orbs and influences of the

stars, and in the meantime to be ignorant of Christ, the bright Morning Star (*Rev. 22:16*)? What is it to understand the nature of minerals or precious stones, and not to know Christ the true Cornerstone (*Isa. 28:16*)? It is undervaluing, yes, despising Christ, when with the lodestone we draw iron and straw to us, but neglect him who has tried gold to bestow on us (*Rev. 3:18*).

Use 2: Is it the sign of a godly person to be a Christ-prizer? Then let us test our godliness by this: Do we set a high estimation on Christ?

Question: How shall we know that?

Answer 1: If we are prizers of Christ, then we prefer him in our judgments before other things. We value Christ above honour and riches; the Pearl of Price lies nearest our heart. He who prizes Christ esteems the gleanings of Christ better than the world's vintage. He counts the worst things of Christ better than the best things of the world: 'esteeming the reproach of Christ greater riches than the treasures in Egypt' (*Heb. 11:26*). And is it thus with us? Has the price of worldly things fallen? Gregory Nazianzene solemnly blessed God that he had anything to lose for Christ's sake. But alas, how few Nazianzenes are to be found! You will hear some say they have honourable thoughts of Christ, but they prize their land and estate above him. The young man in the Gospel preferred his bags of gold before Christ. Judas valued thirty pieces of silver above him. May it not be feared, if an hour of trial comes, that there are many who would rather renounce their baptism, and throw off Christ's livery, than hazard the loss of their earthly possessions for him?

Answer 2: If we are the prizers of Christ, we cannot live without him; things which we value we know not how to be without. A man may live without music, but not without food. A child of God can lack health and friends, but he cannot lack Christ. In the absence of Christ, he says, like Job, 'I went mourning without the sun' (*Job 30:28*). I have the starlight of creature comforts, but I need the Sun of righteousness. 'Give me children,' said Rachel, 'or else I die' (*Gen. 30:1*). So the soul says, 'Lord, give me Christ, or I die. One drop of the water of life to quench my thirst.' Let us test by this – do they prize Christ who can manage well enough to be without him? Give a child a rattle, and it will not want gold. If men only have worldly provisions, 'corn and wine', they can be content enough without Christ. Christ is a spiritual Rock (*1 Cor. 10:4*). Just let men have 'oil in the cruse' and they do not care about honey from this rock. If their trade has gone, they complain, but if God takes away the gospel, which is the ark wherein Christ the manna is hidden, they are quiet and tame enough. Do those prize Christ who can sit down content without him?

Answer 3: If we are prizers of Christ, then we shall not complain at any pains to get him. He who prizes gold will dig for it in the mine: 'My soul followeth hard after God' (*Psa. 63:8*). Plutarch reports of the Gauls, an ancient people in France, that after they had tasted the sweet wine of the Italian grape, they enquired after the country, and never rested till they had arrived at it. He in whose eye Christ is precious never rests till he has gained him: 'I sought him whom my soul loveth; I held him, and would not let him go' (*Song 3:1,4*).

Test by this! Many say they have Christ in high veneration, but they are not industrious in the use of means to obtain him. If Christ would drop as a ripe fig into their mouth, they could be content to have him, but they will not put themselves to too much trouble to get him. Does he who will not take medicine or exercise prize his health?

Answer 4: If we are prizers of Christ, then we take great pleasure in Christ. What joy a man takes in that which he counts his treasure! He who prizes Christ makes him his greatest joy. He can delight in Christ when other delights have gone: 'Although the fig tree shall not blossom, yet I will rejoice in the Lord' (*Hab. 3:17,18*). Though a flower in a man's garden dies, he can still delight in his money and jewels. He who esteems Christ can solace himself in Christ when there is an autumn on all other comforts.

Answer 5: If we are prizers of Christ, then we will part with our dearest pleasures for him. Paul said of the Galatians that they so esteemed him that they were ready to pull out their own eyes and give them to him (*Gal. 4:15*). He who esteems Christ will pull out that lust which is his right eye. A wise man will throw away a poison for a stimulant. He who sets a high value on Christ will part with his pride, unjust gain and sinful fashions (*Isa. 30:32*). He will set his feet on the neck of his sins.

Test by this! How can they be said to prize Christ who will not leave a vanity for him? Not a spot on the face, nor an oath, nor an intemperate cup. What scorn and contempt they put on the Lord Jesus who prefer a damning pleasure before a saving Christ!

Answer 6: If we are prizers of Christ, we shall think we cannot have him at too dear a rate. We may buy gold too dearly but we cannot purchase Christ too dearly. Though we part with our blood for him, it is no dear bargain. The apostles rejoiced that they were graced so much as to be disgraced for Christ (*Acts 5:41*). They esteemed their fetters more precious than bracelets of gold. Do not let him who refuses to bear his cross say that he prizes Christ: 'When persecution ariseth because of the word, by and by he is offended' (*Matt. 13:21*).

Answer 7: If we are prizers of Christ, we will be willing to help others to get a part in him. That which we esteem excellent, we are desirous our friend should have a share in it. If a man has found a spring of water, he will call others that they may drink and satisfy their thirst. Do we commend Christ to others? Do we take them by the hand and lead them to Christ? This shows how few prize Christ, because they do not make more effort that their relations should have a part in him. They get land and riches for their posterity, but have no care to leave them the Pearl of Price as their portion.

Answer 8: If we are prizers of Christ, then we prize him in health as well as in sickness; when we are enlarged, as well as when we are straitened. A friend is prized at all times; the Rose of Sharon is always sweet. He who values his Saviour aright has as precious thoughts of him in a day of prosperity as in a day of adversity. The wicked make use of Christ only when they are in straits -- as the elders of Gilead went to Jephthah when they were in distress (*Judges 11:7*). Themistocles complained of the Athenians that they only ran to him as they did to a tree, to shelter them in a storm. Sinners desire Christ only for shelter. The Hebrews never chose their judges except when they were in some imminent danger. Godless persons never look for Christ except at death, when they are in danger of hell.

Use 3: As we would prove to the world that we have the impress of godliness on us, let us be prizers of Jesus Christ; he is elect, precious. Christ is the wonder of beauty. Pliny said of the mulberry tree that there is nothing in it but what is therapeutic and useful: the fruit, leaves and bark. So there is nothing in Christ but what is precious. His name is precious, his virtues precious, his blood precious – more precious than the world.

Oh, then, let us have endearing thoughts of Christ, let him be accounted our chief treasure and delight. This is the reason why millions perish – because they do not prize Christ. Christ is the door by which men are to enter heaven (*John 10:9*). If they do not know this door or are so proud that they will not stoop to go in at it, how can they be saved? That we may have Christ-admiring thoughts, let us consider:

1. We cannot prize Christ at too high a rate. We may prize other things above their value. That is our sin. We commonly overrate the creature; we think there is more in it than there is; therefore God makes our gourd wither, because we overprize it. But we cannot raise our esteem of Christ high enough; he is beyond all value. There is no ruby or diamond but the jeweller can set a fair price on it. He can say it is worth so much and no more. But Christ's worth can never be fully known. No seraphim can set a due value on him; his are unsearchable riches (*Eph. 3:8*). Christ is more precious than the soul, than the angels, than heaven.

2. Jesus Christ has highly prized us. He took our flesh upon him (*Heb. 2:16*). He made his soul an offering for us (*Isa. 53:10*). How precious our salvation was to Christ! Shall not we prize and adore him who has put such a value upon us?

3. Not to prize Christ is great imprudence. Christ is our guide to glory. It is folly for a man to slight his guide. He is our physician (*Mal. 4:2*). It is folly to despise our physician.

What! To set light by Christ for things of no value? 'Ye fools and blind' (*Matt. 23:17*). How is a fool tested but by showing him an apple and a piece of gold? If he chooses the apple before the gold, he is judged to be a fool and his estate is beggared. How many such idiots there are who prefer husks before manna, the gaudy, empty things of this life before the Prince of Glory! Will not Satan beggar them at last for fools?

4. Some slight Christ now and say, 'There is no beauty that we should desire him' (Isa. 53:2). There is a day coming shortly when Christ will as much slight them. He will set as light by them as they do by him. He will say, 'I know you not' (*Luke 13:27*). What a slighting word that will be, when men cry, 'Lord Jesus, save us', and he says, 'I was offered to you but you would have none of me (*Psa. 81:11*); you scorned me, and now I will set light by you and your salvation. Depart from me, I do not know you.' This is all that sinners get by rejecting the Lord of life. Christ will slight at the day of judgment those who have slighted him in the day of grace.

SECTION 8: A GODLY MAN IS AN EVANGELICAL WEEPER

David sometimes sang with his harp, and sometimes the organ of his eye wept: 'I water my couch with my tears' (*Psa. 6:6*). Christ calls his spouse his 'dove' (*Song 2:14*). The dove is a weeping creature. Grace dissolves and liquefies the soul, causing a spiritual thaw. The sorrow of the heart runs out at the eye (*Psa. 31:9*).

The Rabbis report that the same night on which Israel departed from Egypt towards Canaan, all the idols of Egypt were broken down by lightning and earthquake. So at that very time at which men go forth from their natural condition towards heaven, all the idols of sin in the heart must be broken down by repentance. A melting heart is the chief branch of the covenant of grace (*Ezek. 36:26*), and the product of the Spirit: 'I will pour upon the house of David the spirit of grace, and they shall look upon me whom they have pierced, and they shall mourn for him' (*Zech. 12:10*).

Question: But why is a godly man a weeper? Is not sin pardoned, which is the ground of joy? Has he not had a transforming work upon his heart? Why, then, does he weep?

Answer: A godly man finds enough reasons for weeping:

1. He weeps for indwelling sin, the law in his members (*Rom. 7:23*), the outbursts and first risings of sin. His nature is a poisoned fountain. A regenerate person grieves that he carries that about him which is enmity to God; his heart is like a wide sea in which there are innumerable creeping things (*Psa. 104:25*) – vain, sinful thoughts. A child of God laments hidden wickedness; he has more evil in him than he knows of. There are those windings in his heart which he cannot trace, an unknown world of sin: 'Who can understand his errors?' (*Psa. 19:12*).

2. A godly man weeps for clinging corruption. If he could get rid of sin, there would be some comfort, but he cannot shake off this viper. Sin cleaves to him like leprosy to the wall (*Lev. 14:39*). Though a child of God forsakes his sin, yet sin will not forsake him. 'Concerning the rest of the beasts, they had their dominion taken away: yet their lives were prolonged for a season' (*Dan. 7:12*). So though the dominion of sin is taken away, yet its life is prolonged for a season; and while sin lives, it molests. The Persians were daily enemies to the Romans and would invade their frontiers. So sin 'wars against the soul' (*1 Pet. 2:11*). And there is no cessation of arms till death. Will not this cause tears?

3. A child of God weeps that he is sometimes overcome by the prevalence of corruption: 'The evil which I would not, that I do' (*Rom. 7:19*). Paul was like a man carried downstream.

How often a saint is overpowered by pride and passion! When David had sinned, he steeped his soul in the brinish tears of repentance. It cannot but grieve a regenerate person to think he should be so foolish as, after he has felt the smart of sin, still to put this fire in his bosom again.

4. A godly heart grieves that he can be no more holy. It troubles him that he shoots so short of the rule and standard which God has set. 'I should', says he, 'love the Lord with all my heart. But how defective my love is! How far short I come of what I should be, no, of what I might have been! What can I see in my life but either blanks or blots?'

5. A godly man sometimes weeps out of the sense of God's love. Gold is the finest and most solid of all the metals, yet it is soonest melted in the fire. Gracious hearts, which are golden hearts, are the soonest melted into tears by the fire of God's love. I once knew a holy man, who was walking in his garden and shedding plenty of tears when a friend came on him accidentally and asked him why he wept. He broke forth into this pathetic expression: 'Oh, the love of Christ, the love of Christ!' Thus have we seen the cloud melted into water by the sunbeams.

6. A godly person weeps because the sins he commits are in some sense worse than the sins of other men. The sin of a justified person is very odious:

(i) Because he acts contrary to his own principles. He sins not only against the rule, but against his principles, against his knowledge, vows, prayers, hopes, experiences. He knows how dear sin will cost him, yet he adventures upon the forbidden fruit.

(ii) The sin of a justified person is odious, because it is a sin of unkindness (*1 Kings 11:9*). Peter's denying of Christ was a sin against love. Christ had enrolled him among the

[57]

apostles. He had taken him up into the Mount of Trans-figuration and shown him the glory of heaven in a vision. Yet after all this signal mercy, it was base ingratitude that he should deny Christ. This made him go out and 'weep bitterly' (*Matt. 26:75*). He baptized himself, as it were, in his own tears. The sins of the godly go nearest to God's heart. Others' sins anger God; these grieve him. The sins of the wicked pierce Christ's sides, the sins of the godly wound his heart. The unkindness of a spouse goes nearest to the heart of her husband.

(iii) The sin of a justified person is odious, because it reflects more dishonour upon God: 'By this deed thou hast given great occasion to the enemies of the Lord to blaspheme' (*2 Sam. 12:14*). The sins of God's people put black spots on the face of religion. Thus we see what cause there is why a child of God should weep even after con-version. 'Can whoever sows such things refrain from tears?'

Now this sorrow of a godly man for sin is not a despairing sorrow. He does not mourn without hope. 'Iniquities prevail against me' (*Psa. 65:3*) – there is the holy soul weeping. 'As for our transgressions, thou shalt purge them away' – there is faith triumphing.

Divine sorrow is excellent. There is as much difference between the sorrow of a godly man and one who is wicked as between the water of a spring which is clear and sweet, and the water of the sea which is salt and brackish. A godly man's sorrow has these three qualifications:

(a) It is inward. It is a sorrow of soul. Hypocrites 'disfigure their faces' (*Matt. 6:16*). Godly sorrow goes deep. It is a 'pricking at the heart' (*Acts 2:37*). True sorrow is a spiritual martyrdom, therefore called 'soul affliction' (*Lev. 23:29*).

(b) Godly sorrow is ingenuous. It is more for the evil that is in sin than the evil which follows after. It is more for the spot than the sting. Hypocrites weep for sin only as it brings affliction. I have read of a fountain that never sends out streams except on the evening before a famine. Hypocrites never send forth the streams of their tears except when God's judgments are approaching.

(c) Godly sorrow is influential. It makes the heart better: 'by the sadness of the countenance the heart is made better' (*Eccles. 7:3*). Divine tears not only wet but wash; they purge out the love of sin.

Use 1: How far from being godly are those who scarcely ever shed a tear for sin! If they lose a near relation, they weep; but though they are in danger of losing God and their souls, they do not weep. How few know what it is to be in an agony for sin or what a broken heart means! Their eyes are not like the 'fishpools in Heshbon', full of water (*Song 7:4*), but rather like the mountains of Gilboa, which had no dew upon them (*2 Sam. 1:21*). It was a greater plague for Pharaoh to have his heart turned into stone than to have his rivers turned into blood.

Others, if they sometimes shed a tear, are still never the better. They go on in wickedness, and do not drown their sins in their tears.

Use 2: Let us strive for this divine characteristic: be weepers. This is 'a repentance not to be repented of' (*2 Cor. 7:10*). It is reported of Mr Bradford, the martyr, that he was of a melting spirit; he seldom sat down to his meal but some tears trickled down his cheeks. There are two lavers to wash away sin: blood and tears. The blood of Christ washes away the guilt of sin; tears wash away the filth. Repenting tears are precious. God puts them in his bottle (*Psa. 56:8*). They are beautifying. A tear in the eye adorns more than a ring on the finger. Oil makes the face shine (*Psa. 104:15*). Tears make the heart shine; tears are comforting. A sinner's mirth turns to melancholy. A saint's mourning turns to music. Repentance may be compared to myrrh, which though it is better to the taste, is comforting to the spirits. Repentance may be bitter to the fleshy part but it is most refreshing to the spiritual. Wax that melts is fit for the seal. A melting soul is fit to take the stamp of all heavenly blessing. Let us give Christ the water of our tears and he will give us the wine of his blood.

SECTION 9: A GODLY MAN IS A LOVER OF THE WORD

'O how love I thy law' (*Psa. 119:97*).

A: *A godly man loves the Word written*
Chrysostom compares the Scripture to a garden set with knots and flowers. A godly man delights to walk in this garden and sweetly solace himself. He loves every branch and part of the Word:

1. He loves the counselling part of the Word, as it is a directory and rule of life. The Word is the mercurial statue which points us to our duty. It contains in it things to be believed and practised. A godly man loves the aphorisms of the Word.

2. He loves the threatening part of the Word. The Scripture is like the Garden of Eden: as it has a tree of life in it, so it has a flaming sword at its gates. This is the threatening of the Word. It flashes fire in the face of every person who goes on obstinately in wickedness. 'God shall wound the hairy scalp of such an one as goeth on still in his trespasses' (*Psa. 68:21*). The Word gives no indulgence to evil. It will not let a man halt between God and sin. The true mother would not let the child be divided (*1 Kings 3:26*), and God will not have the heart divided. The Word thunders out threatenings against the very appearance of evil. It is like that flying roll full of curses (*Zech. 5:1*).

[60]

A godly man loves the menaces of the Word. He knows there is love in every threat. God would not have us perish; he therefore mercifully threatens us, so that he may scare us from sin. God's threats are like the buoy, which shows the rocks in the sea and threatens death to such as come near. The threat is a curbing bit to check us, so that we may not run in full career to hell. There is mercy in every threat.

3. He loves the consolatory part of the Word – the promises. He goes feeding on these as Samson went on his way eating the honeycomb (*Judges 14:8,9*). The promises are all marrow and sweetness. They are our Bezar stone when we are fainting; they are the conduits of the water of life. 'In the multitude of my thoughts within me thy comforts delight my soul' (*Psa. 94:19*). The promises were David's harp to drive away sad thoughts; they were the breast which gave him the milk of divine consolation.

A godly man shows his love to the Word written:

(i) By diligently *reading* it. The noble Bereans 'searched the Scriptures daily' (*Acts 17:11*). Apollos was mighty in the Scriptures (*Acts 18:24*). The Word is our Magna Carta for heaven; we should be daily reading over this charter. The Word shows what is truth and what is error. It is the field where the pearl of price is hidden. How we should dig for this pearl! A godly man's heart is the library to hold the Word of God; it dwells richly in him (*Col. 3:16*). It is reported of Melanchthon that when he was young, he always carried the Bible with him and read it greedily. The Word has a double work: to teach us and to judge us. Those who will not be taught by the Word shall be judged by the Word. Oh, let us make ourselves familiar with the Scripture! What if it should be as in the times of Diocletian, who commanded by proclamation that the Bible be burned? Or as in Queen Mary's days, when it spelled death to have a Bible in English? By diligent conversing with Scripture, we may carry a Bible in our heads.

(ii) By frequently *meditating* on it: 'It is my meditation all the day' (*Psa. 119:97*). A pious soul meditates on the truth and holiness of the Word. He not only has a few transient thoughts, but leaves his mind steeping in the Scripture. By meditation, he sucks from this sweet flower and ruminates on holy truths in his mind.

(iii) By *delighting* in it. It is his recreation: 'Thy words were found, and I did eat them; and thy word was unto me the joy and rejoicing of mine heart' (*Jer. 15:16*). Never did a man take such delight in a dish that he loved as the prophet did in the Word. And indeed, how can a saint choose but take great pleasure in the Word? All that ever he hopes to be worth is contained in it. Does not a son take pleasure in reading his father's will and testament, in which he bequeaths his estate to him?

(iv) By *hiding* it: 'Thy word have I hid in mine heart' (*Psa. 119:11*) – as one hides a treasure so that it should not be stolen. The Word is the jewel; the heart is the cabinet where it must be locked up. Many hide the Word in their memory, but not in their heart. And why would David enclose the Word in his heart? 'That I might be kept from sinning against thee.' As a man would carry an antidote about him when he comes near an infected place, so a godly man carries the Word in his heart as a spiritual antidote to preserve him from the infection of sin. Why have so many been poisoned with error, others with moral vice, but because they have not hidden the Word as a holy antidote in their heart?

(v) By *defending* it. A wise man will not let his land be taken from him but will defend his title. David looked upon the Word as his land of inheritance: 'Thy testimonies have I taken as an heritage for ever' (*Psa. 119:111*). And do you think he would let his inheritance be wrested out of his hands? A godly man will not only dispute for the Word but die for it: 'I saw under the altar the souls of them that were slain for the word of God'(*Rev. 6:9*).

(vi) By *preferring* it above things most precious: (a) Above food: 'I have esteemed the words of his mouth more than my necessary food' (*Job. 23:12*). (b) Above riches: 'The law of thy mouth is better unto me than thousands of gold and silver' (*Psa. 119:72*). (c) Above worldly honour. Memorable is the story of King Edward the Sixth. On the day of his coronation, when they presented three swords before him, signifying to him that he was monarch of three kingdoms, the king said, 'There is still one sword missing.' On being asked what that was, he answered, 'The Holy Bible, which is the "sword of the Spirit" and is to be preferred before these ensigns of royalty.'

(vii) By *talking* about it: 'My tongue shall speak of thy word' (*Psa. 119:172*). As a covetous man talks of his rich purchase, so a godly man speaks of the Word. What a treasure it is, how full of beauty and sweetness! Those whose mouths the devil has gagged, who never speak of God's Word, indicate that they never reaped any good from it.

(viii) By *conforming* to it. The Word is his sundial, by which he sets his life, the balance in which he weighs his actions. He copies out the Word in his daily walk: 'I have kept the faith' (*2 Tim. 4:7*). St Paul kept the doctrine of faith, and lived the life of faith.

Question: Why is a godly man a lover of the Word?

Answer 1: Because of the excellence of the Word.

1. The Word written is our pillar of fire to guide us. It shows us what rocks we are to avoid; it is the map by which we sail to the new Jerusalem.

2. The Word is a spiritual mirror through which we may see our own hearts. The mirror of nature, which the heathen had, revealed spots in their lives, but this mirror reveals spots in the imagination; that mirror revealed the spots of their unrighteousness, this reveals the spots of our righteousness. 'When the commandment came, sin revived, and I died' (*Rom. 7:9*). When the Word came like a mirror, all my opinion of self-righteousness died.

3. The Word of God is a sovereign comfort in distress. While we follow this cloud, the rock follows us. 'This is my comfort in my affliction: for thy word hath quickened me' (*Psa. 119:50*). Christ is the fountain of living water, the Word is the golden pipe through which it runs. What can revive at the hour of death but the word of life (*Phil. 2:16*)?

B: A godly man loves the Word, because of the efficacy it has had upon him
This day-star has risen in his heart, and ushered in the Sun of righteousness.

A godly man loves the Word preached, which is a commentary upon the Word written. The Scriptures are the sovereign oils and balsams; the preaching of the Word is the pouring of them out. The Scriptures are the precious spices; the preaching of the Word is the beating of these spices, which causes a wonderful fragrance and delight. The Word preached is 'the rod of God's strength' (*Psa. 110:2*) and 'the breath of his lips' (*Isa. 11:4*). What was once said of the city of Thebes, that it was built by the sound of Amphius' harp, is much more true of soul conversion. It is built by the sound of the gospel harp. Therefore the preaching of the Word is called 'the power of God to salvation' (*1 Cor. 1:24*). By this, Christ is said (now) to speak to us from heaven (*Heb. 12:25*). This ministry of the Word is to be preferred before the ministry of angels.

A godly man loves the Word preached, partly from the good he has found by it – he has felt the dew fall with this manna – and partly because of God's institution. The Lord has appointed this ordinance to save him. The king's image makes the coin current. The stamp of divine authority on the Word preached makes it an instrument conducive to men's salvation.

Use: Let us test by this characteristic whether we are godly: Are we lovers of the Word?

1. Do we love the Word written?   What sums of money the martyrs gave for a few leaves of the Bible! Do we make the Word our bosom friend? As Moses often had 'the rod of God' in his hand, so we should have 'the Book of God' in our hand. When we want direction, do we consult this sacred oracle? When we find corruptions strong, do we make use of this 'sword of the Spirit' to hew them down? When we are disconsolate, do we go to this bottle of the water of life for comfort? Then we are lovers of the Word! But alas, how can they who are seldom conversant with the Scriptures say they love them? Their eyes begin to be sore when they look at a Bible. The two testaments are hung up like rusty armour which is seldom or never made use of. The Lord wrote the law with his own finger, but though God took pains to write, men will not take pains to read. They would rather look at a pair of cards than at a Bible.

2. Do we love the Word preached?   Do we prize it in our judgments? Do we receive it into our hearts? Do we fear the loss of the Word preached more than the loss of peace and trade? Is it the removal of the ark that troubles us?

Again, do we attend to the Word with reverential devotion? When the judge is giving his charge on the bench, all attend. When the Word is preached, the great

[65]

God is giving us his charge. Do we listen to it as to a matter of life and death? This is a good sign that we love the Word.

Again, do we love the holiness of the Word (*Psa. 119:140*)? The Word is preached to beat down sin and advance holiness. Do we love it for its spirituality and purity? Many love the Word preached only for its eloquence and notion. They come to a sermon as to a music lecture (*Ezek. 33:31,32*) or as to a garden to pick flowers, but not to have their lusts subdued or their hearts bettered. These are like a foolish woman who paints her face but neglects her health.

Again, do we love the convictions of the Word? Do we love the Word when it comes home to our conscience and shoots its arrows of reproof at our sins? It is the minister's duty sometimes to reprove. He who can speak smooth words in the pulpit, but does not know how to reprove, is like a sword with a fine hilt without an edge. 'Rebuke them sharply' (*Titus 2:15*). Dip the nail in oil, reprove in love, but strike the nail home. Now Christian, when the Word touches on your sin and says, 'Thou art the man', do you love the reproof? Can you bless God that 'the sword of the Spirit' has divided between you and your lusts? This is indeed a sign of grace and shows that you are a lover of the Word.

A corrupt heart loves the comforts of the Word, but not the reproofs: 'They hate him that rebuketh in the gate' (*Amos 5:10*). 'Their eyes flash with fire!' Like venomous creatures that at the least touch spit poison, 'when they heard these things, they were cut to the heart, and they gnashed on him with their teeth' (*Acts 7:54*). When Stephen touched them to the quick, they were mad and could not endure it.

Question: How shall we know that we love the reproofs of the Word?

Answer 1: When we desire to sit under a heart-searching ministry. Who cares for medicines that will not work? A godly man does not choose to sit under a ministry that will not work upon his conscience.

Answer 2: When we pray that the Word may meet with our sins. If there is any traitorous lust in our heart, we would have it found out and executed. We do not want sin covered, but cured. We can open our breast to the bullet of the Word and say, 'Lord, smite this sin.'

Answer 3: When we are thankful for a reproof: 'Let the righteous smite me; it shall be a kindness: and let him reprove me; it shall be an excellent oil, which shall not break my head' (*Psa. 141:5*). David was glad of a reproof. Suppose a man were in the mouth of a lion, and another should shoot the lion and save the man, would he not be thankful? So, when we are in the mouth of sin, as of a lion, and the minister by a reproof shoots this sin to death, shall we not be thankful? A gracious soul rejoices when the sharp lance of the Word has pierced his abscess. He wears a reproof like a jewel on his ear: 'As an earring of gold, so is a wise reprover upon an obedient ear' (*Prov. 25:12*). To conclude, it is convincing preaching which must do the soul good. A nipping reproof prepares for comfort, as a nipping frost prepares for the sweet flowers of spring.

SECTION 10: A GODLY MAN HAS THE SPIRIT OF GOD RESIDING IN HIM

'The Holy Ghost which dwelleth in us' (*2 Tim. 1:14; Gal. 4:6*). The schoolmen raise the question whether a man receives the Holy Ghost himself or not. Montanus held that the godly so have God's Spirit in them that they partake of his essence, and have become one person with himself. But this amounts to no less than blasphemy. Then it would follow that every saint was to be worshipped.

I conceive that the Spirit is in the godly, in whom he flows in measure. They have his presence and receive his sacred influences. When the sun comes into a room, it is not the body of the sun that is there but the beams that sparkle from it. Indeed, some divines have thought that the godly have more than the influx of the Spirit, though to say how it is more is ineffable, and is fitter for some seraphic pen to describe than mine. The Spirit of God reveals himself in a gracious soul in two ways:

1. By his motions
These are some of that sweet perfume that the Spirit breathes upon the heart, by which it is raised into a kind of angelic frame.

Question 1: But how may we distinguish the motions of the Spirit from a delusion?

Answer: The motions of the Spirit are always consonant with the Word. The Word is the chariot in which the Spirit of God rides; whichever way the tide of the Word runs, that way the wind of the Spirit blows.

Question 2: How may the motions of the Spirit in the godly be distinguished from the impulses of a natural conscience?

Answer 1: A natural conscience may sometimes provoke to the same thing as the Spirit does, but not from the same principle. Natural conscience is a spur to duty, but it drives a man to do his duties for fear of hell – as the galley-slave tugs at the oar for fear of being beaten – whereas the Spirit moves a child of God from a more noble principle. It makes him serve God out of choice, and esteem duty his privilege.

Answer 2: The impulses of a natural conscience drive men only to easier duties of religion, in which the heart is less exercised, like perfunctory reading or praying. But the motions of the Spirit in the godly go further, causing them to do the most irksome duties, like self-reflection, self-humbling; yes, perilous duties, like confessing Christ's name in times of danger. Divine motions in the heart are like new wine which seeks vent. When God's Spirit possesses a man, he carries him full sail through all difficulties.

2. By his virtues
These are various:

(i) God's Spirit has a *teaching* virtue; the Spirit teaches convincingly (*John 16:8*). He so teaches as to persuade.

(ii) God's Spirit has a *sanctifying* virtue. The heart is naturally polluted, but when the Spirit comes into it, he works sin out and grace in. The Spirit of God was represented by the dove, an emblem of purity. The Spirit makes the heart a temple of purity and a paradise for pleasantness. The holy oil of consecration was nothing but a prefiguring of the Spirit (*Exod. 30:25*). The Spirit sanctifies a man's fancy, causing it to mint holy meditations. He sanctifies his will, biasing it to good, so that now it shall be as delightful to serve God as before it was to sin against him. Sweet powders perfume the linen. So God's Spirit in a man perfumes him with holiness and makes his heart a map of heaven.

(iii) God's Spirit has a *vivifying* virtue: 'the Spirit giveth life' (*2 Cor. 3:6*). As the blowing in an organ makes it sound, so the breathing of the Spirit causes life and motion. When the prophet Elijah stretched himself upon the dead child, it revived (*1 Kings 17:22*); so God's Spirit stretching himself upon the soul infuses life into it.

As our life is from the Spirit's operations, so is our liveliness: 'the Spirit lifted me up' (*Ezek. 3:14*). When the heart is bowed down and is listless to duty, the Spirit of God lifts it up. He puts a sharp edge upon the affections; he makes love ardent, hope lively. The Spirit removes the weights of the soul and gives it wings: 'Or ever I was aware, my soul made me like the chariots of Amminadib' (*Song 6:12*). The wheels of the soul were pulled off before and it drove on heavily, but when the Spirit of the Almighty possesses a man, now he runs swiftly in the ways of God and his soul is like the chariots of Amminadib.

(iv) God's Spirit has a *jurisdictive* virtue; he rules and governs. God's Spirit sits paramount in the soul; he gives check to the violence of corruption; he will not allow a man to be vain and loose like others. The Spirit of God will not be put out of office; he exercises his authority over the heart, 'bringing into captivity every thought to the obedience of Christ' (*2 Cor. 10:5*).

(v) The Spirit has a *mollifying* virtue, therefore he is compared to fire which softens the wax. The Spirit turns flint into flesh: 'I will give you an heart of flesh' (*Ezek. 36:26*). How shall this be effected? 'I will put my spirit within you' (*v.27*). While the heart is hard, it lies like a log, and is not wrought upon either by judgments or by mercies, but when God's Spirit comes in, he makes a man's heart as tender as his eye and now it is made yielding to divine impressions.

(vi) The Spirit of God has a *corroborating* virtue; he infuses strength and assistance for work; he is a Spirit of power (*2 Tim. 1:7*). God's Spirit carries a man above himself: 'strengthened with might by his Spirit in the inner man' (*Eph. 3:16*). The Spirit confirms faith and animates courage. He lifts one end of the cross, and makes it lighter to bear. The Spirit gives not only a sufficiency of strength, but a redundance.

Question: How shall we know whether we are acting in the strength of God's Spirit, or in the strength of our own abilities?

Answer 1: When we humbly cast ourselves upon God for assistance, as David going out against Goliath cast himself upon God for help: 'I come to thee in the name of the Lord' (*1 Sam. 17:45*).

Answer 2: When our duties are divinely qualified, we do them with pure aims.

Answer 3: When we have found God going along with us, we give him the glory for everything (*1 Cor. 15:10*). This clearly evinces that the duty was carried on by the strength of God's Spirit more than by any innate abilities of our own.

(vii) God's Spirit has a *comforting* virtue. Sadness may arise in a gracious heart (*Psa. 43:5*). As the heaven, though it is a bright and lucid body, still has interposed clouds, this sadness is caused usually through the malice of Satan, who, if he cannot destroy us, will disturb us. But God's Spirit within us sweetly cheers and revives. He is called the *parakletos*, 'the Comforter' (*John 14:16*). These comforts are real and infallible. Hence it is called 'the seal of the Spirit' (*Eph. 1:13*). When a deed is sealed, it is firm and unquestionable. So when a Christian has the seal of the Spirit, his comforts are confirmed. Every godly man has these revivings of the Spirit in some degree; he has the seeds and beginnings of joy, though the flower is not fully ripe and blown.

Question: How does the Spirit give comfort?

Answer 1: By showing us that we are in a state of grace. A Christian cannot always see his riches. The work of grace may be written in the heart, like shorthand which a Christian cannot read. The Spirit gives him a key to open these dark characters, and spell out his adoption, whereupon he has joy and peace. 'We have received the Spirit which is of God; that we might know the things that are freely given to us of God' (*1 Cor. 2:12*).

Answer 2: The Spirit comforts by giving us some ravishing apprehensions of God's love: 'the love of God is shed abroad in our hearts by the Holy Ghost' (*Rom. 5:5*). God's love is a box of precious ointment, and it is only the Spirit who can break this box open, and fill us with its sweet perfume.

Answer 3: The Spirit comforts by taking us to the blood of Christ. As when a man is weary and ready to faint, we take him to the water, and he is refreshed, so when we are fainting under the burden of sin, the Spirit takes us to the fountain of Christ's blood: 'In that day there shall be a fountain opened . . . ' (*Zech. 13:1*). The Spirit enables us to drink the waters of justification which run out of Christ's sides. The Spirit applies whatever Christ has purchased; he shows us that our sins are done away in Christ, and though we are spotted in ourselves, we are undefiled in our Head.

Answer 4: The Spirit comforts by enabling conscience to comfort. The child must be taught before it can speak. The Spirit opens the mouth of conscience, and helps it to speak and witness to a man that his state is good, whereupon he begins to receive comfort: 'conscience also bearing me witness in the Holy Ghost' (*Rom. 9:1*). Conscience draws up a certificate for a man, then the Holy Ghost comes and signs the certificate.

Answer 5: The Spirit conveys the oil of joy through two golden pipes:

1. The Ordinances. As Christ in prayer had his countenance changed (*Luke 9:29*) and there was a glorious lustre upon his face, so often in the use of holy ordinances the godly have such raptures of joy and soul transfigurations that they have been carried above the world, and despised all things below.

2. *The Promises.*   The promises are comforting: (i) For their sureness (*Rom. 4:16*). God in the promises has put his truth in pawn. (ii) For their suitableness, being calculated for every Christian's condition. The promises are like a herb garden. There is no disease but some herb may be found there to cure it. But the promises of themselves cannot comfort. Only the Spirit enables us to suck these honeycombs. The promises are like a still full of herbs, but this still will not drop unless the fire is put under it. So when the Spirit of God (who is compared to fire) is put to the still of the promises, then they distil consolation into the soul. Thus we see how the Spirit is in the godly by his virtues.

Objection: But is being filled with the Spirit the sign of a godly man? Are not the wicked said to partake of the Holy Ghost (*Heb. 6:4*)?

Answer: Wicked men may partake of the Spirit's working, but not of his indwelling. They may have God's Spirit move upon them; the godly have him enter into them (*Ezek. 3:24*).

Objection: But the unregenerate taste the heavenly gift (*Heb. 6:4*).

Answer: It is with them as it is with cooks who may have a smack and taste of the meat they are dressing, but they are not nourished by it. Tasting there is opposed to eating. The godly have not only a drop or taste of the Spirit, but he is in them like a river of living water (*John 7:38*).

Use 1: It brands those as ungodly who have none of God's Spirit: 'if any man have not the Spirit of Christ, he is none of his' (*Rom. 8:9*). And if he is none of Christ's, then whose is he? To what regiment does he belong? It is the misery of a sinner that he has none of God's Spirit. I think it is very offensive to hear men who never had God's Spirit say, 'Take not thy holy spirit from us' (*Psa. 51:11*). Will those who are drunkards and swearers say they have God's Spirit in them? Do those who are malicious and unclean have God's Spirit? It would be blasphemy to say these have the Spirit. Will the blessed Spirit leave his celestial palace to come and live in a prison? A sinner's heart is a gaol, both for darkness and obnoxiousness, and will God's free Spirit be confined to a prison (*Psa. 51:12*)? A sinner's heart is the emblem of hell. What should God's Spirit do there? Wicked hearts are not a temple, but a pigsty, where the unclean spirit makes his abode – 'the prince of the power of the air, the spirit that now worketh in the children of disobedience' (*Eph. 2:2*). We would be loath to live in a house haunted by evil spirits; a sinner's heart is haunted. 'After the sop Satan entered' (*John 13:27*). Satan abuses the godly, but enters into the wicked. When the devils went into the herd of swine, they ran violently down a steep place into the sea (*Matt. 8:32*). Why is it that men run so greedily to the commission of sin, but because the devil has entered into these swine?

Secondly, this cuts off from godliness those who not only lack the Spirit, but deride him – like those Jews who said, 'These men are full of new wine' (*Acts 2:13*). And indeed, so the apostles were – they were full of the wine of the Spirit. How God's Spirit is scoffed at by the sons of Belial! These (say they) are 'men of the Spirit.' O wretches, to make those tongues which should be organs of God's praise instruments to blaspheme! Have you none to throw your squibs at but the Spirit? Deriding the Spirit comes very near to despising him. How can men be sanctified but by the Spirit? Therefore to reproach him is to make merry with their own damnation.

Use 2: As you would be listed in the number of the godly, strive for the blessed indwelling of the Spirit. Pray with Melanchthon, 'Lord, inflame my soul with thy Holy Spirit'; and with the spouse, 'Awake, O north wind; and come, thou south; blow upon my garden' (*Song 4:16*). As a mariner would desire a wind to drive him to sea, so beg for the prosperous gales of the Spirit and the promise may add wings to prayer. 'If ye then, being evil, know how to give good gifts unto your children: how much more shall your heavenly Father give the Holy Spirit to them that ask him?' (*Luke 11:13*). God's Spirit is a rich jewel. Go to God for him: 'Lord, give me thy Spirit. Where is the jewel you promised me? When shall my soul be like Gideon's fleece, wet with the dew of heaven?'

Consider how necessary the Spirit is. Without him we can do nothing acceptable to God:

1. We cannot pray without him. He is a Spirit of supplications (*Zech. 12:10*). He helps both the inventiveness and the affection: 'The Spirit helps us with sighs and groans' (*Rom. 8:26*).

2. We cannot resist temptation without him: 'ye shall receive power, after that the Holy Ghost is come upon you' (*Acts 1:8*). He who has the tide of corrupt nature and the wind of temptation must of necessity be carried down the stream of sin if the contrary wind of the Spirit does not blow.

3. We cannot be fruitful without the Spirit. 'The golden rain from heaven waters the thirsty hearts.' Why is the Spirit compared to dew and rain, but to show us how unable we are to bring forth a crop of grace unless the dew of God falls upon us?

4. Without the Spirit, no ordinance is effectual to us. Ordinances are the conduit pipes of grace, but the Spirit is the spring. Some are content that they have a 'Levite to their priest' (*Judges 17:13*), but never look any further. As if a merchant should be content that his ship has good tackling and is well manned, though it never has a gale of wind. The ship of ordinances will not carry us to heaven, though an angel is the pilot, unless the wind of God's Spirit blows. The Spirit is the soul of the Word without which it is but a dead letter. Ministers may prescribe medicine, but it is God's Spirit who must make it work. Our hearts are like David's body when it grew old: 'they covered him with clothes, but he gat no heat' (*1 Kings 1:1*). So though the ministers of God ply us with prayers and counsel as with hot clothes, yet we are cold and chilly till God's Spirit comes; and then we say, like the disciples, 'Did not our heart burn within us?' (Luke 24:32). Oh, therefore, what need we have of the Spirit!

Thirdly, you who have the blessed Spirit manifested by his energy and vital operations:

1. Acknowledge God's distinguishing love. The Spirit is an earmark of election (*1 John 3:24*). Christ gave the bag to Judas but not his Spirit. The Spirit is a love token. Where God gives his Spirit as a pawn, he gives himself as a portion. The Spirit is a comprehensive blessing; he is put for all good things (*Matt. 7:11*). What would you be without the Spirit but like so many carcasses? Without this, Christ would not profit you. The blood of God is not enough without the breath of God. Oh then, be thankful for the Spirit. This lodestone will never stop drawing you till it has drawn you up to heaven.

2. If you have this Spirit, do not grieve him (*Eph. 4:30*). Shall we grieve our Comforter?

Question: How do we grieve the Spirit?

Answer 1: When we unkindly repel his motions. The Spirit sometimes whispers in our ears and calls to us as God did to Jacob, 'Arise, go up to Bethel' (*Gen. 35:1*). So the Spirit says, 'Arise, go to prayer, retire to meet your God.' Now when we stifle these motions and entertain temptations to vanity, this is grieving the Spirit. If we check the motions of the Spirit, we shall lose the comforts of the Spirit.

Answer 2: We grieve the Spirit when we deny the work of the Spirit in our hearts. If someone gives another person a token and he should deny it and say he never received it, this would be to abuse the love of his friend. So, Christian, when God has given you his Spirit, witnessed by those meltings of heart and passionate desires for heaven, yet you deny that you ever had any renewing work of the Spirit in you, this is base ingratitude and grieves the good Spirit. Renounce the sinful works of the flesh, but do not deny the gracious work of the Spirit.

SECTION 11: A GODLY MAN IS A HUMBLE MAN

He is like the sun in the zenith, which when it is at the highest, shows lowest. St Augustine calls humility the mother of the grace. But before I show you who the humble man is, I shall lay down three distinctions:

1. I distinguish between being humbled and humble
A man may be humbled and not humble. A sinner may be humbled by affliction. His condition is low but not his disposition. A godly man is not only humbled but humble. His heart is as low as his condition.

2. I distinguish between outward and inward humility
There is a great deal of difference between humble behaviour and a humble spirit.

(i) A person may behave humbly towards others, yet be proud. Who more humble than Absalom in his outward behaviour? 'When any man came near to do him obeisance, Absalom took him by the hand and kissed him' (*2 Sam. 15:5*). But though he acted humbly, he aspired to the crown: 'As soon as ye hear the sound of the trumpet, then ye shall say, Absalom reigneth in Hebron' (v.10). Here was pride dressed in humility's mantle.

(ii) A person may behave humbly towards God yet be proud. 'Ahab put on sackcloth and fasted and went softly' (*1 Kings 21:27*), but his heart was not humble. A man may bow his head like a bullrush, yet lift up the ensigns of pride in his heart.

3. *I distinguish between humility and policy*

Many make a show of humility to achieve their own ends. The Papists seem to be the most humble, mortified saints but it is rather subtlety than humility. For by this means, they get the revenues of the earth into their possession. All this they may do and yet have no godliness.

Question: How may a Christian know that he is humble and consequently godly?

Answer 1: A humble soul is emptied of all swelling thoughts of himself. Bernard calls humility a self-annihilation. 'Thou wilt save the humble' (*Job 22:29*). In the Hebrew it is 'him that is of low eyes'. A humble man has lower thoughts of himself than others can have of him. David, though a king, still looked upon himself as a worm: 'I am a worm, and no man' (*Psa. 22:6*). Bradford, a martyr, still subscribes himself a sinner. 'If I be righteous, yet will I not lift up my head' (*Job 10:15*) – like the violet which is a sweet flower, but hangs down the head.

Answer 2: A humble soul thinks better of others than of

himself: 'let each esteem other better than themselves' (*Phil. 2:3*). A humble man values others at a higher rate than himself, and the reason is because he can see his own heart better than he can another's. He sees his own corruption and thinks surely it is not so with others; their graces are not so weak as his; their corruptions are not so strong. 'Surely', he thinks, 'they have better hearts than I.' A humble Christian studies his own infirmities and another's excellences and that makes him put a higher value upon others than himself. 'Surely I am more brutish than any man' (*Prov. 30:2*). And Paul, though he was the chief of the apostles, still calls himself 'less than the least of all saints' (*Eph. 3:8*).

Answer 3: A humble soul has a low esteem of his duties. Pride is apt to breed in our holy things as the worm breeds in the sweetest fruit and froth comes from the most generous wine. A humble person bemoans not only his sins but also his duties. When he has prayed and wept, 'Alas,' he says, 'how little I have done! God might damn me for all this.' He says, like good Nehemiah, 'Remember me, O my God, concerning this also, and spare me' (*Neh. 13:22*). 'Remember, Lord, how I have poured out my soul, but spare me and pardon me.' He sees that his best duties weigh many grains too light; therefore he desires that Christ's merits may be put into the scales. The humble saint blushes when he looks at his copy. He sees he cannot write evenly, nor without blotting. This humbles him to think that his best duties run to seed. He drops poison upon his sacrifice. 'Oh,' he says, 'I dare not say I have prayed or wept; those which I write down as duties, God might write down as sins.'

Answer 4: A humble man is always preferring bills of indictment against himself. He complains, not of his condition, but of his heart. 'Oh, this evil heart of unbelief!'

'Lord,' says Hooper, 'I am hell, but thou art heaven.' A hypocrite is for ever telling how good he is. A humble soul is for ever saying how bad he is. Paul, that highflown saint, was caught up into the third heaven, but how this bird of paradise bemoans his corruptions! 'O wretched man that I am! . . . ' (*Rom. 7:24*). Holy Bradford subscribes himself, 'the hardhearted sinner'. The more knowledge a humble Christian has, the more he complains of ignorance; the more faith, the more he bewails his unbelief.

Answer 5: A humble man will justify God in an afflicted condition: 'Howbeit thou art just in all that is brought upon us' (*Neh. 9:33*). If men oppress and calumniate, the humble soul acknowledges God's righteousness in the midst of severity: 'Lo, I have sinned' (*2 Sam. 24:17*). 'Lord, my pride, my barrenness, my sermon surfeiting have been the procuring cause of all these judgments.' When clouds are round about God, yet 'righteousness is the habitation of his throne' (*Psa. 97:2*).

Answer 6: A humble soul is a Christ-magnifier (*Phil. 1:20*). He gives the glory of all his actions to Christ and free grace. King Canute took the crown off his own head and set it upon a crucifix. So a humble saint takes the crown of honour from his own head and sets it upon Christ's. And the reason is the love that he bears to Christ. Love can part with anything to the object loved. Isaac loved Rebekah and he gave away his jewels to her (*Gen. 24:53*). The humble saint loves Christ entirely, therefore can part with anything to him. He gives away to Christ the honour and praise of all he does. Let Christ wear those jewels.

Answer 7: A humble soul is willing to take a reproof for sin. A wicked man is too high to stoop to a reproof. The prophet Micaiah used to tell King Ahab of his sin, and the

King said, 'I hate him' (*1 Kings 22:8*). Reproof to a proud man is like pouring water on lime, which grows the hotter. A gracious soul loves the one who reproves: 'rebuke a wise man, and he will love thee' (*Prov. 9:8*). The humble-spirited Christian can bear the reproach of an enemy and the reproof of a friend.

Answer 8: A humble man is willing to have his name and gifts eclipsed, so that God's glory may be increased. He is content to be outshone by others in gifts and esteem, so that the crown of Christ may shine the brighter. This is the humble man's motto: 'Let me decrease; let Christ increase.' It is his desire that Christ should be exalted, and if this is effected, whoever is the instrument, he rejoices. 'Some preach Christ of envy' (*Phil. 1:15*). They preached to take away some of Paul's hearers. 'Well,' says he, 'Christ is preached; and I therein do rejoice' (*v.18*). A humble Christian is content to be laid aside if God has any other tools to work with which may bring him more glory.

Answer 9: A humble saint likes that condition which God sees best for him. A proud man complains that he has no more; a humble man wonders that he has so much: 'I am not worthy of the least of all thy mercies' (*Gen. 32:10*). When the heart lies low, it can stoop to a low condition. A Christian looking at his sins wonders that it is no worse with him; he does not say his mercies are small, but his sins are great. He knows that the worst piece God carves him is better than he deserves; therefore he takes it thankfully upon his knees.

Answer 10: A humble Christian will stoop to the meanest person and the lowest office; he will visit the poorest member of Christ. Lazarus' sores are more precious to him than Dives' purple. He does not say, 'Stand by, come not near to me, for I am holier than thou' (*Isa. 65:5*), but 'condescends to men of low estate' (*Rom. 12:16*).

Use 1: If humility is the inseparable character of a godly man, let us test our hearts by this touchstone. Are we humble? Alas, where does their godliness appear who are swollen with pride and ready to burst? But though men are proud, they will not confess it. This bastard of pride is born but none are willing to father it. Therefore let me ask a few questions and let conscience answer:

1. Are not those who are given to boasting proud? 'Your glorying is not good' (*1 Cor. 5:6*). (i) Those who glory in their riches; their hearts swell with their estates. St Bernard calls pride the rich man's cousin. 'Thine heart is lifted up because of thy riches' (*Ezek. 28:5*). (ii) Those who glory in their apparel. Many dress themselves in such fashions as to make the devil fall in love with them. Black spots, gaudy attire, naked breasts, what are these but the flags and banners which pride displays? (iii) Those who glory in their beauty. The body is but dust and blood kneaded together. Solomon says, 'Beauty is vain' (*Prov. 31:30*). Yet some are so vain as to be proud of vanity. (iv) Those who glory in their gifts. These trappings and ornaments do not set them off in God's eyes. An angel is a knowledgeable creature, but take away humility from an angel, and he is a devil.

2. Are not those who have a high opinion of their own excellences proud? Those who look at themselves in the magnifying mirror of self-love appear in their own eyes better than they are. Simon Magus gave out that he was some great one (*Acts 8:9*). Alexander felt the need to be the son of Jupiter and of the race of the gods. Sapor, King of Persia, styles himself 'Brother of the Sun and Moon'. 'He tosses aside his paintpots and his words one-and-a-half feet long' (*Horace*). I have read of a pope who trod upon the neck of Frederick the Emperor and as a cloak for his pride cited that text, 'Thou shalt tread upon the lion, and the dragon shalt thou trample under feet' (*Psa. 91:13*). There is no idol like self; the proud man bows down to this idol.

3. *Are not those who despise others proud?* 'The Pharisees trusted in themselves that they were righteous, and despised others' (*Luke 18:9*). The Chinese people say that Europe has one eye and they have two, and all the rest of the world is blind. A proud man looks upon others with such an eye of scorn as Goliath did upon David: 'when the Philistine looked about, and saw David, he disdained him' (*1 Sam. 17:42*). They who stand upon the pinnacle of pride look upon other men as no bigger than crows.

4. *Are not those who trumpet their own praise proud?* 'Before these days rose up Theudas, boasting himself to be somebody' (*Acts 5:36*). A proud man is the herald of his own good deeds; he blazes his own fame, and therein lies his vice, to paint his own virtue.

5. *Are not those who take the glory due to God to themselves proud?* 'Is not this great Babylon, that I have built?' (*Dan. 4:30*). So says the proud man, 'Are not these the prayers I have made? Are not these the works of charity I have done?' When Herod had made an oration and the people cried him up for a god (*Acts 12:22*), he was well content to have that honour done to him. Pride is the greatest sacrilege; it robs God of his glory.

6. *Are not those who are never pleased with their condition proud?* They speak harshly of God, taxing his care and wisdom, as if he had not dealt well with them. A proud man

[83]

God himself cannot please but, like Momus, he is for ever finding fault, and flying in the face of heaven.

Oh, let us search if there is none of this leaven of pride in us. Man is naturally a proud piece of flesh; this sin runs in the blood. Our first parents fell by their pride. They aspired to deity. There are the seeds of this in the best, but the godly do not allow themselves in it. They strive to kill this weed by mortification. But certainly where this sin reigns and prevails, it cannot stand with grace. You may as well call him who lacks discretion a prudent man, as him who lacks humility a godly man.

Use 2: Strive for this characteristic: be humble. It is an apostolic exhortation, 'be clothed with humility' (*1 Pet. 5:5*). Put it on as an embroidered robe. It is better to lack anything rather than humility. It is better to lack gifts rather than humility. No, it is better to lack 'the comforts of the Spirit' rather than lack humility. 'What doth the Lord require of thee, but to walk humbly with thy God?' (*Mic. 6:8*).

1. The more value any man has, the more humble he is. Feathers fly up, but gold descends. The golden saint descends in humility. Some of the ancients have compared humility to the Celidonian stone, which is little for substance, but of rare virtue.

2. God loves a humble soul. It is not our high birth, but our low hearts that God delights in. A humble spirit is in God's view: 'to this man will I look, even to him that is poor and of a contrite spirit' (*Isa. 66:2*). A humble heart is God's palace: 'I dwell in the high and holy place, with him also that is of a contrite and humble spirit' (*Isa. 57:15*). Great personages, besides their houses of state, have lesser houses which upon occasion they retreat to. Besides God's house of state in heaven, he has the humble soul for his retiring house, where he takes up his rest, and solaces himself. Let Italy boast that it is, for pleasure, the garden of the world. A humble heart glories in this, that it is the presence chamber of the great King.

3. The times we live in are humbling. The Lord seems to say to us now, as he did to Israel, 'Put off thy ornaments from thee, that I may know what to do unto thee' (*Exod. 33:5*). 'My displeasure is breaking forth, I have eclipsed the light of the sanctuary, I have stained the waters with blood, I have shot the arrow of pestilence, therefore lay down your pride, put off your ornaments.' Woe to them that lift themselves up, when God is casting them down. When should people be humble if not under the rod? 'Humble yourselves under the mighty hand of God' (*1 Pet. 5:6*). When God afflicts his people, and cuts them short in their privileges, it is time then to 'sow sackcloth on their skin and defile their horn (or honour) in the dust' (*Job 16:15*).

4. What a horrid sin pride is! St Chrysostom calls it 'the mother of hell'. Pride is a complicated evil, as Aristotle said. Justice comprehends all virtue in itself; so pride comprehends all vice. It is a spiritual drunkenness; it flies up like wine into the brain and intoxicates it. It is idolatry; a proud man is a self-worshipper. It is revenge; Haman plotted Mordecai's death because he would not bow the knee.

How odious this sin is to God (*1 Pet. 5:5*)! 'Every one that is proud in heart is an abomination to the Lord' (*Prov. 16:5*).

5. The mischief of pride. It is the breakneck of souls: 'Surely Moab shall be as Sodom . . . This shall they have for their pride' (*Zeph. 2:9,10*). 'The doves', says Pliny, 'take a pride in their feathers, and in their flying high; at last they fly so high that they are a prey to the hawk.' Men fly so high in pride that at last they are a prey to the devil, the prince of the air.

6. *Humility raises one's esteem in the eyes of others.* All give respect to the humble: 'Before honour is humility' (*Prov. 15:33*).

Question: What means may we use to be humble?

Answer 1: Let us set before us the golden pattern of Christ. He commenced doctor in humility: 'But made himself of no reputation, and was made in the likeness of men' (*Phil. 2:7*). O what abasement it was for the Son of God to take our flesh! No, that Christ should take our nature when it was in disgrace, being stained with sin – this was the wonder of humility. Look at a humble Saviour, and let the plumes of pride fall.

Answer 2: Study God's immensity and purity; a sight of glory humbles. Elijah wrapped his face in a mantle when God's glory passed before him (*1 Kings 19:13*). The stars vanish when the sun appears.

Answer 3: Let us study ourselves. First, our dark side. By looking at our faces in the mirror of the Word, we see our spots. What a world of sin swarms in us! We may say with Bernard, 'Lord, I am nothing but sin or sterility, either sinfulness or barrenness.'
Secondly, our light side. Is there any good in us?

1. *How disproportionate it is to the means of grace we have enjoyed!* There is still something lacking in our faith (*1 Thess.3:10*). O Christian, do not be proud of what you have, but be humble for what you lack.

2. The grace we have is not of our own growth. We are beholden to Christ and free grace for it. As he said of that axe which fell in the water, 'Alas, master, for it was borrowed' (*2 Kings 6:5*), so I may say of all the good and excellence in us, 'It is borrowed'. Would it not be folly to be proud of a ring that is loaned? 'For who maketh thee to differ from another? And what hast thou that thou didst not receive?' (*1 Cor. 4:7*). The moon has no cause to be proud of her light when she borrows it from the sun.

3. How far short we come of others! Perhaps other Christians are giants in grace; they are in Christ not only before us, but above us. We are but like the foot in Christ's body; they are like the eye.

4. Our beauty is spotted. The church is said to be 'fair as the moon' (*Song 6:10*), which when it shines brightest has a dark spot in it. Faith is mixed with infidelity. A Christian has that in his very grace which may humble him.

5. If we would be humble, let us contemplate our mortality Shall dust exalt itself? The thoughts of the grave should bury our pride. They say that when there is a swelling in the body, the hand of a dead man stroking that part cures the swelling. The serious meditation of death is enough to cure the swelling of pride.

SECTION 12: A GODLY MAN IS A PRAYING MAN

This is in the text, 'Everyone that is godly shall pray unto thee'. As soon as grace is poured in, prayer is poured out: 'but I give myself unto prayer' (*Psa. 109:4*). In the Hebrew it is, 'but I prayer'. Prayer and I are all one. Prayer is the soul's traffic with heaven. God comes down to us by his Spirit, and we go up to him by prayer. Caligula placed his images in the Capitol whispering in Jupiter's ear; prayer whispers in God's ear. A godly man cannot live without prayer. A man cannot live unless he takes his breath, nor can the soul, unless it breathes forth its desires to God. As soon as the babe of grace is born, it cries; no sooner was Paul converted than 'behold, he prayeth' (*Acts 9:11*). No doubt he prayed before, being a Pharisee, but it was either superficially or superstitiously. But when the work of grace had been done in his soul, behold, now he prays. A godly man is on the mount of prayer every day; he begins the day with prayer; before he opens his shop, he opens his heart to God. We burn sweet perfumes in our houses; a godly man's house is 'a house of perfume'; he airs it with the incense of prayer; he engages in no business without seeking God. Scipio never entered the Senate House without first ascending the Capitol, where he did his devotions. A godly man consults God in everything; he asks his leave and his blessing. The Greeks asked counsel at their oracles; so a godly man enquires at the divine oracle (*Gen. 24:12; 1 Sam. 23:3,4*). A true saint continually shoots up his heart to heaven by sacred ejaculations.

Question: Is prayer a sign of a godly man? May not a hypocrite pray eloquently and with seeming devotion?

Answer: He may: 'they seek me daily' (*Isa. 58:2*). But a hypocrite does not pray 'in the Spirit' (*Eph. 6:18*). A man may have the gift of prayer, and not have the spirit of prayer.

Question: How shall we know that we have the spirit of prayer?

Answer: When the prayer which we make is spiritual.

Question: What is it to make a spiritual prayer?

Answer 1: When we pray with knowledge. Under the law, Aaron was to 'light the lamps' when he burned the incense on the altar (*Exod. 30:7*). Incense typified prayer, and the lighting of the lamps typified knowledge. When the incense of prayer burns, the lamp of knowledge must be lit: 'I will pray with the understanding' (*1 Cor. 14:15*). We must know the majesty and holiness of God, so that we may be deeply affected with reverence when we come before him. We must put up such petitions as are exactly adequate and agreeable to God's will. 'Be not rash with thy mouth, to utter any thing before God' (*Eccles. 5:2*). The Lord would not have the blind offered to him (*Mal. 1:8*). How can we pray with affection when we do not pray with judgment? The Papists pray in an unknown tongue. Christ may reply to them as he did to the mother of Zebedee's children, 'Ye know not what ye ask' (*Matt. 20:22*). He that prays he knows not how, shall be heard he knows not when.

Answer 2: A spiritual prayer is when the heart and spirit pray; there are not only words but desires. It is excellent when a man can say, 'Lord, my heart prays.' Hannah 'prayed in her heart' (*1 Sam. 1:13*). The sound of a trumpet comes from within and the excellent music of prayer comes from within the heart. If the heart does not accompany duty, it is speaking, not praying.

Answer 3: A spiritual prayer is a fervent prayer: 'The effectual fervent prayer . . . availeth much' (*Jas. 5:16*). The heart, like the mainspring, should carry the affections in a most zealous and rapid manner; fervency is the wing of prayer by which it ascends to heaven. Prayer is expressed by sighs and groans (*Rom. 8:26*). It is not so much the gifts of the Spirit as the groans of the Spirit which God likes. Prayer is called a 'wrestling' (*Gen. 32:24*) and a 'pouring out of the soul' (*1 Sam. 1:15*). Prayer is compared to incense (*Psa. 141:2*). Incense without fire makes no sweet smell.

Prayer without fervency is like incense without fire. Christ prayed with 'strong crying and tears' (*Heb. 5:7*); crying prayer prevails. When the heart is inflamed in prayer, a Christian is carried as it were in a fiery chariot up to heaven.

Answer 4: A spiritual prayer is such as comes from a broken heart: 'The sacrifices of God are a broken spirit' (*Psa. 51:17*). The incense was to be beaten to typify the breaking of the heart in prayer. It is not the voluble tongue but the melting heart which God accepts. 'Oh,' says a Christian, 'I cannot pray like others.' As Moses said to the Lord, 'I am not eloquent'. But can you weep and sigh? Does your soul melt out at your eyes? God accepts broken expressions when they come from broken hearts. I have read of a plant that bears no fruit, but it weeps forth a kind of gum which is very costly. So, though you do not flourish with those gifts and expressions like others, yet if you can weep forth tears from a contrite heart, these are exceedingly precious to God, and he will put them in his bottle. Jacob wept in prayer and had 'power over the angel' (*Hos. 12:4*).

Answer 5: A spiritual prayer is a believing prayer: 'whatever ye shall ask in prayer, believing, ye shall receive' (*Matt. 21: 22*). The reason why so many prayers suffer shipwreck is because they split against the rock of unbelief. Praying without faith is shooting without bullets. When faith takes prayer by the hand, then we draw near to God. We should come to God in prayer like the leper: 'Lord, if thou wilt, thou canst make me clean' (*Matt. 8:2*). It is a disparagement to deity to have such a whisper in the heart, that 'God's ear is heavy and cannot hear' (*Isa. 59:1*). What is said of the people of Israel may be applied to prayer – 'They could not enter in because of unbelief' (*Heb. 3:19*).

Answer 6: A spiritual prayer is a holy prayer: 'Wherefore lift up pure hands' (*1 Tim. 2:8*). Prayer must be offered on the altar of a pure heart. Sin lived in makes the heart hard and God's ear deaf. Sin stops the mouth of prayer. It does what the thief does to the traveller – puts a gag in his mouth so that he cannot speak. Sin poisons and infests prayer. A wicked man's prayer is sick of the plague, and will God come near him? The lodestone loses its virtue when it is spread with garlic; so does prayer when it is polluted with sin. 'If I regard iniquity in my heart, the Lord will not hear me' (*Psa. 66:18*). It is foolish to pray against sin and then to sin against prayer. A spiritual prayer, like the spirits of wine, must be refined and taken off the lees and dregs of sin: 'that they may offer unto the Lord an offering in righteousness' (*Mal. 3:3*). If the heart is holy, this altar will sanctify the gift.

Answer 7: A spiritual prayer is a humble prayer: 'Lord, thou hast heard the desire of the humble' (*Psa. 10:17*). Prayer is the asking of an alms, which requires humility: 'the publican, standing afar off, would not lift up so much as his eyes unto heaven, but smote upon his breast, saying, God be merciful to me a sinner' (*Luke 18:13*). God's incomprehensible glory may even amaze us and strike a holy consternation into us when we approach near to him: 'O my God, I blush to lift up my face to thee' (*Ezra 9:6*). It is comely to see a poor nothing lie prostrate at the feet of its Maker. 'Behold now, I have taken upon me to speak unto the Lord, which am but dust and ashes' (*Gen. 18:27*). The lower the heart descends, the higher the prayer ascends.

Answer 8: A spiritual prayer is when we pray in the name of Christ. To pray in the name of Christ is not only to name Christ in prayer, but to pray in the hope and confidence of Christ's mediation. As a child claims his estate in the right of his father who purchased it, so we come for mercy in the name of Christ, who has purchased it for us in his blood. Unless we pray thus, we do not pray at all; no, we rather provoke God. As it was with Uzziah, when he wanted to offer incense without a priest, God was angry and struck him with leprosy (*2 Chron. 26:16–19*). So when we do not come in Christ's name in prayer, we offer up incense without a priest, and what can we expect but to meet with wrath?

Answer 9: A spiritual prayer is when we pray out of love to prayer. A wicked man may pray, but he does not love prayer. 'Will he delight himself in the Almighty?' (*Job 27:10*). A godly man is carried on the wings of delight. He is never so well as when he is praying. He is not forced with fear but fired with love. 'I will make them joyful in my house of prayer' (*Isa. 56:7*).

Answer 10: A spiritual prayer is when we have spiritual goals in prayer. There is a vast difference between a spiritual prayer and a carnal desire. The goals of a hypocrite are secular and carnal. He looks asquint in prayer. It is not the sense of his spiritual needs that moves him but rather lust. 'Ye ask amiss, that ye may consume it upon your lusts' (*Jas. 4:3*). The sinner prays more for food than for grace. This, God does not interpret as praying but as howling: 'They howled upon their beds; they assemble for corn and wine' (*Hos. 7:14*). 'Give me only riches' (*Ovid*).

Prayers which lack a good aim lack a good answer. A godly man has spiritual goals in prayer. He sends out his prayer as a merchant sends out his ship, so that he may have large returns of spiritual blessings. His design in prayer is that his heart may be more holy and that he may have more communion with God. A godly man engages in the trade of prayer so that he may increase the stock of grace.

Answer 11: A spiritual prayer is accompanied with the use of means. There must be works as well as prayer. When Hezekiah was sick he did not only pray for recovery, but he laid 'a lump of figs to the boil' (*Isa. 38:21*). Thus it is in the case of the soul when we pray against sin and avoid temptations. When we pray for grace and use opportunities to the full, this is laying a fig on the boil which will make us recover. To pray for holiness and neglect the means is like winding up the clock and taking off the weights.

Answer 12: A spiritual prayer is that which leaves a spiritual mood behind upon the heart. A Christian is better after prayer. He has gained more strength over sin, as a man by exercise gets strength. The heart after prayer keeps a tincture of holiness, as the vessel favours and relishes the wine that is put into it. Having been with God on the mount, Moses' face shone. So, having been on the mount of prayer, our graces shine and our lives shine. This is the sign of a godly man – he prays in the Spirit. This is the right kind of praying. The gift of prayer is ordinary, like culinary fire. But spiritual prayer is more rare and excellent, like elemental fire which comes from heaven.

Use 1: Is a godly man of a praying spirit? Then this excludes from being godly:

1. Those who do not pray at all. Their houses are un-hallowed houses. It is made the note of a reprobate that 'he calls not upon God' (*Psa. 14:4*). Does that poor creature who never asks for alms think that he will get any? Do those who never seek mercy from God think that they will receive it? Truly, then God should befriend them more than he did his own Son. 'He offered up prayers and supplications with strong cries' (*Heb. 5:7*). None of God's children are tongue-tied. 'Because ye are sons, God hath sent forth the Spirit of his Son into your hearts, crying, Abba, Father' (*Gal. 4:6*). Creatures by the instinct of nature cry to God: 'the young ravens which cry' (*Psa. 147:9*). 'The lions seek their meat from God' (*Psa. 104:21*). Not to cry to God is worse than brutish.

2. *Others pray, but it is seldom* – like that profane atheist of whom Heylin speaks, who told God that he was no common beggar; he had never troubled him before and if he would hear him now, he would never trouble him again.

3. *Others pray, but not 'in the Holy Ghost'* (*Jude 20*). They are more like parrots than weeping doves. Their hearts do not melt in prayer: they exercise their inventiveness more than their affection.

Use 2: As you would prove the new birth, cry 'Abba, Father'; be men of prayer. Pray at least twice a day. In the temple there was the morning and evening sacrifice. Daniel prayed three times a day. No, he so loved prayer that he would not neglect prayer to save his life (*Dan. 6:10*). Luther spent three hours every day in prayer.

Objection: But what need is there of prayer, when God has made so many promises of blessings?

Answer: Prayer is the condition annexed to the promise. Promises turn upon the hinge of prayer: 'I will yet for this be inquired of by the house of Israel' (*Ezek. 36:37*). A king promises a pardon, but it must be sued for. David had a promise that God would build him a house, but he sues for the promise by prayer (*2 Sam. 7:25*). Christ himself had all the promises made sure to him, yet he prayed and spent whole nights in prayer.

Therefore if you would be counted godly, be given to prayer. Prayer sanctifies your mercies (*1 Tim. 4:5*). Prayer weeds out sin and waters grace.

That I may encourage Christians and hold up their heads in prayer, as Aaron and Hur held up Moses' hands (*Exod. 17:12*), let me propound these few considerations:

1. Prayer is a seed sown in God's ear. Other seed sown in the ground may be picked up by the birds, but this seed (especially if watered with tears) is too precious to lose.

2. Consider the power of prayer. The apostle, having set out the whole armour of a Christian, brings in prayer as the chief part (*Eph. 6:18*). Without this (says Zanchius), all the rest are of little value. By prayer, Moses divided the Red Sea. Joshua stopped the course of the sun and made it stand still (*Josh. 10: 13*). No, prayer made the Sun of righteousness stand still: 'and Jesus stood still' (*Luke 18:40*). Prayer is the entrance to all blessings, spiritual and temporal. When Aurelius Antonius went against the Germans, he had in his army a regiment of Christians, who upon their earnest prayer obtained rain for the refreshment of his army and because of the power of their prayers, he called them 'the thundering regiment'. Prayer has a power in it to destroy the insolent enemies of the church. We read that 'the two witnesses' have a flame on their lips – fire proceeds out of their mouths which devours their enemies (*Rev. 11:3,5*). This fire is certainly to be interpreted of their prayers. David prayed, 'Lord, turn the counsel of Ahithophel into foolishness' (*2 Sam. 15:31*). This prayer made Ahithophel hang himself. Moses' prayer against Amalek did more than Joshua's sword. Prayer has a kind of omnipotency in it; it has raised the dead, overcome angels, cast out devils. It has influence upon God himself (*Exod. 32:10*). Jacob's prayer held God: 'I will not let thee go, except thou bless me' (*Gen. 32:26*). Prayer finds God free, but leaves him bound.

[95]

3. Jesus Christ prays over our prayers again. He takes the dross out and presents nothing but pure gold to his Father. Christ mingles his sweet odours with the prayers of the saints (*Rev. 5:8*). Think of the dignity of his person – he is God; and the sweetness of his relationship – he is a Son. Oh then, what encouragement there is here for us to pray! Our prayers are put in the hands of a Mediator. Though, as they come from us, they are weak and imperfect, yet as they come from Christ, they are mighty and powerful.

4. The sweet promises which God has made to prayer: 'he will be very gracious unto thee at the voice of thy cry' (*Isa. 30:19*). 'Then shall ye go and pray unto me, and I will hearken unto you. And ye shall seek me, and find me, when ye shall search for me with all your heart' (*Jer. 29:12,13*); and 'before they call, I will answer; and while they are yet speaking, I will hear' (*Isa. 65:24*). These promises keep the head of prayer above water. God is bound with his own promises, as Samson was bound with his own hair.

Let us, then, close ranks and with our Saviour pray yet more earnestly (*Luke 22:44*). Let us be importunate suitors, and resolve with St Bernard that we will not come away from God without God. Prayer is a bomb which will make heaven's gates fly open.

Question: How shall we go about praying aright?

Answer: Implore the Spirit of God: 'praying in the Holy Ghost' (*Jude 20*). The Holy Ghost both indites prayer and inflames it. God understands no other language but that of his Spirit. Pray for the Holy Ghost that you may pray in the Holy Ghost.

SECTION 13: A GODLY MAN IS A SINCERE MAN

'Behold an Israelite indeed, in whose spirit there is no guile'

(*John 1:47*). The word for sincere, *haplous*, signifies 'without pleats and folds'. A godly man is plain-hearted, having no subtle subterfuges. Religion is the livery a godly man wears and this livery is lined with sincerity.

Question: In what does the godly man's sincerity appear?

Answer 1: The godly man is what he seems to be. He is a Jew inwardly (*Rom. 2:29*). Grace runs through his heart, as silver through the veins of the earth. The hypocrite is not what he seems. A picture is like a man, but it lacks breath. The hypocrite is an effigy, a picture; he does not breathe forth sanctity. He is only like an angel on a signpost. A godly man answers to his profession as the transcript to the original.

Answer 2: The godly man strives to approve himself to God in everything: 'We labour, that, whether present or absent, we may be accepted of him' (*2 Cor. 5:9*). It is better to have God approve than the world applaud. Those who ran in the Olympic race strove to have the approval of the judge and umpire of the race. There is a time coming shortly, when a smile from God's face will be infinitely better than all the applause of men. How sweet that word will be, 'Well done, thou good and faithful servant' (*Matt. 25:21*). A godly man is ambitious of God's testimonial letters. The hypocrite desires the praise of men. Saul was for the approval of the people (*1 Sam. 15:30*) A godly man approves his heart to God, who is both the spectator and the judge.

Answer 3: The godly man is ingenuous in laying open his sins: 'I acknowledged my sin unto thee, and mine iniquity have I not hid' (*Psa. 32:5*). The hypocrite veils and smothers his sin. He does not cut off his sin but conceals it. Like a patient that has some loathsome disease in his body, he will rather die than confess his disease. But a godly man's sincerity is seen in this: he will confess and shame himself for sin: 'Lo, I have sinned, and I have done wickedly' (*2 Sam. 24:17*). No, a child of God will confess sin in particular. An unsound Christian will confess sin whole-sale, he will acknowledge he is a sinner in general, whereas David does, as it were, point with his finger to the sore: 'I have done this evil' (*Psa. 51:4*). He does not say, 'I have done evil', but '*this* evil'. He points at his blood-guiltiness.

Answer 4: The godly man has blessed designs in all he does. He propounds this objective in every ordinance – that he may have more acquaintance with God and bring more glory to God. As the herb heliotropium turns about according to the motion of the sun, so a godly man's actions all move towards the glory of God. It is an axiom in philosophy, 'The means are in order to the end'. A godly man's praying and worshipping is so that he may honour God. Though he shoots short, yet he takes correct aim. The hypocrite thinks of nothing but self-interest; the sails of his mill move only when the wind of promotion blows. He never dives into the waters of the sanctuary except to fetch up a piece of gold from the bottom.

Answer 5: The godly man abhors dissimulation with men; his heart goes along with his tongue; he cannot flatter and hate, commend and censure (*Psa. 28:3*). 'Let love be without dissimulation' (*Rom. 12:9*). Dissembled love is worse than hatred; counterfeiting of friendship is no better than a lie (*Psa. 78:36*), for there is a pretence of that which is not. Many are like Joab: 'He took Amasa by the beard to kiss him and smote him with his sword in the fifth rib, and he died' (*2 Sam. 20:9,10*). 'Horrible poisons lie hidden under sweet honey.'

There is a river in Spain where the fish seem to be of a golden colour but take them out of the water and they are like other fish. All is not gold that glitters; there are some who pretend much kindness, but they are like great veins which have little blood. If you lean upon them, they are like a leg out of joint. For my part I seriously question a man's sincerity with God, if he flatters and lies to his friend. 'He that hideth hatred with lying lips is a fool' (*Prov. 10:18*). By all that has been said, we may test whether we have this mark of a godly man – being sincere.

Sincerity (as I conceive it) is not strictly a grace but rather the ingredient in every grace. Sincerity is that which qualifies grace and without which grace is not true: 'Grace be with all them that love our Lord Jesus Christ in sincerity' (*Eph. 6:24*). Sincerity qualifies our love; sincerity is to grace what the blood and spirits are to the body. There can be no life without the blood, so no grace without sincerity.

Use: As we would be reputed godly, let us strive for this characteristic of sincerity.

1. Sincerity renders us lovely in God's eyes. God says of the sincere soul, as of Zion, 'This is my rest for ever: here will I dwell; for I have desired it' (*Psa. 132:14*). A sincere heart is God's paradise of delight. 'Noah found grace in God's eyes.' Why, what did God see in Noah? He was girt with the girdle of sincerity (*Gen. 6:9*). Noah was perfect in his generation. Truth resembles God and when God sees a sincere heart, he sees his own image, and he cannot choose but fall in love with it: 'He that is upright in his way is God's delight' (*Prov. 11:20*).

2. Sincerity makes our services find acceptance with God. The church of Philadelphia had only 'a little strength'; her grace was weak, her services slender; yet of all the churches Christ wrote to, he found the least fault with her. What was the reason? Because she was most sincere: 'Thou hast kept fast my word, and hast not denied my name' (*Rev. 3:8*). Though we cannot pay God all we owe, yet a little in current coin is accepted. God takes sincerity for full payment. A little gold, though rusty, is better than alchemy, be it never so bright. A little sincerity, though rusted over with many infirmities, is of more value with God than all the glorious flourishes of hypocrites.

3. Sincerity is our safety.   False hearts that will step out of God's way and use carnal policy, when they think they are most safe, are least secure. 'He that walketh uprightly walketh surely' (*Prov. 10:9*). A sincere Christian will do nothing but what the Word warrants, and that is safe, as to the conscience. No, often the Lord takes care of the outward safety of those who are upright in their way: 'I laid me down and slept' (*Psa. 3:5*). David was now beleaguered by enemies, yet God so encamped about him by his providence that he could sleep as securely as in a garrison. 'The Lord sustained me.' The only way to be safe is to be sincere.

4. Sincerity is gospel perfection: 'Hast thou considered my servant Job, that there is none like him in the earth, a perfect and an upright man?' (*Job 1:8*). Though a Christian is full of infirmities and, like a child that is put out to nurse, weak and feeble, God still looks on him as if he were completely righteous. Every true saint has the Thummim of perfection on his breastplate.

5. Sincerity is what the devil attacks most.   Satan's spite was not so much at Job's estate, as his integrity; he would have wrested the shield of sincerity from him, but Job held that fast (*Job 27:6*). A thief does not fight for an empty purse, but for money. The devil would have robbed Job of the jewel of a good conscience, and then he would have been poor Job indeed. Satan does not oppose profession, but sincerity. Let men go to church and make glorious pretences of holiness. Satan does not oppose this; this does him no hurt and them no good; but if men want to be sincerely pious, then Satan musters up all his forces against them. Now what the devil most assaults, we must strive most to maintain. Sincerity is our fort royal, where our chief treasure lies. This fort is most shot at, therefore let us be more careful to preserve it. While a man keeps his castle, his castle will keep him. While we keep sincerity, sincerity will keep us.

6. *Sincerity is the beauty of a Christian.* Wherein does the beauty of a diamond lie, but in this, that it is a true diamond? If it is counterfeit, it is worth nothing. So wherein does the beauty of a Christian lie, but in this, that he has truth in the inward parts (*Psa. 51:6*)? Sincerity is a Christian's ensign of glory; it is both his breastplate to defend him and his crown to adorn him.

7. *The vileness of hypocrisy.* The Lord would have no leaven offered up in sacrifice; leaven typified hypocrisy (*Luke 12:1*). The hypocrite does the devil double service; under the visor of piety, he can sin more and be less suspected: 'Woe unto you, scribes and Pharisees, hypocrites! for ye devour widows' houses, and for a pretence make long prayers' (*Matt. 23:14*). Who would think that those who pray for so many hours on end would be guilty of extortion? Who would suspect of false weights the man who has the Bible so often in his hand? Who would think that the one who seems to fear an oath would slander? Hypocrites are the worst sort of sinners; they reflect infinite dishonour upon religion. Hypocrisy for the most part ends in scandal, and that brings an evil report on the ways of God. One man breaking in renders the honest suspect. One scandalous hypocrite makes the world suspect that all

professing Christians are like him. The hypocrite was born to spite religion and bring it into disrepute.

The hypocrite is a liar; he worships God with his knee, and his passions with his heart, like those who 'feared the Lord, and served their own gods' (*2 Kings 17:33*).

The hypocrite is an impudent sinner. He knows his heart is false, yet he goes on. Judas knew himself to be a hypocrite; he asks, 'Master, is it I?' Christ replies, 'Thou hast said it' (*Matt. 26:25*). Yet so shameless was he as to persist in his falseness and betray Christ. All the plagues and curses written in the Book of God are the hypocrite's portion; hell is his place of rendezvous (*Matt. 24:51*). Hypocrites are the chief guests the devil expects and he will make them as welcome as fire and brimstone can make them.

8. If the heart is sincere, God will wink at many failings: 'He hath not beheld iniquity in Jacob' (*Numb. 23:21*). God's love does not make him blind; he can see infirmities. But how? Not with an eye of revenge, but pity, as a physician sees a disease in his patient so as to heal him. God does not see iniquity in Jacob so as to destroy him, but to heal him: 'He went on frowardly. I have seen his ways, and will heal him' (*Isa. 57:17,18*). How much pride, vanity, passion, does the Lord pass by in his sincere ones! He sees the integrity, and pardons the infirmity. How much God overlooked in Asa! The 'high places were not removed', yet it is said, 'The heart of Asa was perfect all his days' (*2 Chron. 15:17*). We esteem a picture, though it is not drawn full length. So though the graces of God's people are not drawn to their full length – no, have many scars and spots – yet having something of God in sincerity, they shall find mercy. God loves the sincere and it is the nature of love to cover infirmity.

9. Nothing but sincerity will give us comfort in an hour of trouble. King Hezekiah thought he was dying, yet this revived him, that conscience drew up a certificate for him: 'Remember, O Lord, how I have walked before thee in truth . . . ' (*Isa. 38:3*). Sincerity was the best flower in his crown. What a golden shield this will be against Satan! When he roars at us by his temptations, and sets our sins before us on our death-bed, then we shall answer, 'It is true, Satan; these have been our misdeeds, but we have bewailed them; if we have sinned, it was against the bent and purpose of our heart.' This will stop the devil's mouth and make him retreat; therefore strive for this jewel of sincerity. 'If our heart condemn us not, then have we confidence toward God' (*1 John 3:21*). If we are cleared at the petty sessions in our conscience, then we may be confident we shall be acquitted at the great assizes on the day of judgment.

SECTION 14: A GODLY MAN IS A HEAVENLY MAN

Heaven is in him before he is in heaven. The Greek word for saint, *hagios*, signifies a man taken away from the earth. A person may live in one place, yet belong to another. He may live in Spain yet be a free citizen of England. Pomponius lived in Athens yet was a citizen of Rome. So a godly man is a while in the world, but he belongs to the Jerusalem above. That is the place to which he aspires. Every day is Ascension Day with a believer. The saints are called 'stars' for their sublimity; they have gone above into the upper region: 'The way of life is above to the wise' (*Prov. 15:24*). A godly man is heavenly in six ways:

1. In his election.
2. In his disposition.
3. In his communication.
4. In his actions.
5. In his expectation.
6. In his conduct.

1. A godly man is heavenly in his election

He chooses heavenly objects. David chose to be a resident in God's house (*Psa. 84:10*). A godly person chooses Christ and grace before the most illustrious things under the sun. What a man is, that is his choice; and this choosing of God is best seen in a critical hour. When Christ and the world come into competition, and we part with the world to keep Christ and a good conscience, that is a sign we have chosen 'the better part' (*Luke 10:42*).

2. A godly man is heavenly in his disposition

He sets his affections on things above (*Col. 3:2*). He sends his heart to heaven before he gets there; he looks upon the world as but a beautiful prison and he cannot be much in love with his fetters, though they are made of gold. A holy person contemplates glory and eternity; his desires have got wings and have fled to heaven. Grace is in the heart like fire, which makes it sparkle upwards in divine desires and ejaculations.

3. A godly man is heavenly in his communication

His words are sprinkled with salt to season others (*Col. 4:6*). As soon as Christ had risen from the grave, he was 'speaking of the things pertaining to the kingdom of God' (*Acts 1:3*). No sooner has a man risen from the grave of unregeneracy than he is speaking of heaven: 'The words of a wise man's mouth are gracious' (*Eccles. 10:12*). He speaks in such a heavenly manner as if he were already in heaven. The love he has for God will not allow him to be silent. The spouse being sick of love, her tongue was like the pen of a ready writer: 'My beloved is white and ruddy, his head is as the most fine gold . . . ' (*Song 5:10,11*). If there is wine in the house, the bush will be hung outside, and where there is a principle of godliness in the heart, it will vent itself at the lips; the bush will be hung up.

How can they be termed godly:

(i) Who are possessed with a dumb devil? They never have any good discourse. They are fluent and discursive enough in secular things: they can speak of their wares and drugs, they can tell what a good crop they have, but in matters of religion they are as if their tongue cleaved to the roof of their mouth. There are many people in whose company you cannot tell what to make of them, whether they are Turks or atheists, for they never speak a word of Christ.

(ii) Whose tongues are set on fire by hell? Their lips do not drop honey but poison, to the defiling of others. Plutarch says that speech ought to be like gold, which is of most value when it has least dross in it. Oh, the unclean, malicious words that some people utter! What an unsavoury stench comes from these dunghills! Those lips that gallop so fast in sin need David's bridle (*Psa. 39:1*). Can the body be healthy when the tongue is black? Can the heart be holy when the devil is in the lips? A godly man speaks 'the language of Canaan'. 'They that feared the Lord spake often one to another' (*Mal. 3:16*).

4. A godly man is heavenly in his actions

The motions of the planets are celestial. A godly man is sublime and sacred in his motions; he works out salvation; he puts forth all his strength, as they did in the Greek Olympics, so that he may obtain the garland made of the flowers of paradise. He prays, fasts, watches, he offers violence to heaven, he is divinely actuated, he carries on God's interest in the world, he does angels' work, he is seraphic in his actions.

5. A godly man is heavenly in his expectation

His hopes are above the world (*Psa. 39:7*): 'In hope of eternal life' (*Titus 1:2*). A godly man casts anchor within the

[105]

veil. He hopes to have his fetters of sin filed off; he hopes for such things as eye has not seen; he hopes for a kingdom when he dies, a kingdom promised by the Father, purchased by the Son, assured by the Holy Ghost. As an heir lives in hope of the time when such a great estate shall fall to him, so a child of God, who is a co-heir with Christ, hopes for glory. This hope comforts him in all varieties of condition: 'we rejoice in hope of the glory of God' (*Rom. 5:2*).

(i) This hope comforts a godly man in affliction; hope lightens and sweetens the most severe dispensations. A child of God can laugh with tears in his eyes; the time is shortly coming when the cross shall be taken off his shoulders and a crown set on his head. A saint at present is miserable, with a thousand troubles; in an instant, he will be clothed with robes of immortality, and advanced above seraphim.

(ii) This hope comforts a godly man in death: 'the righteous hath hope in his death' (*Prov. 14:32*). If one should ask a dying saint, when all his earthly comforts have gone, what he had left, he would say, 'the helmet of hope'. I have read of a woman martyr who, when the persecutors commanded that her breasts should be cut off, said, 'Tyrant, do your worst; I have two breasts which you can not touch, the one of faith and the other of hope'. A soul that has this blessed hope is above the desire of life or the fear of death. Would anyone be troubled at exchanging a poor lease for an inheritance that will be for him and his heirs? Who would worry about parting with life, which is a lease that will soon run out, to be possessed of a glorious inheritance in light?

6. A godly man is heavenly in his conduct

He casts such a lustre of holiness as adorns his profession. He lives as if he had seen the Lord with his bodily eyes. What zeal, sanctity, humility, shines forth in his life! A godly person emulates not only the angels, but imitates Christ himself (*1 John 2:6*). The Macedonians celebrate the birthday of Alexander, on which day they wear his picture round their necks, set with pearl and rich jewels. So a godly man carries the lively picture of Christ about him in the heavenliness of his deportment: 'our conversation is in heaven' (*Phil. 3:20*).

Use 1: Those who are eaten up with the world will be rejected, as ungodly, at the bar of judgment. To be godly and earthly is a contradiction: 'For many walk, of whom I now tell you even weeping, that they are the enemies of the cross of Christ, whose god is their belly, who mind earthly things' (*Phil. 3:18,19*). We read that the earth swallowed up Korah alive (*Numb. 16:32*). This judgment is on many – the earth swallows up their time, thoughts and discourse. They are buried twice; their hearts are buried in the earth before their bodies. How sad it is that the soul, that princely thing, which is made for communion with God and angels, should be put to the mill to grind, and made a slave to the earth! How like the prodigal the soul has become, choosing rather to converse with swine and feed upon husks than to aspire after communion with the blessed Deity! Thus does Satan befool men, and keep them from heaven by making them seek a heaven here.

Use 2: As we would prove ourselves to be 'born of God', let us be of a sublime, heavenly temper. We shall never go to heaven when we die unless we are in heaven while we live. That we may be more noble and raised in our affections, let us seriously weigh these four considerations:

1. God himself sounds a retreat to us to call us off the world: 'Love not the world' (*1 John 2:15*). We may use it as a posy of flowers to smell, but it must not lie like a bundle of myrrh between our breasts: 'be not conformed to this world' (*Rom. 12:2*). Do not hunt after its honours and profits. God's providences, like his precepts, are to beat us off the world. Why does he send war and epidemics? What does the heat of this great anger mean? Surely dying times are to make men die to the world.

2. Consider how much below a Christian it is to be earthly-minded. We laugh sometimes at children when we see them busying themselves with toys, blowing bubbles in the air out of a shell, kissing their dolls, etc., when in the meantime we do the same! At death, what will all the world be which we so hug and kiss, but like a rag doll? It will yield us no more comfort then. How far it is below a heaven-born soul to be taken up with these things! No, when such as profess to be ennobled with a principle of piety and to have their hopes above, have their hearts below, how they disparage their heavenly calling and spot their silver wings of grace by beliming them with earth!

3. Consider what a poor, contemptible thing the world is. It is not worth setting the affections on; it cannot fill the heart. If Satan should take a Christian up to the mount of temptation and show him all the kingdoms and glory of the world, what could he show him but a fancy, an apparition? Nothing here can be proportionate to the immense soul of man. 'In the fulness of his sufficiency he shall be in straits' (*Job 20:22*). Here is want in plenty. The creature will no more fill the soul than a drop will fill the bucket, and that little sweet we suck from the creature is intermixed with some bitterness, like that cup which the Jews gave Christ. 'They gave him to drink wine mingled with myrrh' (*Mark 15:23*). And this imperfect sweet will not last long: 'the world passeth away' (*1 John 2:17*). The creature merely salutes us, and is soon on the wing. The world rings changes. It is never constant except in its disappointments.

How quickly we may remove our lodgings and make our pillow in the dust! The world is but a great inn where we are to stay a night or two and be gone. What madness it is so to set our heart upon our inn as to forget our home!

4. Consider what a glorious place heaven is. We read of an angel coming down from heaven who 'set his right foot upon the sea, and his left foot on the earth' (*Rev. 10:2*). Had we only once been in heaven, and viewed its superlative glory, how we might in holy scorn trample with one foot on the earth and with the other foot on the sea! Heaven is called a better country: 'But now they desire a better country, that is, an heavenly' (*Heb. 11:16*). Heaven is said to be a better country, in opposition to the country where we are now staying. What should we seek but that better country?

Question: In what sense is heaven a better country?

Answer 1: In that country above there are better delights. There is the tree of life, the rivers of pleasure. There is amazing beauty, unsearchable riches; there are the delights of angels; there is the flower of joy fully blown; there is more than we can ask or think (*Eph. 3:20*). There is glory in its full dimensions and beyond all hyperbole.

Answer 2: In that country there is a better dwelling house:

(i) It is a house 'not made with hands' (*2 Cor. 5:1*). To denote its excellence, there was never any house but was made with hands, but the house above surpasses the art of man or angel; none besides God could lay a stone in that building.

(ii) It is 'eternal in the heavens'. It is not a guest house but a mansion house. It is a house that will never be out of repair. 'Wisdom hath builded her house, she hath hewn out her seven pillars' (*Prov. 9:1*), which can never moulder.

Answer 3: In that country there are better provisions; in our Father's house there is bread enough. Heaven was typified by Canaan, which flowed with milk and honey. There is the royal feast, the spiced wine; there is angels' food; there they serve up those rare foods and dainties, such as exceed not only our expressions, but our faith.

Answer 4: In that country there is better society. There is God blessed forever. How infinitely sweet and ravishing will a smile of his face be! The king's presence makes the court. There are the glorious cherubim. In this terrestrial country where we now live, we are among wolves and serpents; in that country above, we shall be among angels. There are 'the spirits of just men made perfect' (*Heb. 12:23*). Here the people of God are clouded with infirmities; we see them with spots on their faces; they are full of pride, passion, censoriousness. In that Jerusalem above we shall see them in their royal attire, decked with unparalleled beauty, not having the least tincture or shadow of sin on them.

Answer 5: In that country there is a better air to breathe in. We go into the country for air; the best air is only to be had in that better country: (i) It is a more temperate air; the climate is calm and moderate; we shall neither freeze with the cold nor faint with the heat. (ii) It is a brighter air; there is a better light shining there. The Sun of righteousness enlightens that horizon with his glorious beams: 'the Lamb is the light thereof' (*Rev. 21:23*). (iii) It is a purer air. The fens, which are full of black vapours, we count a bad air and unwholesome to live in. This world is a place of bogs and fens, where the noxious vapours of sin arise, which make it pestilential and unwholesome to live in; but in that country above, there are none of these vapours, but a sweet perfume of holiness. There is the smell of the orange-tree and the pomegranate. There is the myrrh and cassia coming from Christ, which send forth a most odoriferous scent.

Answer 6: In that country there is a better soil. The land or soil is better:

(i) For its *altitude*. The earth, lying low, is of a baser pedigree; the element which is nearest heaven is purer and more excellent, like the fire. That country above is the high country; it is seated far above all the visible orbs (*Psa. 24:3*).

(ii) For its *fertility*; it bears a richer crop. The richest harvest on earth is the golden harvest, but the country above yields noble commodities. There are pearls celestial; there is the spiritual vine; there is the honeycomb of God's love dropping; there is the water of life, the hidden manna. There is fruit that does not rot, flowers that never fade. There is a crop which cannot be totally reaped; it will always be reaping time in heaven, and all this the land yields without the labour of ploughing and sowing.

(iii) For its *inoffensiveness*. There are no briars there. The world is a wilderness where there are wicked men, and the 'best of them is a brier' (*Micah 7:4*). They tear the people of God in their spiritual liberties, but in the country above there is not one briar to be seen; all the briars are burned.

(iv) For the *rarity* of the prospect; all that a man sees there is his own. I account that the best prospect where a man can see furthest on his own ground.

Answer 7: In that country there is better unity. All the inhabitants are knit together in love. The poisonous weed of malice does not grow there. There is harmony without division, and charity without envy. In that country above, as in Solomon's temple, no noise of hammer is heard.

Answer 8: In that country there is better employment; while we are here, we are complaining of our wants, weeping over our sins, but there we shall be praising God. How the birds of paradise will chirp when they are in that celestial country! There the morning stars will sing together, and all the saints of God will shout for joy.

Oh, what should we aspire after but this country above? Such as have their eyes opened, will see that it infinitely excels. An ignorant man looks at a star and it appears to him like a little silver spot, but the astronomer, who has his instrument to judge the dimension of a star, knows it to be many degrees bigger than the earth. So a natural man hears of the heavenly country that it is very glorious, but it is at a great distance. And because he has not a spirit of discernment, the world looks bigger in his eye. But such as are spiritual artists, who have the instrument of faith to judge heaven, will say it is by far the better country and they will hasten there with the sails of desire.

SECTION 15: A GODLY MAN IS A ZEALOUS MAN

Grace turns a saint into a seraph. It makes him burn in holy zeal. Zeal is a mixed affection, a compound of love and anger. It carries forth our love to God and anger against sin in the most intense manner. Zeal is the flame of the affections; a godly man has a double baptism – of water and fire. He is baptized with a spirit of zeal; he is zealous for God's honour, truth, worship: 'My zeal hath consumed me' (*Psa. 119:139*). It was a crown set on Phineas' head that he was zealous for his God (*Numb. 25:13*). Moses is touched with a coal from God's altar and in his zeal he breaks the tablets (*Exod. 32:19*). Our blessed Saviour in his zeal whips the buyers and sellers out of the temple: 'The zeal of thine house hath eaten me up' (*John 2:17*).

But there is a preternatural heat – something looking like zeal, which it is not. A comet looks like a star. I shall therefore show some differences between a true and a false zeal:

1. A false zeal is a blind zeal

'They have a zeal of God, but not according to knowledge' (*Rom. 10:2*). This is not the fire of the spirit, but wildfire. The Athenians were very devout and zealous, but they did not know for what. 'I found an altar with this inscription, To the unknown God' (*Acts 17:23*). Thus the Papists are zealous in their way, but they have taken away the key of knowledge.

2. A false zeal is a self-seeking zeal

Jehu cries, 'Come, see my zeal for the Lord' (*2 Kings 10:16*). But it was not zeal, but ambition; he was fishing for a crown. Demetrius pleads for the goddess Diana, but it was not her temple, but her silver shrines he was zealous for (*Acts 19:25–27*). Such zealots Ignatius complains of in his time, that they made a trade of Christ and religion by which to enrich themselves. It is probable that many in King Henry VIII's time were eager to pull down the abbeys, not out of any zeal against popery, but that they might build their own houses upon the ruins of those abbeys, like eagles which fly aloft but their eyes are down upon their prey. If blind zeal is punished sevenfold, hypocritical zeal shall be punished seventy-sevenfold.

3. A false preposterous zeal is a misguided zeal

It occurs most in things which are not commanded. It is the sign of a hypocrite to be zealous for traditions and careless of institutions. The Pharisees were more zealous about washing their cups than their hearts.

4. A false zeal is fired with passion

James and John, when they wished to call for fire from heaven, were rebuked by our Saviour: 'Ye know not what manner of spirit ye are of' (*Luke 9:55*). It was not zeal, but anger. Many have espoused the cause of religion, rather out of faction and fancy than out of zeal for the truth.

But the zeal of a godly man is a true and holy zeal which evidences itself in its effects:

1. True zeal cannot bear an injury done to God

Zeal makes the blood rise when God's honour is impeached. 'I know thy works, and thy labour, and thy patience, and how thou canst not bear them which are evil' (*Rev. 2:2*). He who zealously loves his friend cannot hear him spoken against and be silent.

2. True zeal will encounter the greatest difficulties

When the world holds out a Gorgon's head of danger to discourage us, zeal casts out fear. It is quickened by opposition. Zeal does not say, 'There is a lion in the way'. Zeal will charge through an army of dangers, it will march in the face of death. Let news be brought to Paul that he was waylaid; 'in every city bonds and afflictions' awaited him. This set a keener edge upon his zeal: 'I am ready not to be bound only, but also to die for the name of the Lord Jesus' (*Acts 21:13*). As sharp frosts by force of contrast make the fire burn hotter, so sharp oppositions only inflame zeal the more.

3. As true zeal has knowledge to go before it, so it has sanctity to follow after it

Wisdom leads the van of zeal, and holiness brings up the rear. A hypocrite seems to be zealous, but he is vicious. The godly man is white and ruddy; white in purity as well as ruddy in zeal. Christ's zeal was hotter than the fire, and his holiness purer than the sun.

4. Zeal that is genuine loves truth when it is despised and opposed

'They have made void thy law. Therefore I love thy

commandments above gold' (*Psa. 119:126,127*). The more others deride holiness, the more we love it. What is religion the worse for others disgracing it? Does a diamond sparkle the less because a blind man disparages it? The more outrageous the wicked are against the truth, the more courageous the godly are for it. When Michal scoffed at David's religious dancing before the ark, he said, 'If this is to be vile, I will yet be more vile' (*2 Sam. 6:22*).

5. True zeal causes fervency in duty: 'fervent in spirit' (Rom. 12:11)

Zeal makes us hear with reverence, pray with affection, love with ardency. God kindled Moses' sacrifice from heaven: 'there came a fire out from before the Lord, and consumed upon the altar the burnt offering' (*Lev. 9:24*). When we are zealous in devotion, and our heart waxes hot within us, here is a fire from heaven kindling our sacrifice. How odious it is for a man to be all fire when he is sinning, and all ice when he is praying! A pious heart, like water seething hot, boils over in holy affections.

6. True zeal is never out of breath

Though it is violent, it is perpetual. No waters can quench the flame of zeal, it is torrid in the frigid zone. The heat of zeal is like the natural heat coming from the heart, which lasts as long as life. That zeal which is not constant was never true.

Use 1: How opposite to godliness are those who cry down zeal, and count it a religious frenzy! They are for the light of knowledge, but not for the heat of zeal. When Basil was earnest in preaching against the Arian heresy, it was interpreted as folly and dotage. Religion is a matter requiring zeal; the kingdom of heaven will not be taken except by violence (*Matt. 11:12*).

Objection: But why so much fervour in religion? What becomes then of prudence?

Answer: Though prudence is to direct zeal, yet it is not to destroy it. Because sight is requisite, must the body therefore have no heat? If prudence is the eye in religion, zeal is the heart.

Question: But where is moderation?

Answer: Though moderation in things of indifference is commendable, and doubtless it would greatly tend to settling the peace of the church, yet in the main articles of faith, wherein God's glory and our salvation lie at stake, here moderation is nothing but sinful neutrality. It was Calvin's advice to Melanchthon that he should not so affect the name of moderate that at length he lost all his zeal.

Objection: But the apostle urges moderation: 'Let your moderation be known to all' (*Phil. 4:5*).

Answer:

1. The apostle is speaking there of moderating our passion. The Greek word for 'moderation' signifies candour and meekness – the opposite of rash anger. And so the word is rendered in another place 'patient' (*1 Tim. 3:3*). By moderation, then, is meant meekness of spirit. That is made clear by the subsequent words, 'The Lord is at hand' – as if the apostle had said, 'Avenge not yourselves, for the Lord is at hand.' He is ready to avenge your personal wrongs, but this in no way hinders a Christian from being zealous in matters of religion.

2. What strangers they are to godliness who have no zeal for the glory of God! They can see his ordinances despised, his worship adulterated, yet their spirits are not at all stirred in them. How many are of a dull, lukewarm temper, zealous for their own secular interest, but with no zeal for the things of heaven! Hot in their own cause, but cool in God's. The Lord most abominates lukewarm nominal Christians. I almost said that he is sick of them. 'I would thou wert cold or hot' (anything but lukewarm); 'because thou art neither cold nor hot, I will spue thee out of my mouth' (*Rev. 3:15,16*). A lukewarm Christian is only half-baked, just like Ephraim: 'Ephraim is a cake not turned' (*Hos. 7:8*). To keep up a form of religion without zeal is to be like those bodies that the angels assumed, which moved but had no life in them. I would ask these tepid, neutral professing Christians this question, If religion is not a good cause, why did they undertake it at first? If it is, why do they go about it so faintly? Why have they no more holy ardour of soul? These persons would gladly go to heaven on a soft bed, but are loath to be carried there in a fiery chariot of zeal. Remember, God will be zealous against those who are not zealous; he provides the fire of hell for those who lack the fire of zeal.

Use 2: As you would be found in the catalogue of the godly, strive for zeal. It is better to be of no religion than not to be zealous in religion. Beware of carnal policy. This is one of those three things which Luther feared would be the death of religion. Some men have been too wise to be saved. Their discretion has quenched their zeal. Beware of sloth, which is an enemy to zeal: 'be zealous therefore, and repent' (*Rev. 3:19*). Christians, what do you reserve your zeal for? Is it for your gold that perishes, or for your passions that will make you perish? Can you bestow your zeal better than upon God? How zealous men have been in a false religion! 'They lavish gold out of the bag, and weigh silver in the balance' (*Isa. 46:6*). The Jews did not spare any cost in their idolatrous worship. No, they 'cause their sons and daughters to pass through the fire to Molech' (*Jer. 32:35*). They were so zealous in their idol worship that they would sacrifice their sons and daughters to their false gods. How far the purblind heathen went in their false zeal! When the tribunes of Rome complained that they wanted gold in their treasuries to offer to Apollo, the Roman matrons plucked off their chains of gold and rings and bracelets and gave them to the priests to offer up sacrifice. Were these so zealous in their sinful worship, and will you not be zealous in the worship of the true God? Can you lose anything by your zeal? Shall it not be superabundantly recompensed? What is heaven worth? What is a sight of God worth? Was not Jesus Christ zealous for you? He sweated drops of blood, he conflicted with his Father's wrath. How zealous he was for your redemption, and have you no zeal for him? Is there anything you yourselves hate more than dulness and slothfulness in your servants? You are weary of such servants. Do you dislike a dull spirit in others, and not in yourselves? What are all your duties without zeal but mere fancies and nonentities?

Do you know what a glorious thing zeal is? It is the lustre that sparkles from grace; it is the flame of love; it resembles the Holy Ghost: 'There appeared cloven tongues like fire, which sat upon each of them, and they were all filled with the Holy Ghost' (*Acts 2:3,4*). Tongues of fire were an emblem to represent that fire of zeal which the Spirit poured upon them.

Zeal makes all our religious performances prevail with God. When the iron is red hot it enters best and when our services are red hot with zeal, they pierce heaven soonest.

SECTION 16: A GODLY MAN IS A PATIENT MAN

'Ye have heard of the patience of Job' (*Jas. 5:11*). Patience is a star which shines in a dark night. There is a twofold patience:

1. Patience in waiting

If a godly man does not obtain his desire immediately, he will wait till the mercy is ripe: 'My soul waiteth for the Lord' (*Psa. 130:6*). There is good reason why God should have the timing of our mercies: 'I the Lord will hasten it in his time' (*Isa. 60:22*). Deliverance may delay beyond our time, but it will not delay beyond God's time.

Why should we not wait patiently for God? We are servants; it becomes servants to be in a waiting posture. We wait for everything else; we wait for the fire till it burns; we wait for the seed till it grows (*Jas. 5:7*). Why cannot we wait for God? God has waited for us (*Isa. 30:18*). Did he not wait for our repentance? How often did he come year after year before he found fruit? Did God wait for us, and cannot we wait for him? A godly man is content to await God's leisure; though the vision is delayed, he will wait for it (*Hab. 2:3*).

2. Patience in bearing trials

This patience is twofold: (a) Either in regard to man, when we bear injuries without revenging, or (b) in regard to God, when we bear his hand without repining. A good man will not only *do* God's will, but *bear* his will: 'I will bear the indignation of the Lord' (*Mic. 7:9*). This patient bearing of God's will is not:

(i) *A stoical apathy*; patience is not insensitivity under God's hand; we ought to be sensitive.

(ii) *Enforced patience*, to bear a thing because we cannot help it, which (as Erasmus said) is rather necessity than patience. But patience is a cheerful submission of our will to God: 'The will of the Lord be done' (*Acts 21:14*). A godly man acquiesces in what God does, as being not only good but best for himself. The great quarrel between God and us is, Whose will shall stand? Now the regenerate will falls in with the will of God. There are four things opposite to this patient frame of soul:

(a) *Disquiet of spirit*, when the soul is discomposed and pulled off the hinges, insomuch that it is unfit for holy duties. When the strings of a lute are snarled up, the lute is not fit to make music. So when a Christian's spirit is perplexed and disturbed, he cannot make melody in his heart to the Lord.

(b) *Discontent*, which is a sullen, dogged mood. When a man is not angry at his sins, but at his condition, this is different from patience. Discontent is the daughter of pride.

(c) *Prejudice*, which is a dislike of God and his ways, and a falling off from religion. Sinners have hard thoughts of God, and if he just touches them on a sore spot, they will at once go away from him and throw off his livery.

(d) *Self-vindication*, when instead of being humbled under God's hand, a man justifies himself, as if he had not deserved what he suffers. A proud sinner stands upon his own defence, and is ready to accuse God of unrighteousness, which is as if we should tax the sun with darkness. This is far from patience. A godly man subscribes to God's wisdom and submits to his will. He says not only, 'Good is the word of the Lord' (*Isa. 39:8*), but 'Good is the rod of the Lord'.

Use: As we would demonstrate ourselves to be godly, let us be eminent in this grace of patience: 'the patient in spirit is better than the proud in spirit' (*Eccles. 7:8*). There are some graces which we shall have no need of in heaven. We shall have no need of faith when we have full vision, nor patience when we have perfect joy, but in a dark sorrowful night there is need of these stars to shine (*Heb. 10:36*). Let us show our patience in bearing God's will. Patience in bearing God's will is twofold:

1. When God removes any comfort from us.
2. When God imposes any evil on us.

1. We must be patient when God removes any comfort from us. If God takes away any of our relations – 'I take away the desire of thine eyes with a stroke' (*Ezek. 24:16*) – it is still our duty patiently to acquiesce in the will of God. The loss of a dear relation is like pulling away a limb from the body. 'A man dies every time he loses his own kith and kin.' But grace will make our hearts calm and quiet, and produce holy patience in us under such a severe dispensation. I shall lay down eight considerations which may act like spiritual medicine to kill the worm of impatience under the loss of relations:

(i) The Lord never takes away any comfort from his people without giving them something better. The disciples parted with Christ's corporal presence and he sent them the Holy Ghost. God eclipses one joy and augments another. He simply makes an exchange; he takes away a flower and gives a diamond.

(ii) When godly friends die, they are in a better condition; they are taken away 'from the evil to come' (*Isa. 57:1*). They are out of the storm and have gone to the haven: 'Blessed are the dead which die in the Lord' (*Rev. 14:13*). The godly have a portion promised them upon their marriage to Christ, but the portion is not paid till the day of their death. The saints are promoted at death to communion with God; they have what they so long hoped for, and prayed for. Why, then, should we be impatient at our friends' promotion?

(iii) You who are a saint have a friend in heaven whom you cannot lose. The Jews have a saying at their funerals, 'Let your consolation be in heaven'. Are you mourning somebody close to you? Look up to heaven and draw comfort from there; your best kindred are above. 'When my father and my mother forsake me, then the Lord will take me up' (*Psa. 27:10*). God will be with you in the hour of death: 'though I walk through the valley of the shadow of death, thou art with me' (*Psa. 23:4*). Other friends you cannot keep. God is a friend you cannot lose. He will be your guide in life; your hope in death; your reward after death.

(iv) Perhaps God is correcting you for a fault, and if so, it becomes you to be patient. It may be your friend had more of your love than God and therefore God took away such a relation, so that the stream of your love might run back to him again. A gracious woman had been deprived, first of her children, then of her husband. She said, 'Lord, thou hast a plot against me; thou intendest to have all my love'. God does not like to have any creature set upon the throne of our affections; he will take away that comfort, and then he shall lie nearest our heart. If a husband bestows a jewel on his wife, and she so falls in love with that jewel as to forget her husband, he will take away the jewel so that her love may return to him again. A dear relation is this jewel. If we begin to idolize it, God will take away the jewel so that our love may return to him again.

(v) A godly relation is parted with, but not lost. That is lost which we have no hope ever of seeing again. Religious friends have only gone a little ahead of us. A time will shortly come when there shall be a meeting without parting (*1 Thess. 5:10*). How glad one is to see a long-absent friend! Oh, what glorious applause there will be, when old relations meet together in heaven, and are in each other's embraces! When a great prince lands at the shore, the guns go off in token of joy; when godly friends have all landed at the heavenly shore and congratulate one another on their happiness, what stupendous joy there will be! What music in the choir of angels! How heaven will ring with their praises! And that which is the crown of all, those who were joined in the flesh here shall be joined nearer than ever in the mystic body, and shall lie together in Christ's bosom, that bed of perfume (*1 Thess. 4:17*).

(vi) We have deserved worse at God's hand. Has he taken away a child, a wife, a parent? He might have taken away his Spirit. Has he deprived us of a relation? He might have deprived us of salvation. Does he put wormwood in the cup? We have deserved poison. 'Thou hast punished us less than our iniquities deserve' (*Ezra 9:13*). We have a sea of sin, and only a drop of suffering.

(vii) The patient soul enjoys itself most sweetly. An impatient man is like a troubled sea that cannot rest (*Isa. 57:20*). He tortures himself upon the rack of his own griefs and passions, whereas patience calms the heart, as Christ did the sea, when it was rough. Now there is a sabbath in the heart, yes, a heaven. 'In your patience possess ye your souls' (*Luke 21:19*). By faith a man possesses God and by patience he possesses himself.

(viii) How patient many of the saints have been, when the Lord has broken the very staff of their comfort in bereaving them of relations. The Lord took away Job's children and he was so far from murmuring that he fell to blessing: 'the Lord hath taken away; blessed be the name of the Lord' (*Job 1:21*). God foretold the death of Eli's sons: 'in one day they shall die, both of them' (*1 Sam. 2:34*). But how patiently he took this sad news: 'It is the Lord: let him do what seemeth him good' (*1 Sam. 3:18*). See the difference between Eli and Pharaoh! Pharaoh said, 'Who is the Lord?' (*Exod. 5:2*). Eli said, 'It is the Lord.' When God struck two of Aaron's sons dead, 'Aaron held his peace' (*Lev. 10:2,3*). Patience opens the ear but shuts the mouth. It opens the ear to hear the rod but shuts the mouth so that it has not a word to say against God. See here the patterns of patience; and shall we not copy them? These are heart-quietening considerations when God sets a death's-head upon our comforts and removes dear relations from us.

2. We must be patient when God inflicts any evil on us. 'Patient in tribulation' (*Rom. 12:12*).

(i) God sometimes lays heavy affliction on his people: 'thy hand lies sore upon me' (*Psa. 38:2*). The Hebrew word for 'afflicted' signifies 'to be melted'. God seems to melt his people in a furnace.

(ii) God sometimes lays various afflictions on the saints: 'he multiplieth my wounds' (*Job 9:17*). As we have various ways of sinning, so the Lord has various ways of afflicting. Some he deprives of their estates; others he chains to a sick bed; others he confines to a prison. God has various arrows in his quiver which he shoots.

(iii) Sometimes God lets the affliction lie for a long time: 'there is no more any prophet; neither is there among us any that knoweth how long' (*Psa. 74:9*). As it is with diseases – some are chronic and linger and hang about the body several years on end – so it is with afflictions. The Lord is pleased to exercise many of his precious ones with chronic afflictions, which they suffer for a long time. Now in all these cases, it becomes the saints to rest patiently in the will of God. The Greek word for 'patient' is a metaphor and alludes to one who stands invincibly under a burden. This is the right notion of patience, when we bear affliction invincibly without fainting or fretting.

The test of a pilot is seen in a storm; so the test of a Christian is seen in affliction. That man has the right art of navigation who, when the boisterous winds blow from heaven, steers the ship of his soul wisely, and does not dash upon the rock of impatience. A Christian should always maintain decorum, not behaving himself in an unseemly manner or disguising himself with intemperate passion when the hand of God lies upon him. Patience adorns suffering. Affliction in Scripture is compared to a net: 'Thou broughtest us into the net' (*Psa. 66:11*). Some have escaped the devil's net, yet the Lord allows them to be taken in the net of affliction. But they must not be 'as a wild bull in a net' (*Isa. 51:20*), kicking and flinging against their Maker, but lie patiently till God breaks the net and makes a way for their escape. I shall propound four cogent arguments to encourage patience under those evils which God inflicts on us:

(a) Afflictions are for our profit, for our benefit: 'he for our profit' (*Heb. 12:10*). We pray that God would take such a course with us as may do our souls good. When God is afflicting us, he is hearing our prayers; he does it 'for our profit'. Not that afflictions in themselves profit us, but as God's Spirit works with them. For as the waters of Bethesda could not give health of themselves unless the angel descended and stirred them (*John 5:4*), so the waters of affliction are not in themselves healing till God's Spirit co-operates and sanctifies them to us. Afflictions are profitable in many ways:

(i) They make men sober and wise. Physicians have mental patients bound in chains and put on a frugal diet to bring them to the use of reason. Many run stark mad in prosperity; they know neither God nor themselves. The Lord therefore binds them with cords of affliction, so that he may bring them to their right minds. 'If they be held in cords of affliction, then he sheweth them their transgressions. He openeth also their ear to discipline' (*Job 36:8–10*).

(ii) Afflictions are a friend to grace:

(1) They beget grace. Beza acknowledged that God laid the foundation of his conversion during a violent sickness in Paris.

(2) They augment grace. The people of God are beholden to their troubles; they would never have had so much grace, if they had not met with such severe trials. Now the waters run and the spices flow forth. The saints thrive by affliction as the Lacedemonians grew rich by war. God makes grace flourish most in the fall of the leaf.

(iii) Afflictions quicken our pace on the way to heaven. It is with us as with children sent on an errand. If they meet with apples or flowers by the way, they linger and are in no great hurry to get home, but if anything frightens them,

[125]

then they run with all the speed they can to their father's house. So in prosperity, we gather the apples and flowers and do not give much thought to heaven, but if troubles begin to arise and the times grow frightful, then we make more haste to heaven and with David 'run the way of God's commandments' (*Psa. 119:32*).

(b) God intermixes mercy with affliction. He steeps his sword of justice in the oil of mercy. There was no night so dark but Israel had a pillar of fire in it. There is no condition so dismal but we may see a pillar of fire to give us light. If the body is in pain and conscience is at peace, there is mercy. Affliction is for the prevention of sin; there is mercy. In the ark there was 'a rod and a pot of manna', the emblem of a Christian's condition: 'mercy interlined with judgment (*Psa. 101:1*). Here is the rod and manna.

(c) Patience proves that there is much of God in the heart. Patience is one of God's titles: 'the God of patience' (*Rom. 15:5*). If you have your heart cast in this blessed mould, it is a sign that God has imparted much of his own nature to you; you shine with some of his beams.

Impatience proves that there is much unsoundness of heart. If the body is of such a type that every little scratch of a pin makes the flesh fester, you say, 'Surely this man's flesh is very unsound.' So impatience with every petty annoyance and quarrelling with providence is the sign of a disturbed Christian. If there is any grace in such a heart, they who can see it must have good eyes. But he who is of a patient spirit is a graduate in religion and participates in much of the divine nature.

(d) The end of affliction is glorious. The Jews were captive in Babylon but what was the end? They departed from Babylon with vessels of silver, gold and precious things (*Ezra 1:6*). So, what is the end of affliction? It ends in endless glory (*Acts 14:22; 2 Cor. 4:17*). How this may rock our impatient hearts quiet! Who would not willingly travel along a little dirty path and ploughed lands, at the end of which is a fair meadow and in that meadow a goldmine?

Question: How shall I get my heart tuned to a patient mood?

Answer: Get faith; all our impatience proceeds from unbelief. Faith is the breeder of patience. When a storm of passion begins to arise, faith says to the heart, as Christ did to the sea, 'Peace, be still', and there is at once a calm.

Question: How does faith work patience?

Answer: Faith argues the soul into patience. Faith is like that town clerk in Ephesus who allayed the contention of the multitude and argued them soberly into peace (*Acts 19:35,36*). So when impatience begins to clamour and make a hubbub in the soul, faith appeases the tumult and argues the soul into holy patience. Faith says, 'Why art thou disquieted, O my soul?' (*Psa. 42:5*). 'Are you afflicted ? Is it not your Father who has done it? He is carving and polishing you and making you fit for glory. He smites that he may save. What is your trial? Is it sickness? God shakes the tree of your body so that some fruit may fall, even "the peaceable fruit of righteousness" (*Heb. 12:11*). Are you driven from your home? God has prepared a city for you (*Heb. 11:16*). Do you suffer reproach for Christ's sake? "The spirit of glory and of God resteth upon you" (*1 Pet. 4:14*).' Thus faith argues and disputes the soul into patience.

Pray to God for patience. Patience is a flower of God's planting. Pray that it may grow in your heart, and send forth its sweet perfume. Prayer is a holy charm, to charm down the evil spirit. Prayer composes the heart and puts it in tune, when impatience has broken the strings and put everything into confusion. Oh, go to God. Prayer delights God's ear; it melts his heart; it opens his hand. God cannot

[127]

THE GODLY MAN'S PICTURE

deny a praying soul. Seek him with importunity and either he will remove the affliction or, which is better, he will remove your impatience.

SECTION 17: A GODLY MAN IS A THANKFUL MAN

Praise and thanksgiving is the work of heaven and he begins that work here which he will always be doing in heaven. The Jews have a saying – the world subsists by three things: the law, the worship of God and thankfulness. As if where thankfulness was missing, one of the pillars of the world had been taken away and it was ready to fall. The Hebrew word for 'praise' comes from a root that signifies 'to shoot up'. The godly man sends up his praises like a volley of shots towards heaven. David was modelled after God's heart and how melodiously he warbled out God's praises! Therefore he was called 'the sweet psalmist of Israel' (*2 Sam. 23:1*). Take a Christian at his worst, yet he is thankful. The prophet Jonah was a man of waspish spirit. The sea was not so stirred with the tempest as Jonah's heart was stirred with passion (*Jonah 1:13*). Yet through this cloud you might see grace appear. He had a thankful heart: 'I will sacrifice unto thee with the voice of thanksgiving; I will pay that that I have vowed' (*Jonah 2:9*). To illustrate this more clearly, I shall lay down these four particulars:

1. Praise and thanksgiving is a saint-like work
We find in Scripture that the godly are still called upon to praise God: 'ye that fear the Lord, bless the Lord' (*Psa. 135:20*). 'Let the saints be joyful in glory: let the high praises of God be in their mouth' (*Psa. 149:5,6*). Praise is a work proper to a saint:

(i) None but the godly can praise God aright. As all do not have the skill to play the lute, so not everyone can sound

forth the harmonious praises of God. Wicked men are bound to praise God, but they are not fit to praise him. None but a living Christian can tune God's praise. Wicked men are dead in sin; how can they who are dead lift up God's praises? 'The grave cannot praise thee' (*Isa. 38:18*). A wicked man stains and eclipses God's praise. If an unclean hand works in damask or flowered satin, it will slur its beauty. God will say to the sinner, 'What hast thou to do, to take my covenant in thy mouth?' (*Psa. 50:16*).

(*ii*) *Praise is not comely for any but the godly*: 'praise is comely for the upright' (*Psa. 33:1*). A profane man stuck with God's praises is like a dunghill stuck with flowers. Praise in the mouth of a sinner is like an oracle in the mouth of a fool. How uncomely it is for anyone to praise God if his whole life dishonours God! It is as indecent for a wicked man to praise God as it is for a usurer to talk of living by faith, or for the devil to quote Scripture. The godly alone are fit to be choristers in God's praises. It is called 'the garment of praise' (*Isa. 61:3*). This garment fits handsomely only on a saint's back.

2. Thanksgiving is a more noble part of God's worship
Our wants may send us to prayer but it takes a truly honest heart to bless God. The raven cries; the lark sings. In petition we act like men; in thanksgiving we act like angels.

3. Thanksgiving is a God-exalting work
'Whoso offereth praise glorifieth me' (*Psa. 50:23*). Though nothing can add the least mite to God's essential glory, yet praise exalts him in the eyes of others. Praise is a setting forth of God's honour, a lifting up of his name, a displaying of the trophy of his goodness, a proclaiming of his excellence, a spreading of his renown, a breaking open of the box of ointment, whereby the sweet savour and perfume of God's name is sent abroad into the world.

[129]

4. Praise is a more distinguishing work

By this a Christian excels all the infernal spirits. Do you talk of God? So can the devil; he brought Scripture to Christ. Do you profess religion? So can the devil; he transforms himself into an angel of light. Do you fast? He never eats. Do you believe? The devils have a faith of assent; they believe, and tremble (*Jas. 2:19*). But as Moses worked such a miracle as none of the magicians could reproduce, so here is a work Christians may be doing, which none of the devils can do, and that is the work of thanksgiving. The devils blaspheme, but do not bless. Satan has his fiery darts but not his harp and viol.

Use 1: See here the true genius and complexion of a godly man. He is much in doxologies and praises. It is a saying of Lactantius that he who is unthankful to his God cannot be a good man. A godly man is a God-exalter. The saints are temples of the Holy Ghost (*1 Cor. 3:16*). Where should God's praises be sounded, but in his temples? A good heart is never weary of praising God: 'his praise shall continually be in my mouth' (*Psa. 34:1*). Some will be thankful while the memory of the mercy is fresh, but afterwards leave off. The Carthaginians used at first to send the tenth of their yearly revenue to Hercules, but by degrees they grew weary and left off sending. David, as long as he drew his breath, would chirp forth God's praise: 'I will sing praises unto my God while I have any being' (*Psa. 146:2*). David would not now and then give God a snatch of music, and then hang up the instrument, but he would continually be celebrating God's praise. A godly man will express his thankfulness in every duty. He mingles thanksgiving with prayer: 'in every thing by prayer with thanksgiving let your requests be made known unto God' (*Phil. 4:6*). Thanksgiving is the more divine part of prayer. In our petitions we express our own necessities; in our thanksgivings we declare God's excellences. Prayer goes up as incense, when it is perfumed with thanksgiving.

And as a godly man expressses thankfulness in every duty, he does so in every condition. He will be thankful in adversity as well as prosperity: 'In every thing give thanks' (*1 Thess. 5:18*). A gracious soul is thankful and rejoices that he is drawn nearer to God, though it be by the cords of affliction. When it goes well with him, he praises God's mercy; when it goes badly with him, he magnifies God's justice. When God has a rod in his hand, a godly man will have a psalm in his mouth. The devil's smiting of Job was like striking a musical instrument; he sounded forth praise: 'The Lord hath taken away; blessed be the name of the Lord' (*Job. 1:21*). When God's spiritual plants are cut and bleed, they drop thankfulness; the saints' tears cannot drown their praises.

If this is the sign of a godly man, then the number of the godly appears to be very small. Few are in the work of praise. Sinners cut God short of his thank offering: 'Where are the nine?' (*Luke 17:17*). Of ten lepers healed there was but one who returned to give praise. Most of the world are sepulchres to bury God's praise. You will hear some swearing and cursing but few who bless God. Praise is the yearly rent that men owe, but most are behindhand with their rent. God gave King Hezekiah a marvellous deliverance, 'but Hezekiah rendered not again according to the benefit done unto him' (*2 Chron. 32:25*). That 'but' was a blot on his escutcheon. Some, instead of being thankful to God, 'render evil for good'. They are the worse for mercy: 'Do ye thus requite the Lord, O foolish people and unwise?' (*Deut. 32:6*). This is like the toad that turns the most wholesome herb to poison. Where shall we find a grateful Christian? We read of the saints 'having harps in their hands' (*Rev 5:8*) – the emblem of praise. Many have tears in their eyes and complaints in their mouths, but few have harps in their hand and are blessing and praising the name of God.

Use 2: Let us scrutinize ourselves and examine by this characteristic whether we are godly: Are we thankful for mercy? It is a hard thing to be thankful.

Question: How may we know whether we are rightly thankful?

Answer 1: When we are careful to register God's mercy: 'David appointed certain of the Levites to record, and to thank and praise the Lord God of Israel' (*1 Chron. 16:4*). Physicians say that the memory is the first thing that decays. It is true in spiritual matters: 'They soon forgat his works' (*Psa. 106:13*). A godly man enters his mercies, as a physician does his remedies, in a book, so that they may not be lost. Mercies are jewels that should be locked up. A child of God keeps two books always by him: one to write his sins in, so that he may be humble; the other to write his mercies in, so that he may be thankful.

Answer 2: We are rightly thankful when our hearts are the chief instrument in the music of praise: 'I will praise the Lord with my whole heart' (*Psa. 111:1*). David would tune not only his viol, but also his heart. If the heart does not join with the tongue, there can be no comfort. Where the heart is not engaged, the parrot is as good a chorister as the Christian.

Answer 3: We are rightly thankful when the favours which we receive endear our love to God the more. David's miraculous preservation from death drew forth his love to God: 'I love the Lord' (*Psa. 116:1*). It is one thing to love our mercies; it is another thing to love the Lord. Many love their deliverance but not their deliverer. God is to be loved more than his mercies.

Answer 4: We are rightly thankful when, in giving our praise to God, we take all worthiness from ourselves: 'I am not worthy of the least of all the mercies thou hast shewed unto thy servant' (*Gen. 32:10*). As if Jacob had said, 'Lord, the worst bit thou carvest me is better than I deserve.' Mephibosheth bowed himself and said, 'What is thy servant, that thou shouldst look upon such a dead dog as I am?' (*2 Sam. 9:8*). So when a thankful Christian makes a survey of his blessings and sees how much he enjoys that others better than he lack, he says, 'Lord, what am I, a dead dog, that free grace should look upon me, and that thou shouldest crown me with such loving kindness?'

Answer 5: We are rightly thankful when we put God's mercy to good use. We repay God's blessings with service. The Lord gives us health, and we spend and are spent for Christ (*2 Cor. 12:15*). He gives us an estate, and we honour the Lord with our substance (*Prov. 3:9*). He gives us children, and we dedicate them to God and educate them for God. We do not bury our talents but trade them. This is to put our mercies to good use. A gracious heart is like a piece of good ground that, having received the seed of mercy, produces a crop of obedience.

Answer 6: We are rightly thankful when we can have our hearts more enlarged for spiritual than for temporal mercies: 'Blessed be God, who hath blessed us with all spiritual blessings' (*Eph. 1:3*). A godly man blesses God more for a fruitful heart than a full crop. He is more thankful for Christ than for a kingdom. Socrates was wont to say that he loved the king's smile more than his gold. A pious heart is more thankful for a smile of God's face than he would be for the gold of the Indies.

Answer 7: We are rightly thankful when mercy is a spur to duty. It causes a spirit of activity for God. Mercy is not like the sun to the fire, to dull it, but like oil to the wheel, to make it run faster. David wisely argues from mercy to duty:

'Thou hast delivered my soul from death. I will walk before the Lord in the land of the living' (*Psa. 116:8,9*). It was a saying of Bernard, 'Lord, I have two mites, a soul and a body, and I give them both to thee.'

Answer 8: We are rightly thankful when we motivate others to this angelic work of praise. David does not only wish to bless God himself, but calls upon others to do so: 'Praise ye the Lord' (*Psa. 111:1*). The sweetest music is that which is in unison. When many saints join together in unison, then they make heaven ring with their praises. As one drunkard will be calling upon another, so in a holy sense, one Christian must be stirring up another to the work of thankfulness.

Answer 9: We are rightly thankful when we not only speak God's praise but live his praise. It is called an expression of gratitude. We give thanks when we live thanks. Such as are mirrors of mercy should be patterns of piety. 'Upon Mount Zion shall be deliverance, and there shall be holiness' (*Obad. 17*). To give God oral praise and dishonour him in our lives is to commit a barbarism in religion, and is to be like those Jews who bowed the knee to Christ and then spat on him (*Mark 15:19*).

Answer 10: We are rightly thankful when we propagate God's praises to posterity. We tell our children what God has done for us: in such a want he supplied us; from such a sickness he raised us up; in such a temptation he helped us. 'O God, our fathers have told us, what work thou didst in their days, in the times of old' (*Psa. 44:1*). By transmitting our experiences to our children, God's name is eternalized, and his mercies will bring forth a plentiful crop of praise when we have gone. Heman puts the question, 'Shall the dead praise thee?' (*Psa. 88:10*). Yes, in the sense that when we are dead, we praise God because, having left the chronicle of God's mercies with our children, we start them on thankfulness and so make God's praises live when we are dead.

Use 3: Let us prove our godliness by gratefulness: 'Give unto the Lord the glory due unto his name' (*Psa. 29:2*).

1. 'It is a good thing to be thankful: 'It is good to sing praises unto our God' (*Psa. 147:1*). It is bad when the tongue (that organ of praise) is out of tune and jars by murmuring and discontent. But it is a good thing to be thankful. It is good, because this is all the creature can do to lift up God's name; and it is good because it tends to make us good. The more thankful we are, the more holy. While we pay this tribute of praise, our stock of grace increases. In other debts, the more we pay, the less we have; but the more we pay this debt of thankfulness, the more grace we have.

2. Thankfulness is the rent we owe to God. 'Kings of the earth, and all people; let them praise the name of the Lord' (*Psa. 148:11,13*), Praise is the tribute or custom to be paid into the King of heaven's exchequer. Surely while God renews our lease, we must renew our rent.

3. The great cause we have to be thankful. It is a principle grafted in nature, to be thankful for benefits. The heathen praised Jupiter for their victories.

What full clusters of mercies hang on us when we go to enumerate God's mercies! We must, with David, confess ourselves to be nonplussed: 'Many, O Lord my God, are thy wonderful works which thou hast done, they cannot be reckoned up in order' (*Psa. 40:5*). And as God's mercies are past numbering, so they are past measuring. David takes the longest measuring line he could get. He measures from earth to the clouds, no, above the clouds, yet this measure would not reach the heights of God's mercies: 'Thy mercy is great above the heavens' (*Psa. 108:4*). Oh, how God has enriched us with his silver showers! A whole constellation of mercies has shone in our hemisphere.

(i) What temporal favours we have received! Every day we see a new tide of mercy coming in. The wings of mercy have covered us, the breast of mercy has fed us: 'the God which fed me all my life long unto this day' (*Gen. 48:15*). What snares laid for us have been broken! What fears have blown over! The Lord has made our bed, while he has made others' graves. He has taken such care of us, as if he had no-one else to take care of. Never was the cloud of providence so black, but we might see a rainbow of love in the cloud. We have been made to swim in a sea of mercy, and does not all this call for thankfulness?

(ii) That which may put another string into the instrument of our praise and make it sound louder is to consider what spiritual blessings God has conferred on us. He has given us water from the upper springs; he has opened the wardrobe of heaven and fetched us out a better garment than any of the angels wear. He has given us the best robe and put on us the ring of faith, by which we are married to him. These are mercies of the first magnitude, which deserve to have an asterisk put on them. And God keeps the best wine till last. Here he gives us mercies only in small quantities; the greatest things are laid up. Here there are some honey drops and foretastes of God's love; the rivers of pleasure are reserved for paradise. Well may we take the harp and viol and triumph in God's praise. Who can tread on these hot coals of God's love and his heart not burn in thankfulness?

4. Thankfulness is the best policy. There is nothing lost by it. To be thankful for one mercy is the way to have more. It is like pouring water into a pump which fetches out more. Musicians love to sound their trumpets where there is the best echo, and God loves to bestow his mercies where there is the best echo of thankfulness.

5. Thankfulness is a frame of heart that God delights in. If repentance is the joy of heaven, praise is the music. Bernard calls thankfulness the sweet balm that drops from a Christian.

Four sacrifices God is very pleased with: the sacrifice of Christ's blood; the sacrifice of a broken heart; the sacrifice of alms; and the sacrifice of thanksgiving. Praise and thanksgiving (says Mr Greenham) is the most excellent part of God's worship, for this shall continue in the heavenly choir when all other exercises of religion have ceased.

6. What a horrid thing ingratitude is! It gives a dye and tincture to every other sin and makes it crimson. Ingratitude is the spirit of baseness: 'They that eat thy bread have laid a wound under thee' (*Obad. 7*). Ingratitude is worse than brutish (*Isa. 1:3*). It is reported of Julias Caesar that he would never forgive an ungrateful person. Though God is a sin-pardoning God, he scarcely knows how to pardon for this. 'How shall I pardon thee for this? thy children have forsaken me, when I had fed them to the full, they then committed adultery' (*Jer. 5:7*). Draco (whose laws were written in blood) published an edict that if any man had received a benefit from another, and it could be proved against him that he had not been grateful for it, he should be put to death. An unthankful person is a monster in nature, a paradox in Christianity. He is the scorn of heaven and the plague of earth. An ungrateful man never does well except in one thing – that is, when he dies.

7. Not being thankful is the cause of all the judgments which have lain on us. Our unthankfulness for health has been the cause of so much mortality. Our gospel unthankfulness and sermon-surfeiting has been the reason why God has put so many lights under a bushel. As Bradford said, 'My unthankfulness was the death of King Edward VI.' Who will spend money on a piece of ground that produces nothing but briars? Unthankfulness stops the golden phial of God's bounty, so that it will not drop.

Question: What shall we do to be thankful?

Answer 1: If you wish to be thankful, get a heart deeply humbled with the sense of your own vileness. A broken heart is the best pipe to sound forth God's praise. He who studies his sins wonders that he has anything and that God should shine on such a dunghill: 'Who was before a blasphemer, and a persecutor, but I obtained mercy' (*1 Tim. 1:13*). How thankful Paul was! How he trumpeted forth free grace! A proud man will never be thankful. He looks on all his mercies as either of his own procuring or deserving. If he has an estate, this he has got by his wits and industry, not considering that scripture, 'Thou shalt remember the Lord thy God: for it is he that giveth thee power to get wealth' (*Deut. 8:18*). Pride stops the current of gratitude. O Christian, think of your unworthiness; see yourself the least of saints and the chief of sinners, and then you will be thankful.

Answer 2: Strive for sound evidences of God's love to you. Read God's love in the impress of holiness upon your hearts. God's love poured in will make the vessels of mercy run over with thankfulness: 'Unto him that loved us, be glory and dominion for ever' (*Rev. 1:5,6*). The deepest springs yield the sweetest water. Hearts deeply aware of God's love yield the sweetest praises.

SECTION 18: A GODLY MAN IS A LOVER OF THE SAINTS

The best way to discern grace in oneself is to love grace in others: 'We know that we have passed from death unto life, because we love the brethren' (*1 John 3:14*). What is religion but religation – a knitting together of hearts? Faith knits us to God and love knits us one to another. There is a twofold love to others:

1. A civil love.   A godly man has a love of civility to all: 'Abraham stood up, and bowed to the children of Heth' (*Gen. 23:7*). Though they were extraneous and not within the pale of the covenant, yet Abraham was affable to them. Grace sweetens and refines nature: 'be courteous' (*1 Pet. 3:8*). We are to have a love of civility to all:

(i) Because they are of the same clay, of the same lump and mould with ourselves and are a piece of God's intricate needlework.

(ii) Because our sweet deportment towards them may be a means to win them over and put them in love with the ways of God. Morose, rude behaviour often alienates the hearts of others and hardens them most against holiness, whereas loving behaviour is very obliging and may be like a lodestone to draw them to religion.

2. A pious and a holy love.   This, a godly man has chiefly for those who are 'of the household of faith' (*Gal. 6:10*). The first was a love of courtesy, this of delight. Our love to the saints (says Augustine) should be more than to our natural relations, because the bond of the Spirit is closer than that of blood. This love to the saints which shows a man to be godly must have seven ingredients in it:

(i) Love to the saints must be *sincere*: 'Let us not love in word, neither in tongue, but in deed and in truth' (*1 John 3:18*). The honey that drops from the comb is pure; so love

[139]

must be pure, without deceit. Many are like Naphtali: 'He giveth goodly words' (*Gen. 49:21*). Pretended love is like a painted fire, which has no heat in it. Some hide malice under a false veil of love. I have read of Antoninus the Emperor that where he made a show of friendship, he intended the most mischief.

(ii) Love to the saints must be *spiritual*. We must love them because they are saints, not out of self-respect because they are affable or have been kind to us.

But we must love them from spiritual considerations, because of the good that is in them. We are to reverence their holiness, else it is a carnal love.

(iii) Love to the saints must be *extensive*; we must love all who bear God's image:

(a) Though they have many infirmities. A Christian in this life is like a good face full of freckles. You who cannot love another because of his imperfections have never yet seen your own face in the mirror. Your brother's infirmities may make you pity him; his graces must make you love him.

(b) We must love the saints though in some things they do not coalesce and agree with us. Another Christian may differ from me in lesser matters, either because he has more light than I, or because he has less light. If he differs from me because he has more light, then I have no reason to censure him. If because he has less light, then I ought to bear with him as the weaker vessel. In things of an indifferent nature, there ought to be Christian forbearance.

(c) We must love the saints though their graces outvie and surpass ours. We ought to bless God for the eminence of another's grace, because hereby religion is honoured. Pride is not quite slain in a believer. Saints themselves are apt to grudge and repine at each other's excellences. Is it not strange that the same person should hate one man for his sin and envy another for his virtue? Christians need to look to their hearts. Love is right and genuine when we can rejoice in the graces of others though they seem to eclipse ours.

(iv) Love to the saints must be *appreciating*. We must esteem their persons above others: 'He honoureth them that fear the Lord' (*Psa. 15:4*). We are to look upon the wicked as lumber, but upon the saints as jewels. These must be had in high veneration.

(v) Love to the saints must be *social*. We should delight in their company: 'I am a companion of all them that fear thee' (*Psa. 119:63*). It is a kind of hell to be in the company of the wicked, where we cannot choose but hear God's name dishonoured. It was a capital crime to carry the image of Tiberius, engraved on a ring or coin, into any sordid place. Those who have the image of God engraved on them should not go into any sinful, sordid company. I have only ever read of two living people who desired to keep company with the dead, and they were possessed by the devil (*Matt. 8:28*). What comfort can a living Christian have from conversing with the dead (*Jude 12*)? But the society of saints is desirable. This is not to walk 'among the tombs', but 'among beds of spices'. Believers are Christ's garden; their graces are the flowers; their savoury discourse is the fragrant scent of these flowers.

(vi) Love to the saints must be *demonstrative*. We should be ready to do all offices of love to them, vindicate their names, contribute to their necessities and, like the good Samaritan, pour oil and wine into their wounds (*Luke 10: 34,35*). Love cannot be concealed, but is active in its sphere and will lay itself out for the good of others.

(vii) Love to the saints must be *constant*: 'he that dwelleth in love' (*1 John 4:16*). Our love must not only lodge for a night, but we must dwell in love: 'Let brotherly love continue' (*Heb. 13:1*). As love must be sincere without hypocrisy, so it must be constant, without deficiency. Love must be like the pulse, always beating, not like those

Galatians who at one time were ready to pluck out their eyes for Paul (*Gal. 4:15*) and afterwards were ready to pluck out his eyes. Love should expire only with our life. And surely if our love to the saints is thus divinely qualified, we may hopefully conclude that we are enrolled among the godly. 'By this shall all men know that ye are my disciples, if ye have love one to another' (*John 13:35*).

What induces a godly man to love the saints is the fact that he is closely related to them. There ought to be love among relations; there is a spiritual consanguinity among believers. They all have one head, therefore should all have one heart. They are stones of the same building (*1 Pet. 2:5*), and shall not these stones be cemented together with love?

Use 1: If it is the distinguishing mark of a godly man to be a lover of the saints, then how sad it is to see this grace of love in eclipse! This characteristic of godliness is almost blotted out among Christians. England was once a fair garden where the flower of love grew, but surely now this flower is either plucked or withered. Where is that amity and unity which there should be among Christians? I appeal to you, would there be that censuring and despising, that reproaching and undermining one another, if there were love? Instead of bitter tears there are bitter spirits. It is a sign that iniquity abounds when the love of many grows cold. There is that distance among some professing Christians as if they had not received the same Spirit, or as if they did not hope for the same heaven. In primitive times there was so much love among the godly that it set the heathen wondering, and now there is so little that it may set Christians blushing.

Use 2: As we would be written down for saints in God's calendar, let us love the brotherhood (*1 Pet. 2:17*). Those who shall one day live together should love together. What is it that makes a disciple but love (*John 13:35*)? The devil has knowledge, but that which makes him a devil is that he lacks love. To persuade Christians to love, consider:

(i) The saints have that in them which may make us love them. They are the intricate embroidery and workmanship of the Holy Spirit (*Eph. 2:10*). They have those rare lineaments of grace that none but a pencil from heaven could draw. Their eyes sparkle forth beauty, 'their breasts are like clusters of grapes' (*Song 7:7*). This makes Christ himself delight in his spouse: 'The king is held in the galleries' (*Song 7:5*). The church is the daughter of a prince (*Song 7:1*). She is waited on by angels (*Heb 1:14*). She has a palace of glory reserved for her (*John 14:2*), and may not all this draw forth our love?

(ii) Consider how evil it is for saints not to love:

(a) It is *unnatural*. The saints are Christ's lambs (*John 21:15*). For a dog to worry a lamb is usual but for one lamb to worry another is unnatural. The saints are brethren (*1 Peter 3:8*). How barbarous it is for brethren not to love!

(b) Not to love is a *foolish* thing. Have not God's people enemies enough that they should fly in the faces of one another? The wicked confederate against the godly: 'They have taken crafty counsel against thy people' (*Psa. 83:3*). Though there may be a private grudge between such as are wicked, yet they will all agree and unite against the saints. If two greyhounds are snarling at a bone and you put a hare between them, they will leave the bone and chase the hare. So if wicked men have private differences amongst themselves, and the godly are near them, they will leave snarling at one another and chase the godly. Now, when God's people have so many enemies abroad, who watch for their halting and are glad when they can do them a mischief, shall the saints fall out and divide into parties among themselves?

(iii) Not to love is very *unseasonable*. God's people are in a common calamity. They suffer in one cause and for them to disagree is altogether unseasonable. Why does the Lord bring his people together in affliction, except to bring them together in affection? Metals will unite in a furnace. If ever Christians unite, it should be in the furnace of affliction. Chrysostom compares affliction to a shepherd's dog which makes all the sheep run together. God's rod has this loud voice in it: 'Love one another'. How unworthy it is when Christians are suffering together to be then striving together.

(iv) Not to love is very *sinful*.

(a) For saints not to love is to live in contradiction to Scripture. The apostle is continually beating upon this string of love, as if it made the sweetest music in religion: 'This commandment have we from him, That he who loveth God love his brother also' (*1 John 4:21*). (See also *Rom. 13:8; Col. 3:14; 1 Peter 1:22; 1 John 3:11*). Not to love is to walk contrary to the Word. Can he who goes against the rules of medicine be a good physician? Can he who goes against the rules of religion be a good Christian?

(b) Lack of love among Christians greatly silences the spirit of prayer. Hot passions make cold prayers. Where animosities and contentions prevail, instead of praying for one another, Christians will be ready to pray against one another, like the disciples who prayed for fire from heaven on the Samaritans (*Luke 9:54*). And will God, do you think, hear such prayers as come from a wrathful heart? Will he eat our leavened bread? Will he accept those duties which are soured with bitterness of spirit? Shall that prayer which is offered with the strange fire of our sinful passions ever go up as incense?

(c) These heart-burnings hinder the progress of piety in our own souls. The flower of grace will not grow in a wrathful heart. The body may as soon thrive while it has the plague as a soul can that is infected with malice. While Christians are debating, grace is abating. As the spleen grows, health decays. As hatred increases, holiness declines.

(v) Not to love is very *fatal*. The differences among God's people portend ruin. All mischiefs come in at this gap of division (*Matt. 12:25*). Animosities among saints may make God leave his temple: 'the glory of the Lord went up from the cherub, and stood upon the threshold' (*Ezek. 10:4*). Does not God seem to stand upon the threshold of his house as if he were taking wings to fly? And woe to us if God departs from us (*Hos. 9:12*)! If the master leaves the ship, it is nearly sinking indeed. If God leaves a land, it must of necessity sink in ruin.

Question: How shall we attain this excellent grace of love?

Answer 1: Beware of the devil's couriers – I mean such as run on his errand, and make it their work to blow the coals of contention among Christians, and render one party odious to another.

Answer 2: Keep up friendly meetings. Christians should not be shy of one another as if they had the plague.

Answer 3: Let us plead that promise: 'I will give them one heart, and one way' (*Jer. 32:39*). Let us pray that there may be no contests among Christians, except as to who shall love most. Let us pray that God will divide Babylon and unite Zion.

Use 3: Is it a mark of a godly man to love the saints? Then those who hate the saints must stand indicted as ungodly. The wicked have an implacable malice against God's people and how can antipathies be reconciled? To hate saintship is a brand of the reprobate. Those who malign the godly are the curse of creation. If all the scalding drops from God's phial will make them miserable, they shall be so. Never did any who were the haters and persecutors of saints thrive at that trade. What became of Julian, Diocletian, Maximinus, Valerian, Cardinal Crescentius and others? The bowels of some of them came out; others choked in their own blood, that they might be set up as standing monuments of God's vengeance: 'they that hate the righteous shall be desolate' (*Psa. 34:21*).

SECTION 19: A GODLY MAN DOES NOT INDULGE HIMSELF IN ANY SIN

Though sin lives in him, yet he does not live in sin. Every man that has wine in him is not in wine. A godly man may step into sin through infirmity, but he does not keep on that road. 'See if there be any wicked way in me' (*Psa. 139:24*).

Question: What is it to indulge sin?

Answer 1: To give the breast to it and feed it. As a fond parent humours his child and lets him have what he wants, so to indulge sin is to humour sin.

Answer 2: To indulge sin is to commit it with delight: 'they had pleasure in unrighteousness' (*2 Thess. 2:12*).

In this sense, a godly man does not indulge sin. Though sin is in him, he is troubled at it and would gladly get rid of it. There is as much difference between sin in the wicked and the godly as between poison being in a serpent and in a man. Poison in a serpent is in its natural place and is delightful, but poison in a man's body is offensive and he uses antidotes to expel it. So sin in a wicked man is delightful, being in its natural place, but sin in a child of God is burdensome and he uses all means to expel it. The sin is trimmed off. The will is against it. A godly man enters his protest against sin: 'What I do I allow not' (*Rom. 7:15*). A child of God, while he commits sin, hates the sin he commits (*Rom. 7*). In particular there are four sorts of sin which a godly man will not allow himself:

[146]

1. Secret sins. Some are more modest than to commit gross sin. That would be a stain on their reputation. But they will sit brooding upon sin in a corner: 'Saul secretly practised mischief' (*1 Sam. 23:9*). All will not sin on a balcony but perhaps they will sin behind the curtain. Rachel did not carry her father's images like a saddle cloth to be exposed to public view, but she put them under her and sat on them (*Gen. 31:34*). Many carry their sins secretly like a candle in a dark lantern.

But a godly man dare not sin secretly:

(i) He knows that God sees in secret (*Psa. 44:21*). As God cannot be deceived by our subtlety, so he cannot be excluded by our secrecy.

(ii) A godly man knows that secret sins are in some sense worse than others. They reveal more guile and atheism. The curtain-sinner makes himself believe that God does not see: 'Son of man, hast thou seen what the ancients of the house of Israel do in the dark, for they say, The Lord seeth us not' (*Ezek. 8:12*). Those who have bad eyes think that the sun is dim. How it provokes God, that men's atheism should give the lie to his omniscience! 'He that formed the eye, shall he not see?' (*Psa. 94:9*).

(iii) A godly man knows that secret sins shall not escape God's justice. A judge on the bench can punish no offence but what is proved by witnesses. He cannot punish the treason of the heart, but the sins of the heart are as visible to God as if they were written upon the forehead. As God will reward secret duties, so he will revenge secret sins.

2. Gainful sins. Gain is the golden bait with which Satan fishes for souls: 'the sweet smell of money'. This was the last temptation he used with Christ: 'All these things will I give thee' (*Matt. 4:9*). But Christ saw the hook under the bait. Many who have escaped gross sins are still caught in a golden net. To gain the world, they will use indirect routes.

[147]

A godly man dare not travel for riches along the devil's highway. Those are sad gains that make a man lose peace of conscience and heaven at last. He who gets an estate by injustice stuffs his pillow with thorns, and his head will lie very uneasy when he comes to die.

3. *A beloved sin.* There is usually one sin that is the favourite, the sin which the heart is most fond of. A beloved sin lies in a man's bosom as the disciple whom Jesus loved leaned on his bosom (*John 13:23*). A godly man will not indulge a darling sin: 'I kept myself from mine iniquity' (*Psa. 18:23*). 'I will not indulge the sin of my constitution, to which the bias of my heart more naturally inclines.' 'Fight neither with small nor great, save only with the king' (*1 Kings 22:31*). A godly man fights this king sin. The oracle of Apollo answered the people of Cyrrha that if they would live in peace among themselves, they must make continual war with those strangers who were on their borders. If we would have peace in our souls, we must maintain a war against our favourite sin and never leave off till it is subdued.

Question: How shall we know the beloved sin?

Answer 1: The sin which a man does not love to have reproved is the darling sin. Herod could not endure having his incest spoken against. If the prophet meddles with that sin, it shall cost him his head. Men can be content to have other sins declaimed against, but if the minister puts his finger on the sore, and touches this sin, their hearts begin to burn in malice against him. Herodias was an ominous sign.

Answer 2: The sin on which the thoughts run most is the darling sin. Whichever way the thoughts go, the heart goes. He who is in love with a person cannot keep his thoughts off the object. Examine what sin runs most in your mind, what sin is first in your thoughts and greets you in the morning – that is the predominant sin.

Answer 3: The sin which has most power over us and most easily leads us captive is the one beloved by the soul. There are some sins that a man can resist better. If they come for entertainment, he can more easily put them off. But the bosom sin comes as a suitor, and he cannot deny it, but is overcome by it. The young man in the Gospel had repulsed many sins, but there was one sin that soiled him, and that was covetousness. Christians, mark what sin you are most readily led captive by – that is the harlot in your bosom. It is a sad thing that a man should be so bewitched by lust that, if it asks him to part with not only half the kingdom (*Esther 7:2*) but the whole kingdom of heaven, he must part with it, to gratify that lust.

Answer 4: The sin which men use arguments to defend is the beloved sin. He that has a jewel in his bosom will defend it for very life. So when there is any sin in the bosom, men will defend it. The sin we advocate and dispute for is the besetting sin. If the sin is passion, we plead for it: 'I do well to be angry' (*Jonah 4:9*). If the sin is covetousness and we vindicate it and perhaps wrest Scripture to justify it, that is the sin which lies nearest the heart.

Answer 5: The sin which most troubles us, and flies most in the face in an hour of sickness and distress, that is the Delilah sin. When Joseph's brethren were distressed, their sin in selling their brother came to remembrance: 'We are verily guilty concerning our brother, in that we saw the anguish of his soul, when he besought us, and we would not hear; therefore is this distress come upon us' (*Gen. 42:21*). So, when a man is on a sickbed and conscience says, 'You have been guilty of such a sin; you went on in it, and rolled it like honey under your tongue!' Conscience is reading him a sad lecture. That was the beloved sin for sure.

Answer 6: The sin which a man finds most difficulty in giving up is the endeared sin. Of all his sons, Jacob found most difficulty in parting with Benjamin: 'Joseph is not, and Simeon is not, and ye will take Benjamin away' (*Gen. 42:36*). So the sinner says, 'This and that sin I have parted with, but must Benjamin go, must I part with this delightful sin? That goes to the heart.' As with a castle that has several forts about it, the first and second fort are taken, but when it comes to the castle, the governor will rather fight and die than yield that. So a man may allow some of his sins to be demolished, but when it comes to one sin, that is the taking of the castle; he will never agree to part with that. That is the master sin for sure.

The besetting sin is a God-provoking sin. The wise men of Troy counselled Priam to send Helena back to the Greeks, not permitting himself to be abused any longer by the charms of her beauty, because keeping her within the city would lay the foundation of a fatal war. So we should put away our Delilah sin, lest it incense the God of heaven, and make him commence a war against us.

The besetting sin is of all others most dangerous. As Samson's strength lay in his hair, so the strength of sin lies in this beloved sin. This is like a poison striking the heart, which brings death. A godly man will lay the axe of repentance to this sin and hew it down. He sets this sin, like Uriah, in the forefront of the battle, so that it may be slain. He will sacrifice this Isaac, he will pluck out this right eye, so that he may see better to go to heaven.

4. Those sins which the world counts lesser. There is no such thing as little sin, yet some may be deemed less comparatively. But a good man will not indulge himself in these. Such as:

(i) Sins of omission. Some think it no great matter to omit family, or private prayer. They can go for several months and God never hears from them. A godly man will as soon live without food as without prayer. He knows that every creature of God is sanctified by prayer (*1 Tim. 4:5*). The bird may shame many Christians; it never takes a drop, but the eye is lifted up towards heaven.

(ii) A godly man dare not allow himself vain, frothy discourse, much less that which looks like an oath. If God will judge for idle words, will he not much more for idle oaths?

(iii) A godly man dare not allow himself rash censuring. Some think this a small matter. They will not swear, but they will slander. This is very evil. You wound a man in that which is dearest to him. He who is godly turns all his censures upon himself. He judges himself for his own sins, but is very chary and tender of the good name of another.

Use: As you would be numbered among the genealogies of the saints, do not indulge yourselves in any sin. Consider the mischief that one sin lived in will do:

1. One sin gives Satan as much advantage against you as more sins. The fowler can hold a bird by one wing; Satan held Judas fast by one sin.

2. One sin lived in proves that the heart is not sound. He who hides one rebel in his house is a traitor to the crown. The person who indulges one sin is a traitorous hypocrite.

3. One sin will make way for more, as a little thief can open the door to more. Sins are linked and chained together. One sin will draw on more. David's adultery made way for murder. One sin never goes alone. If there is only one nest-egg, the devil can brood on it.

4. *One sin is as much a breach of God's law as more sins*: 'He that shall offend in one point is guilty of all' (*Jas. 2:10*). The king may make a law against felony, treason and murder. If a man is guilty of only one of these, he is as much a transgressor of the law as if he were guilty of all.

5. *One sin lived in prevents Christ from entering.* One stone in the pipe keeps out the water. One sin indulged in obstructs the soul and keeps the streams of Christ's blood from running into it.

6. *One sin lived in will spoil all your good duties.* A drop of poison will spoil a glass of wine. Abimelech, a bastard, destroyed seventy of his brethren (*Judges 9:5*). One bastard sin will destroy seventy prayers. One dead fly will corrupt the box of ointment.

7. *One sin lived in will be a cankerworm to eat out the peace of conscience.* It takes away the manna from the ark and leaves only a rod. 'Alas! What a scorpion lies within!' (*Seneca*). One sin is a pirate to rob a Christian of his comfort. One jarring string puts all the music out of tune. One sin countenanced will spoil the music of conscience.

8. *One sin allowed will damn as well as more sins.* One disease is enough to kill. If a fence is made never so strong, leave open only one gap and the wild beast may enter and tread down the corn. If only one sin is allowed in the soul, you leave open a gap for the devil to enter. It is a simile of Chrysostom that a soldier may have his helmet and his breastplate on, but if only one place has no armour, the bullet may enter there, and he may as well be shot as if he

had no armour on. So if you favour only one sin, you leave a part of your soul unprotected and the bullet of God's wrath may enter there and shoot you. One sin may shut you out of heaven. And as Jerome says, what difference is there between being shut out for more sins and for one? Therefore, beware of cherishing one sin. One millstone will sink a man into the sea as well as a hundred.

9. One sin harboured in the soul will unfit us for suffering. How soon an hour of trial may come. A man who has hurt his shoulder cannot carry a heavy burden, and a man who has any guilt in his conscience cannot carry the cross of Christ. Will he who cannot deny his lust for Christ deny his life for Christ? One unmortified sin in the soul will bring forth the bitter fruit of apostasy.

If, then, you would show yourselves godly, give a certificate of divorce to every sin. Kill the Goliath sin: 'Let not sin reign' (*Rom. 6:12*). In the original it is 'Let not sin king it over you'. Grace and sin may be together, but grace and the love of sin cannot. Therefore parley with sin no longer, but with the spear or mortification, spill the heart blood of every sin.

SECTION 20: A GODLY MAN IS GOOD IN HIS RELA-
TIONSHIPS

To be good in general is not enough, but we must show piety in our relationships.

1. He who is good as a magistrate is godly. The magistrate is God's representative. A godly magistrate holds the balance of justice and gives everyone his right: 'thou shalt not respect persons, neither take a gift: for a gift doth blind the eyes' (*Deut. 16:19*). A magistrate must judge the cause, not the person. He who allows himself to be corrupted by bribes is not a judge but a party. A magistrate must do that which is 'according to law' (*Acts 23:3*). And in order that he may do justice, he must examine the cause. The archer who wishes to shoot right must first see the target.

2. He who is good as a minister is godly. Ministers must be:

(i) *Painstaking.* 'Preach the word; be instant in season, out of season' (*2 Tim. 4:2*). The minister must not be idle. Sloth is as inexcusable in a minister as sleeping in a sentry. John the Baptist was a 'voice crying' (*Matt. 3:3*). A dumb minister is of no more use than a dead physician. A man of God must work in the Lord's vineyard. It was Augustine's wish that Christ might find him at his coming either praying or preaching.

(ii) *Knowledgeable*: 'the priest's lips should keep knowledge, and they should seek the law at his mouth' (*Mal. 2:7*). It was said in honour of Gregory Nazianzene that he was an ocean of divinity. The prophets of old were called 'seers' (*1 Sam. 9:9*). It is absurd to have blind seers. Christ said to Peter, 'Feed my sheep' (*John 21:16*). But how sad it is when the shepherd needs to be fed! Ignorance in a minister is like blindness in an oculist. Under the law, he who had the plague in his head was unclean (*Lev. 13:44*).

(iii) A *plain preacher*, suiting his matter and style to the capacity of his audience (*1 Cor. 14:19*). Some ministers, like eagles, love to soar aloft in abstruse metaphysical notions, thinking they are most admired when they are least understood. They who preach in the clouds, instead of hitting their people's conscience, shoot over their heads.

(iv) *Zealous* in reproving sin: 'rebuke them sharply' (*Titus 1:13*). Epiphanius said of Elijah that he sucked fire out of his mother's breasts. A man of God must suck the fire of zeal out of the breasts of Scripture. Zeal in a minister is as proper as fire on the altar. Some are afraid to reprove, like the swordfish which has a sword in his head but is without a heart. So they carry the sword of the Spirit about them, but have no heart to draw it out in reproof against sin. How many have sown pillows under their people (*Ezek. 13:18*), making them sleep so securely that they never woke till they were in hell!

(v) *Holy* in heart and life:

(a) In heart. How sad it is for a minister to preach that to others which he never felt in his own soul; to exhort others to holiness and himself be a stranger to it. Oh, that this were not too often so! How many blow the Lord's trumpet with foul breath!

(b) In life. Under the law, before the priests served at the altar, they washed in the laver. Such as serve in the Lord's house must first be washed from gross sin in the laver of repentance. The life of a minister should be a walking Bible. Basil said of Gregory Nazianzene that he thundered in his doctrine and lightened in his conduct. A minister must imitate John the Baptist, who was not only 'a voice crying', but 'a light shining' (*John 5:35*). They who live in contradiction to what they preach disgrace this excellent calling. They turn their books into cups. And though they are angels by office, yet they are devils in their lives (*Jer. 23:15*).

3. *He who is good as a husband is godly.* He fills up that relationship with love: 'Husbands, love your wives' (*Eph. 5:25*). The vine twisting its branches about the elm and embracing it may be an emblem of that entire love which should be in the conjugal relationship. A married condition would be sad, if it had cares to embitter it and not love to sweeten it. Love is the best diamond in the marriage ring: 'Isaac loved Rebekah' (*Gen. 24:67*). Unkindnesses in this close relationship are very unhappy. We read in heathen authors that Clytemnestra, the wife of Agamemnon, in order to revenge an injury received from her husband, first

rent the veil of her chastity and afterwards consented to his death. The husband should show his love to his wife by covering infirmities; by avoiding occasions of strife; by sweet, endearing expressions; by pious counsel; by love tokens; by encouraging what he sees amiable and virtuous in her; by mutual prayer; by associating with her, unless detained by urgency of business. The pilot who leaves his ship and abandons it entirely to the merciless waves, declares that he does not value it or reckon there is any treasure in it.

The apostle gives a good reason why there should be mutual love between husband and wife: 'that your prayers be not hindered' (*1 Pet. 3:7*). Where passions prevail, there prayer is either intermitted or interrupted.

4. He who is good as a father is godly

(i) A father must drop holy instructions into his children: 'bring them up in the nurture and admonition of the Lord' (*Eph. 6:4*). This is what Abraham did: 'I know Abraham, that he will command his children and his household, and they shall keep the way of the Lord' (*Gen. 18:19*). Children are young plants which must be watered with good education, so that they may, with Obadiah, fear the Lord 'from their youth up' (*1 Kings 18:12*). Plato said, 'In vain does he expect a harvest who has been negligent in sowing.' Nor can a parent expect to reap any good from a child, where he has not sown the seed of wholesome instruction. And though, notwithstanding all counsel and admonition, the child should die in sin, yet it is a comfort to a godly parent to think that before his child died, he gave it spiritual medicine.

(ii) A parent must pray for his children. Monica, the mother of Augustine, prayed for his conversion, and someone said it was impossible that a son of so many prayers and tears should perish. The soul of your child is in a snare and will you not pray that it may 'recover out of the snare of the devil' (*2 Tim. 2:26*)? Many parents are careful to lay up portions for their children, but they do not lay up prayers for them.

(iii) A parent must give his children discipline: 'Withhold not correction from the child: for if thou beatest him with the rod, he shall not die' (*Prov. 23:13*). The rod beats out the dust and moth of sin. A child indulged and humoured in wickedness will prove a burden instead of a blessing. David pampered Adonijah: 'his father had not displeased him at any time, saying, Why hast thou done so?' (*1 Kings 1:6*). And afterwards he was a grief of heart to his father, and wanted to put him off his throne. Correction is a hedge of thorns to stop children in their full career to hell.

5. *He who is good as a master is godly*
A godly man promotes religion in his family; he sets up piety in his house as well as in his heart: 'I will walk within my house with a perfect heart' (*Psa. 101:2*). 'I and my household will serve the Lord' (*Josh. 24:15*). I find it written in honour of Cranmer that his family was a nursery of piety. A godly man's house is a little church: 'the church which is in his house' (*Col. 4:15*).

(i) A good man makes known the oracles of God to those who are under his roof. He reads the Word and perfumes his house with prayer. It is recorded of the Jews that they had sacrifices in their family as well as in the tabernacle (*Exod. 12:3*).

(ii) A godly man provides necessities. He relieves his servants in health and sickness. He is not like that Amalekite who shook off his servant when he was sick (*1 Sam. 30:13*), but rather like the good centurion, who sought Christ for the healing of his sick servant (*Matt. 8:5*).

(iii) A godly man sets his servants a good example. He is

sober and heavenly in his deportment; his virtuous life is a good mirror for the servants in the family to dress themselves by.

6. He who is good in the relationship of a child is godly

He honours his parents. Philo the Jew placed the fifth commandment in the first table – as if children had not performed their whole devotion to God till they had given honour to their parents. This honouring of parents consists in two things:

(i) In *respecting* their persons, which respect is shown both by humility of speech and by gesture. The opposite of this is when a child behaves himself in an unseemly and proud manner. Among the Lacedemonians, if a child had behaved imperiously towards his parent, it was published by authority that it was lawful for the father to appoint whom he would to be his heir and to disinherit that child.

(ii) *Obeying* their commands: 'Children, obey your parents in the Lord' (*Eph. 6:1*). Duty is the interest which children pay their parents on the capital they have had from them. Christ has set all children a pattern of obedience to their parents: 'He was subject unto them' (*Luke 2:51*). The Rechabites were eminent for this: 'I set before the Rechabites pots full of wine, and said to them, Drink ye wine. But they said, We will drink no wine: for Jonadab the son of Rechab our father commanded us saying, Ye shall drink no wine, neither ye, nor your sons for ever' (*Jer. 35:5,6*). Solon was asked why, among the many laws he made, none was against disobedient children. He answered that it was because he thought none would be so wicked.

God has punished children who have refused to pay the tribute of obedience. Absalom, a disobedient son, was hanged in an oak between heaven and earth, as being worthy of neither. Manlius, an old man, being reduced to much poverty, and having a rich son, entreated him only for charity, but could not obtain it. The son disowned him as his father, using reproachful language. The poor old man let tears fall (as witnesses of his grief) and went away. God, to revenge this disobedience of his son, soon afterwards struck him with madness. He in whose heart godliness lives makes as much conscience of the fifth commandment as of the first.

7. *He who is good as a servant is godly*

'Servants, be subject to them who are your masters according to the flesh, with fear and trembling' (*Col. 3:22; Eph. 6:5*). The goodness of servants lies in:

(i) *Diligence*. Abraham's servant quickly dispatched the business his master entrusted him with (*Gen. 24:33*).

(ii) *Cheerfulness*. Servants must be free-willers, like the centurion's servants: 'If I say to one, Go, he goeth' (*Luke 7:8*).

(iii) *Faithfulness*, which consists in two things: (a) In not defrauding: 'not purloining' (*Titus 2:10*). (b) In keeping counsel. It proves the badness of a stomach, when it cannot retain what is put into it, and the badness of a servant when he cannot retain those secrets which his master has committed to him.

(iv) *Silence*: 'not answering again' (*Titus 2:9*). It is better to correct a fault than to minimize it. And what may stimulate a servant in his work is that encouraging scripture, 'Knowing that of the Lord ye shall receive the reward of the inheritance: for ye serve the Lord Christ' (*Col. 3:24*). If Christ should bid you do a piece of work for him, would you not do it? While you serve your master, you serve the Lord Christ. If you ask what salary you shall have, 'Ye shall receive the reward of the inheritance'.

Use 1: Is it the grand sign of a godly man to be relatively holy? Then the Lord be merciful to us. How few godly ones are to be found! Many put on the coat of profession. They will pray and discourse on points of religion, but 'What meaneth this bleating of the sheep?' (*1 Sam. 15:14*). They are not good in their relationships. How bad it is when Christians are defective in relative piety! Can we call a bad magistrate godly? He perverts equity: 'Do ye judge uprightly, O ye sons of men? Ye weigh the violence of your hands in the earth' (*Psa. 58:1,2*). Can we call a bad parent godly? He never teaches his child the way to heaven. He is like the ostrich which is cruel to her young (*Job 39:16*). Can we call a bad employer godly? Many employers leave their religion at church (as the clerk does his book); they have nothing of God at home; their houses are not Bethels, but Bethavens – not little temples but little hells. How many employers at the last day must plead guilty at the bar. Though they have fed their servants' bellies, they have starved their souls. Can we call a bad child godly? He stops his ear to his parents' counsel. You may as well call him who is disloyal a good subject. Can we call a bad servant godly? He is slothful and wilful; he is more ready to spy a fault in another than to correct it in himself. To call one who is bad in his relationships godly is a contradiction; it is to call evil good (*Isa. 5:20*).

Use 2: As we desire to have God approve of us, let us show godliness in our relationships. Not to be good in our relationships spoils all our other good things. Naaman was an honourable man, but he was a leper (*2 Kings 5:1*). That 'but' spoiled everything. So such a person is a great hearer, but he neglects relative duties. This stains the beauty of all his other actions. As in printing, though the letter is never so well shaped, yet if it is not set in the right place, it spoils the sense. So let a man have many things commendable in him, yet if he is not good in his right place, making conscience of how he walks in his relationships, he does harm to religion. There are many to whom Christ will say at last, as to the young man, 'Yet lackest thou one thing' (*Luke*

18:22). You have misbehaved in your relative capacity. As therefore we cherish our salvation and the honour of religion, let us shine in that orb of relationships where God has placed us.

SECTION 21: A GODLY MAN DOES SPIRITUAL THINGS IN A SPIRITUAL MANNER

'We are the circumcision, which worship God in the spirit' (*Phil. 3:3*). Spiritual worship is pure worship: 'Ye are built up a spiritual house, an holy priesthood, to offer up spiritual sacrifices' (*1 Peter 2:5*) – spiritual not only in the matter, but also in the quality. A wicked man either lives in the total neglect of duty or else discharges it in a dull, careless manner. Instead of 'using the world as if he used it not' (*1 Cor. 7.31*), he serves God as if he did not serve him. A godly man spiritualizes duty; he is not only for the doing of holy things but for the holy doing of things.

Question: What is it to perform spiritual duties spiritually?

Answer: It consists in three things:

1. To do duties from a spiritual principle, namely, a renewed principle of grace. A man may have gifts which attract admiration; he may have the most melting, ravishing expressions; he may speak like an angel come down from heaven; yet his duties may not be spiritual because he lacks the grace of the Spirit. Whatever a moral, unregenerate person does is only nature refined. Though he may do duties better than a godly man, yet not so well – better as to the matter and elegance, yet not so well, as lacking a renewed principle. A crab-tree may bear as well as a pippin; the fruit may be big and lovelier to the eye, yet it is not such good fruit as the other, because it does not come from so good a stock. So an unregenerate person may perform as

[161]

many duties as a child of God, and these may seem to be more glorious to the outward view, but they are harsh and sour, because they do not come from the sweet and pleasant root of grace. A true saint gives God that wine which comes from the pure grape of the Spirit.

2. To perform duties spiritually is to do them with the utmost intention. A Christian is very serious and strives to keep his thoughts close to the work in hand: 'that ye may attend upon the Lord without distraction' (*1 Cor. 7:35*).

Question: But may not a godly man have roving thoughts in duty?

Answer: Yes, sad experience proves it. The thoughts will be dancing up and down in prayer. The saints are called stars and many times in duty they are wandering stars. The heart is like quicksilver which will not settle. It is hard to tie two good thoughts together. We cannot lock our hearts so close but that distracting thoughts, like wind, will get in. Jerome complains about himself. 'Sometimes,' he says, 'when I am doing God's service, I am walking in the galleries or casting up accounts.'

But these wandering thoughts in the godly are not allowed: 'I hate vain thoughts' (*Psa. 119:113*). They come like unwelcome guests who are no sooner spied than they are turned out.

Question: From where do these wandering thoughts arise in the godly?

Answer 1: From the depravity of nature. They are the mud which the heart casts up.

Answer 2: From Satan. The devil, if he cannot hinder us *from* duty, will hinder us *in* duty. When we come before the Lord, he is at our right hand to resist us (*Zech. 3:1*). Like when a man is going to write, and another stands at his elbow and jogs him, so that he cannot write evenly. Satan will set vain objects before the fancy to cause a diversion. The devil does not oppose formality but fervency. If he sees that we are setting ourselves in good earnest to seek God, he will be whispering things in our ears, so that we can scarcely attend to what we are doing.

Answer 3: These wandering thoughts arise from the world. These vermin are bred out of the earth. Worldly business often crowds into our duties, and while we are speaking to God, our hearts are talking with the world: 'They sit before me as my people, but their heart goeth after their covetousness' (*Ezek. 33:31*). While we are hearing the Word or meditating, some worldly business or other commonly knocks at the door and we are called away from the duty while we are doing it. It is the same with us as it was with Abraham when he was going to worship – the birds came down on the sacrifice (*Gen. 15:11*).

Question: How may we get rid of these wandering thoughts, so that we may be more spiritual in duty?

Answer 1: Fix your eyes on God's purity. He whom we serve is a holy God, and when we are worshipping him, he cannot tolerate our conversing with vanity. While a king's subject is speaking to him, will he like him to be playing with a feather? Will God endure light, feathery hearts? How devout and reverent the angels are! They cover their faces and cry, 'Holy, holy'.

Answer 2: Think of the grand importance of the duties we are engaged in. As David said, concerning his building a house for God, 'the work is great' (*1 Chron. 29:1*). When we are hearing the Word, 'the work is great'. This is the Word by which we shall be judged. When we are at prayer, 'the work is great'. We are pleading for the life of our souls, and is this a time to trifle?

Answer 3: Come with affection to duty. The nature of love is to fix the mind upon the object. The thoughts of a man who is in love are on the person he loves, and nothing can distract them. The thoughts of a man who loves the world are always intent on it. If our hearts were more fired with love, they would be more fixed in duty, and oh, what cause we have to love duty! Is not this the direct road to heaven? Do we not meet with God here? Can the spouse be better than in her husband's company? Where can the soul be better than in drawing near to God?

Answer 4: Consider the mischief that these vain distracting thoughts do. They fly-blow our duties; they hinder fervency; they show great irreverence; they tempt God to turn his ear away from us. Why do we think God should heed our prayers, when we ourselves scarcely heed them?

3. To do duties spiritually is to do them in faith: 'By faith Abel offered unto God a better sacrifice than Cain' (*Heb. 11.4*). The holy oil for the tabernacle had several spices put into it (*Exod. 30:34*). Faith is the sweet spice which must be put into duty. It is a wrong done to God to doubt either his mercy or his truth. A Christian may venture his soul upon the public faith of heaven.

Use 1: How far from godliness are those who are unspiritual in their worship, who do not do duties from a renewed principle and with the utmost intention of soul, but merely to stop the mouth of conscience! Many people look no further than the bare doing of duties, but never heed how they are done. God does not judge our duties by length, but by love. When men put God off with the dreggish part of duty, may he not say, like Isaiah, 'Is it such a fast that I have chosen?' (*Isa. 58:5*). 'Are these the duties I required? I called for the heart and spirit and you bring nothing but the carcass of duty. Should I receive comfort in this?'

Use 2: Let us show ourselves godly by being more spiritual in duty. It is not the quantity but the quality; it is not how much we do but how well. A musician is commended, not for playing long but for playing well. We must not only do what God appoints but as God appoints. Oh, how many are unspiritual in spiritual things! They bring their services but not their hearts. They give God the skin, not the fat of the offering. 'God is a Spirit' (*John 4:24*) – and it is the spirituality of duty he is best pleased with: 'spiritual sacrifices, acceptable to God' (*1 Pet. 2:5*). The spirits of the wine are best. So is the spiritual part of duty: 'making melody in your heart to the Lord' (*Eph. 5:19*). It is the heart which makes the music; the spiritualizing of duty gives life to it. Without this it is dead praying, dead hearing – and dead things are not pleasing. A dead flower has no beauty, a dead breast has no sweetness.

Question: What may we do to perform duties in a spiritual manner?

Answer 1: Let the soul be kept pure. Lust besots and dispirits a man. Beware of any tincture of uncleanness (*Jas. 1:21*). Wood that is full of sap will not easily burn, and a heart steeped in sin is not fit to burn in holy devotion. Can he who feeds carnal lust be spiritual in worship? 'Whoredom and wine and new wine take away the heart' (*Hos. 4:11*). Any sin lived in takes away the heart. Such a person has no heart to pray or meditate. The more alive the heart is in sin, the more it dies to duty.

Answer 2: If we wish to be spiritual in duty, let us revolve these two things in our mind:
(i) The profit which comes from a duty performed in a spiritual manner. It enfeebles corruption; it increases grace; it defeats Satan; it strengthens our communion with

God; it breeds peace of conscience; it procures answers of mercy; and it leaves the heart always in better tune.

(ii) The danger of doing duties in an unspiritual manner. They are as if they had not been done. For what the heart does not do is not done. Duties carelessly performed turn ordinances into judgments. Therefore many, though they are often doing duty, go away worse from duty. If medicine is not well made and the ingredients rightly mixed, it is as bad as poison for the body. So if duties are not well performed, they leave the heart harder and more sinful than before.

Unspiritual duties often create temporal judgments: 'the Lord our God made a breach upon us, for that we sought him not after the due order' (*1 Chron. 15:13*). Therefore God makes breaches in families and relationships because people do not worship him in that manner and due order which he requires.

Answer 3: If we want to have our duties spiritual, we must get our hearts spiritual. An earthly heart cannot be spiritual in duty. Let us beg from God a spiritual palate to relish a sweetness in holy things. For lack of spiritual hearts, we come to duty without delight, and go away without profit. If a man wants to have the wheels of his watch move regularly, he must mend the spring. Christian, if you want to move more spiritually in duty, get the spring of your heart mended.

SECTION 22: A GODLY MAN IS THOROUGHLY TRAINED IN RELIGION

He obeys every command of God: 'I have found David a man after mine own heart, which shall fulfil all my will' (*Acts 13:22*). In the Greek it is 'all my wills'. A godly man strives to walk according to the full breadth and latitude of

God's law. Every command has the same stamp of divine authority on it, and he who is godly will obey one command as well as another: 'Then shall I not be ashamed, when I have respect to all thy commandments' (*Psa. 119:6*). A godly man goes through all the body of religion as the sun through all the signs of the Zodiac. Whoever is to play a ten-stringed instrument must strike every string or he will spoil all the music. The ten commandments may be compared to a ten-stringed instrument. We must obey every commandment, strike every string, or we cannot make any sweet music in religion. True obedience is filial. It is fitting that the child should obey the parent in all just and sober commands. God's laws are like the curtains of the tabernacle which were looped together. They are like a chain of gold where all the links are coupled. A conscientious man will not willingly break one link of this chain. If one command is violated, the whole chain is broken: 'whosoever shall keep the whole law, yet offend in one point, he is guilty of all' (*Jas. 2:10*). A voluntary breach of one of God's laws involves a man in the guilt and exposes him to the curse of the whole law. True obedience is entire and uniform. A good heart, like the needle, points the way in which the lodestone draws.

This is one great difference between a child of God and a hypocrite. The hypocrite picks and chooses in religion. He will perform some duties which are easier and gratify his pride or interest, but other duties he takes no notice of: 'Ye pay tithe of mint and anise, and have omitted the weightier matters of the law, judgment, mercy, and faith' (*Matt. 23:23*). To sweat in some duties of religion and freeze in others is the symptom of a disordered Christian. Jehu was zealous in destroying the idolatry of Baal, but let the golden calves of Jeroboam stand (*2 Kings 10:29*). This shows that men are not good in truth when they are good by halves. If your servant should do some of your work you set him, and leave the rest undone, how would you like that? The Lord says, 'Walk before me, and be thou perfect' (*Gen. 17:1*). How are our hearts perfect with God when we prevaricate with him? Some things we will do and other things we leave undone. He is good who is good universally. 'Here I am, Father; command what you will' (*Plautus*).

There are ten duties that God calls for which a godly man will conscientiously perform, and indeed these duties may serve as so many other characteristics and touchstones to test our godliness by:

1. A godly man will often be calling his heart to account
He takes the candle of the Word and searches his innermost being: 'I commune with mine own heart: and my spirit made diligent search' (*Psa. 77:6*). A gracious soul searches whether there is any duty omitted, any sin cherished. He examines his evidences for heaven. As he will not take his gold on trust, so neither will he take his grace. He is a spiritual merchant; he casts up the estate of his soul to see what he is worth. He 'sets his house in order'. Frequent reckonings keep God and conscience friends. A carnal person cannot abide this heart-work; he is ignorant how the affairs go in his soul. He is like a man who is well acquainted with foreign parts but a stranger in his own country.

2. A godly man is much in private prayer
He keeps his hours for private devotion. Jacob, when he was left alone, wrestled with God (*Gen. 32:24*). So when a gracious heart is alone, it wrestles in prayer and will not leave God till it has a blessing. A devout Christian exerises eyes of faith and knees of prayer.

Hypocrites who have nothing of religion besides the frontispiece love to be seen. Christ has characterized them: 'they love to pray in the corners of the streets, that they may be seen' (*Matt. 6:5*). The hypocrite is devout in the temple.

There everyone will gaze at him, but he is a stranger to secret communion with God. He is a saint in the church, but an atheist in private. A good Christian holds secret communication with heaven. Private prayer keeps up the trade of godliness. When private holiness is laid aside, a stab is given to the heart of religion.

3. A godly man is diligent in his calling

He takes care to provide for his family. The church must not exclude the shop. Mr Perkins said: 'Though a man is endued with excellent gifts, hears the Word with reverence and receives the sacrament, yet if he does not practise the duties of his calling, all is sheer hypocrisy.' Religion never did grant a patent for idleness: 'there are some which walk among you disorderly, working not at all; them that are such we command and exhort by our Lord Jesus, that with quietness they work, and eat their own bread' (*2 Thess. 3:11,12*). The bread that tastes most sweet is obtained with most sweat. A godly man would rather fast than eat the bread of idleness. Vain professing Christians talk of living by faith, but do not live in a calling. They are like the lilies of the field: 'they toil not, neither do they spin' (*Matt. 6:28*). An idle person is the devil's tennis ball, which he bandies up and down with temptation till at last the ball goes out of play.

4. A godly man sets bounds to himself in things lawful

He is moderate in matters of recreation and diet. He takes only so much for the restoration of health as may the better dispose him for God's service. Jerome lived abstemiously; his diet was a few dried figs and cold water. And Augustine in his 'Confessions' says: 'Lord, thou hast taught me to go to my food as to a medicine.' If the bridle of reason checks the appetite, much more should the curbing-bit of grace do so. The life of a sinner is brutish; the glutton feeds 'without fear' (*Jude 12*), and the drunkard drinks without reason. Too much oil chokes the lamp, whereas a smaller quantity makes it burn more brightly. A godly man holds the golden bridle of temperance, and will not allow his table to be a snare.

5. A godly man is careful about moral righteousness

He makes conscience of equity as well as piety. The Scripture has linked both together: 'that we might serve him in holiness and righteousness' (*Luke 1:74,75*). Holiness: there is the *first* table; righteousness: there is the *second* table. Though a man may be morally righteous and not godly, yet no-one can be godly unless he is morally righteous. This moral righteousness is seen in our dealings with men. A good man observes that golden maxim, 'Whatsoever ye would that men should do to you, do ye even so to them' (*Matt. 7:12*). There is a threefold injustice in business matters:

(i) Using false weights: 'the balances of deceit are in his hand' (*Hos. 12:7*). Men, by making their weights lighter, make their sin heavier: 'They make the ephah small' (*Amos 8:5*). The ephah was a measure they used in selling. They made the ephah small; they gave but scant measure. A godly man who takes the Bible in one hand dare not use false weights in the other.

(ii) Debasing a commodity: 'they sell the refuse of the wheat' (*Amos 8:6*). They would pick out the best grains of the wheat and sell the worst at the same price as they did the best. 'Thy wine is mixed with water' (*Isa. 1:22*). They adulterated their wine, yet made their customers believe it came from the pure grape.

(iii) Taking a great deal more than the commodity is worth. 'If thou sell ought unto thy neighbour . . . ye shall not oppress one another' (*Lev. 25:14*). A godly man deals exactly but not exactingly. He will sell so as to help himself, but not to damn another. His motto is, 'a conscience void of offence toward God, and toward men' (*Acts 24:16*).

The hypocrite separates these two which God has joined together – righteousness and holiness. He pretends to be pure but is not just. It brings religion into contempt when men hang out Christ's colours, yet will use fraudulent circumvention and, under a mask of piety, neglect morality. A godly man makes conscience of the second table as well as the first.

6. A godly man will forgive those who have wronged him, but revenge is sweet to nature

A gracious spirit passes by affronts, forgets injuries and counts it a greater victory to conquer an enemy by patience than by power. It is truly heroic 'to overcome evil with good' (*Rom. 12:21*). Though I would not trust an enemy, yet I would endeavour to love him. I would exclude him from my creed, but not from my prayer (*Matt. 5:44*).

Question: But does every godly man succeed in forgiving, yes, loving his enemies?

Answer: He does so in a gospel sense. That is:

(a) In so far as there is assent. He subscribes to it in his judgment as a thing which ought to be done: 'with my mind I serve the law of God' (*Rom. 7:25*).

(b) In so far as there is grief. A godly man mourns that he can love his enemies no more: 'O wretched man that I am!' (*Rom. 7:24*). Oh, this base cankered heart of mine, that has received so much mercy and can show so little! I have had talents forgiven me, yet I can hardly forgive pence.

(c) In so far as there is prayer. A godly man prays that God will give him a heart to love his enemies. 'Lord, pluck this root of bitterness out of me, perfume my soul with love, make me a dove without gall.'

(d) In so far as there is effort. A godly man resolves and strives in the strength of Christ against all rancour and virulence of spirit. This is in a gospel sense to love our enemies. A wicked man cannot do this; his malice boils up to revenge.

7. A godly man lays to heart the miseries of the church

'We wept, when we remembered Zion' (Psa. 137:1). I have read of certain trees whose leaves, if cut or touched, the other leaves begin to contract and shrink, and for a time hang down their heads. Such a spiritual sympathy exists among Christians. When other parts of God's church suffer, they feel themselves, as it were, touched in their own persons. Ambrose reports that when Theodosius was terminally ill, he was more troubled about the church of God than about his own sickness. When Aeneas would have saved Anchises' life, he says, 'Far be it from me that I should desire to live when Troy is buried in its ruins.' In music there are two unisons; if you strike one, you perceive that the other is stirring, as if it were affected. When the Lord strikes others, a godly heart is deeply affected: 'my bowels shall sound like an harp' (Isa. 16:11). Though things go well with a child of God in his own private life and he lives in a house of cedar, he still grieves to see things go badly with the public. Queen Esther enjoyed the king's favour and all the delights of the court, yet when a warrant portending bloodshed was signed for the death of the Jews, she mourns and fasts, and ventures her own life to save theirs.

8. A godly man is content with his present condition

If provisions get low, his heart is tempered to his condition. 'Many', says Cato, 'blame me because I am in need, and I blame them because they cannot be in need.' A godly man puts a candid interpretation upon providence. When God brews him a bitter cup, he says, 'This is my diet drink: it is to purge me and do my soul good.' Therefore he is most content (*Phil. 4:11*).

9. A godly man is fruitful in good works (Titus 2:7)

The Hebrew word for godly (*chasid*) signifies 'merciful', implying that to be godly and charitable are of equal force, one and the same. A good man feeds the hungry, clothes the naked: 'He is ever merciful' (*Psa. 37:26*). The more devout sort of the Jews to this day distribute the tenth part of their estate to the poor and they have a proverb among them, 'Give the tenth, and you will grow rich'. The hypocrite is all for faith, nothing for works, like the laurel that makes a flourish but bears no fruit.

10. A godly man will suffer persecution

He will be married to Christ, though he settles no other estate on him than the cross. He suffers out of choice and with a spirit of gallantry (*Heb. 11:35*). Argerius wrote a letter to his friend, headed: 'From the pleasant gardens of the Leonine prison'. The blessed martyrs who put on the whole armour of God blunted the edge of persecution by their courage. The juniper tree makes the coolest shadow and the hottest coal. So persecution makes the coal of love hotter and the shadow of death cooler.

Thus a godly man goes round the whole circle of religious duties and obeys God in whatever he commands.

Objection: But it is impossible for anyone to walk according to the full breadth of God's law, and to follow God fully!

Answer: There is a twofold obeying of God's law. The first is perfect, when all is done that the law requires. This we cannot arrive at in this life. Secondly, there is an incomplete obedience which is accepted in Christ. This consists in four things:

(i) An approving of all God's commands: 'the commandment is holy and just and good . . . I consent unto the law that it is good' (*Rom. 7:12, 16*). There is both assent and consent.

(ii) A sweet delight in God's commands: 'I will delight myself in thy commandments, which I have loved' (*Psa. 119:47*).

(iii) A cordial desire to walk in all God's commands: 'O that my ways were directed to keep thy statutes' (*Psa. 119:5*).

(iv) A real endeavour to tread in every path of the command: 'I turned my feet unto thy testimonies' (*Psa. 119:59*). This, God esteems perfect obedience and is pleased to take it in good part. Zacharias had his failings; he hesitated through unbelief, for which he was struck dumb. Yet it is said that he 'walked in all the commands of the Lord blameless' (*Luke 1:6*), because he cordially endeavoured to obey God in all things. Evangelical obedience is true in its essence, though not perfect in its degree, and where it comes short, Christ puts his mercies into the scales, and then there is full weight.

SECTION 23: A GODLY MAN WALKS WITH GOD

'Noah walked with God' (*Gen. 6:9*). The age in which Noah lived was very corrupt: 'the wickedness of man was great in the earth' (*v. 5*). But the iniquity of the times could not put Noah off his walk: 'Noah walked with God'. Noah is called a 'preacher of righteousness' (*2 Peter 2:5*):

1. Noah preached by doctrine

His preaching (say some of the rabbis) was in this vein: 'Turn from your evil ways, so that the waters of the flood will not come upon you and cut off the whole of Adam's race.'

2. Noah preached by his life

He preached by his humility, patience, sanctity: 'Noah walked with God'.

Question: What is it to walk with God?

Answer: Walking with God imports five things:

1. *Walking as under God's eye*. Noah reverenced a deity. A godly man sets himself as in God's presence, knowing that his judge is looking on: 'I have set the Lord always before me' (*Psa. 16:8*). David's eyes were here.

2. *The familiarity and intimacy that the soul has with God*. Friends walk together and console themselves one with another. The godly make known their requests to God and he makes known his love to them. There is a sweet intercourse between God and his people: 'Our communion (*koinonia*) is with the Father, and with his Son Jesus Christ' (*1 John 1:3*).

3. *Walking above the earth*. A godly man is elevated above all sublunary objects. The person who walks with God must ascend very high. A dwarf cannot walk among the stars, nor can a dwarfish, earthly soul walk with God.

4. *Visible piety*. Walking is a visible posture. Grace must be conspicuous to the onlookers. He who reveals something of God in his behaviour walks with God. He shines forth in biblical conduct.

5. *Continued progress in grace*. It is not only a step but a walk. There is a going on towards perfection. A godly man does not sit down in the middle of his way but goes on till he comes to the 'end of his faith' (*1 Pet. 1:9*). Though a good man may be out of the path, he is not out of the way. He may through infirmity step aside (as Peter did), but he recovers by repentance and goes on in progressive holiness: 'The righteous also shall hold on his way' (*Job 17:9*).

Use 1: See from this how improper it is to describe as godly those who do not walk with God. They want to have

Noah's crown, but they do not love Noah's walk. Most are found in the devil's black walk: 'Many walk, of whom I tell you weeping, that they are the enemies of the cross of Christ' (*Phil. 3:18*).

1. Some will commend walking with God, and say it is the rarest life in the world, but will not set one foot on the way. All who commend wine do not pay the price. Many a father commends virtue to his child but does not set him a pattern.

2. Others walk a few steps in the good old ways, but they retreat back again (*Jer. 6:16*). If the ways of God were not good, why did they enter them? If they were good, why did they forsake them? 'For it had been better for them not to have known the way of righteousness, than, after they have known it, to turn from the holy commandment' (*2 Pet. 2:21*).

3. Others slander walking with God as a melancholy walk, and describe such as are less zealous as more prosperous. This God accounts blasphemy: 'the way of truth shall be evil spoken of' (*2 Pet. 2:2*). In the Greek it is 'it shall be blasphemed'.

4. Others deride walking with God as if it were a way of foolish scrupulosity: 'What? Do you want to join the "holy tribe"? Do you want to be wiser than others?' There are some people who, if it were in their power, would jeer holiness out of the world. The chair of the scornful stands at the mouth of hell (*Prov. 19:29*).

5. Others, instead of walking with God, walk according to the flesh (*2 Pet. 2:10*).

(i) They walk by fleshly opinions.
(ii) They walk according to fleshly lusts.
(i) They walk by fleshly opinions. There are six of these:
(a) That it is best to do what most do, to steer after the course of the world – to be in the mode, not to get a new heart, but to get into a new fashion.

(b) That reason is the highest judge and umpire in matters of religion. We must believe no further than we can see. For a man to become a fool that he may be wise, to be saved purely by the righteousness of another, to keep all by losing all – this the natural man will by no means put in his creed.

(c) That a little religion will serve the turn. The lifeless form may in policy be kept up, but zeal is madness. The world thinks that religion to be best which, like leaf-gold, is spread very thin.

(d) That the way which is exposed to affliction is not good. A stick, though it is straight, seems crooked under water. So religion, if it is under affliction, appears crooked to a carnal eye.

(e) That all a man's concern should be for the present. As that profane cardinal said, he would leave his part in paradise to keep his cardinalship in Paris.

(f) That sinning is better than suffering. It is greater discretion to keep the skin whole than the conscience pure. These are such rules as the crooked serpent has found out – and whoever walks by them 'shall not know peace'.

(ii) They walk according to fleshly lusts. They make provision (turn caterers) for the flesh (*Rom. 13:14*). Such a person was the Emperor Heliogabalus. He so indulged the flesh that he never sat except among sweet flowers, mixed with amber and musk. He attired himself in purple, set with precious stones. He did not burn oil in his lamps, but a costly balsam brought from Arabia, very odoriferous. He bathed himself in perfumed water; he put his body to no other use, but to be a strainer for meat and drink to run through.

Thus sinners walk according to the flesh. If a drunken or unclean lust calls, they gratify it. They brand as cowards all who dare not sin at the same rate as they do. These, instead of walking with God, walk contrary to him. Lust is the compass they sail by. Satan is their pilot and hell the port they are bound for.

Use 2: Let us test whether we have this characteristic of the godly: Do we walk with God? That may be known:

1. By the way we walk in. It is a private, secluded way, in which only some few holy ones walk. Therefore it is called a 'pathway' to distinguish it from the common road: 'in the pathway thereof is no death' (*Prov. 12:28*).

2. By a walk in the fear of God: 'Enoch walked with God' (*Gen. 5:22*). The Chaldean version renders it, 'he walked in the fear of the Lord'. The godly are fearful of that which may displease God: 'how then can I do this great wickedness and sin against God?' (*Gen. 39:9*). This is not a base, servile fear, but:

(i) A fear springing from affection (*Hos. 3:5*). A child fears to offend his father out of the tender affection he has for him. This made holy Anselm say, 'If sin were on one side and hell on the other, I would rather leap into hell than willingly offend my God.'

(ii) A fear joined with faith: 'By faith Noah, moved with fear' (*Heb. 11:7*). Faith and fear go hand in hand. When the soul looks at God's holiness, he fears. When he looks at God's promises, he believes. A godly man trembles, yet trusts. Fear preserves reverence, faith preserves cheerfulness; fear keeps the soul from lightness, faith keeps it from overmuch sadness. By this we may know whether we walk with God, if we walk 'in the fear of God'. We are fearful of infringing his laws, and forfeiting his love. It is a brand set upon sinners: 'There is no fear of God before their eyes' (*Rom. 3:18*). The godly fear and do not offend (*Psa. 4:4*). The wicked offend and do not fear (*Jer. 5:23,24*). Careless and dissolute walking will soon estrange God from us and make him weary of our company: 'what communion hath light with darkness?' (*2 Cor. 6:14*).

Use 3: Let me persuade all who wish to be accounted godly to get into Noah's walk. Though the truth of grace is in the heart, yet its beauty is seen in the walk:

1. Walking with God is very pleasing to God. He who walks with God declares to the world which company he loves most: 'His fellowship is with the Father' (*1 John 1:3*). He counts those the sweetest hours which are spent with God. This is very pleasing and acceptable to God: 'Enoch walked with God' (*Gen. 5:24*). And see how kindly God took this at Enoch's hand: 'he had this testimony, that he pleased God' (*Heb. 11:5*).

2. Close walking with God will be a good means to entice and allure others to walk with him. The apostle exhorts wives so to walk that the husbands might be won by their conduct (*1 Pet. 3:1*). Justin Martyr confessed that he became a Christian by observing the holy and innocent lives of the early saints.

3. Close walking with God would put to silence the adversaries of the truth (1 Pet. 2:15). Careless behaviour puts a sword into wicked men's hands to wound religion. What a sad thing it is when it is said of professing Christians that they are as proud, as covetous and as unjust as others. Will this not expose the ways of God to contempt? But holy and close walking would stop the mouths of sinners, so that they should not be able to speak against God's people without giving themselves the lie. Satan came to Christ and 'found nothing in him' (*John 14:30*). What a confounding thing it will be to the wicked when holiness is the only thing they have to fasten on the godly as a crime. 'We shall not find any occasion against this Daniel, unless we find it against him concerning the law of his God' (*Dan. 6:5*).

4. *Walking with God is a pleasant walk.* The ways of wisdom are called pleasantness (*Prov. 3:17*). Is the light not pleasant? 'They shall walk, O Lord, in the light of thy countenance' (*Psa. 89:15*). Walking with God is like walking among beds of spices which send forth a fragrant perfume. This is what brings peace: 'walking in the fear of the Lord, and in the comfort of the Holy Ghost' (*Acts 9:31*). While we walk with God, what sweet music the bird of conscience makes in our breast! 'They shall sing in the ways of the Lord' (*Psa. 138:5*).

5. *Walking with God is honourable.* It is a credit for one of an inferior rank to walk with a king. What greater dignity can be put upon a mortal man than to converse with his Maker and to walk with God every day?

6. *Walking with God leads to rest:* 'There remaineth therefore a rest to the people of God' (*Heb. 4:9*). The philosopher Aristotle says, 'Motion tends to rest.' Indeed, there is a motion which does not tend to rest. They who walk with their sins shall never have rest: 'they rest not day and night' (*Rev. 4:8*). But they that walk with God shall sit down in the kingdom of God (*Luke 13:29*); just as a weary traveller, when he comes home, sits down and rests. 'To him that overcometh will I grant to sit with me in my throne' (*Rev. 3:21*). A throne denotes honour and sitting denotes rest.

7. *Walking with God is the safet walking.* Walking in the ways of sin is like walking on the banks of a river. The sinner treads on the banks of the bottomless pit, and if death gives him a jog, he tumbles in. But it is safe going in

God's way: 'Then shalt thou walk in thy way safely' (*Prov. 3:23*). He who walks with a guard walks safely. He who walks with God shall have God's Spirit to guard him from sin and God's angels to guard him from danger (*Psa. 91:11*).

8. Walking with God will make death sweet. It was Augustus' wish that he might have a *euthanasia*, a quiet, easy death without much pain. If anything makes our pillow easy at death it will be this, that we have walked with God in our generation. Do we think walking with God can do us any hurt? Did we ever hear any cry out on their deathbed that they have been too holy, that they have prayed too much, or walked with God too much? No, that which has cut them to the heart has been this, that they have not walked more closely with God; they have wrung their hands and torn their hair to think that they have been so bewitched with the pleasures of the world. Close walking with God will make our enemy (death) be at peace with us. When King Ahasuerus could not sleep, he called for the book of records, and read it (*Esther 6:1*). So when the violence of sickness causes sleep to depart from our eyes and we can call for conscience (that book of records) and find written in it, 'On such a day we humbled our souls by fasting; on such a day our hearts melted in prayer; on such a day we had sweet communion with God' – what a reviving this will be! How we may look death in the face with comfort and say, 'Lord, now take us up to thee in heaven. Where we have so often been by affection let us now be by fruition.'

9. Walking with God is the best way to know the mind of God. Friends who walk together impart their secrets one to another: 'The secret of the Lord is with them that fear him' (*Psa. 25:14*). Noah walked with God and the Lord revealed a great secret to him – destroying the old world and saving him in the ark. Abraham walked with God, and God made him one of his privy council (*Gen. 24:40*): 'Shall I hide from Abraham that thing which I do?' (*Gen. 18:17*). God sometimes sweetly unbosoms himself to the soul in prayer and in the holy supper, as Christ made himself known to the disciples in the breaking of bread (*Luke 24:35*).

10. *They who walk with God shall never be wholly left by God.* The Lord may withdraw for a time, to make his people cry after him the more, but he will not leave them altogether: 'I hid my face from thee for a moment; but with everlasting kindness will I have mercy on thee' (*Isa. 54:8*). God will not cast off any of his old acquaintance; he will not part with one that has kept him company. 'Enoch walked with God: and he was not; for God took him' (*Gen. 5:24*). He took him up to heaven. As the Arabic renders it, 'Enoch was lodged in the bosom of divine love.'

Question: What may we do to walk with God?

Answer 1: Get off the old road of sin. He that would walk in a pleasant meadow must turn off the road. The way of sin is full of travellers. There are so many travellers on this road that hell, though it is of a great circumference, would gladly enlarge itself and make room for them (*Isa. 5:14*). This way of sin seems pleasant but the end is damnable. 'I have', says the harlot, 'perfumed my bed with myrrh, aloes and cinnamon' (*Prov. 7:17*). See how with one sweet (the cinnamon) there were two bitters (myrrh and aloes). For that little sweet in sin at present there will be a far greater proportion of bitterness afterwards. Therefore get out of these briars. You cannot walk with God and sin: 'what fellowship hath righteousness with unrighteousness?' (*2 Cor. 6:14*).

Answer 2: If you wish to walk with God, get acquainted with him: 'Acquaint now thyself with him' (*Job 22:21*). Know God in his attributes and promises. Strangers do not walk together.

Answer 3: Get all differences removed. 'Can two walk together, except they are agreed?' (*Amos 3:3*). This agreement and reconciliation is made by faith: 'Whom God hath set forth to be a propitiation through faith in his blood' (*Rom. 3:25*). When once we are friends, then we shall be called up the mount like Moses, and have this dignity conferred on us, to be the favourites of heaven and to walk with God.

Answer 4: If you desire to walk with God, get a liking for the ways of God. They are adorned with beauty (*Prov. 4:18*); they are sweetened with pleasure (*Prov. 3:17*); they are fenced with truth (*Rev. 15:3*); they are accompanied with life (*Acts 2:28*); they are lengthened with eternity (*Hab. 3:6*). Be enamoured with the way of religion and you will soon walk in it.

Answer 5: If you desire to walk with God, take hold of his arm. Those who walk in their own strength will soon grow weary and tire. 'I will go in the strength of the Lord God' (*Psa. 71:16*). We cannot walk with God without God. Let us press him with his promise: 'I will cause you to walk in my statutes' (*Ezek. 36:27*). If God takes us by the hand, then we shall 'walk, and not faint' (*Isa. 40:31*).

SECTION 24: A GODLY MAN STRIVES TO BE AN INSTRU-
MENT FOR MAKING OTHERS GODLY

He is not content to go to heaven alone but wants to take others there. Spiders work only for themselves, but bees work for others. A godly man is both a diamond and a lodestone – a diamond for the sparkling lustre of grace and a lodestone for his attractiveness. He is always drawing others to embrace piety. Living things have a propagating virtue. Where religion lives in the heart, there will be an endeavour to propagate the life of grace in those we converse with: 'My son, Onesimus, whom I have begotten in my bonds' (*Philem. 10*). Though God is the fountain of grace, yet the saints are pipes to transmit living streams to others. This great effort for the conversion of souls proceeds:

1. From the nature of godliness
It is like fire which assimilates and turns everything into its own nature. Where there is the fire of grace in the heart, it will endeavour to inflame others. Grace is a holy leaven, which will be seasoning and leavening others with divine principles. Paul would gladly have converted Agrippa – how he courted him with rhetoric! 'King Agrippa, believest thou the prophets? I know that thou believest' (*Acts 26:27*). His zeal and eloquence had almost captivated the king (*v. 28*). Then Agrippa said to Paul, 'Almost thou persuadest me to be a Christian.'

2. From a spirit of compassion
Grace makes the heart tender. A godly man cannot choose but pity those who are in the gall of bitterness. He sees what a deadly cup is brewing for the wicked. They must, without repentance, be bound over to God's wrath. The fire which rained on Sodom was but a painted fire in comparison with hell fire. This is a fire with a vengeance: 'suffering the vengeance of eternal fire' (*Jude 7*). Now when a godly man sees captive sinners ready to be damned, he strives to convert them from the error of their way: 'Knowing the terror of the Lord, we persuade men' (*2 Cor. 5:11*).

3. From a holy zeal he has for Christ's glory

The glory of Christ is as dear to him as his own salvation. Therefore, that this may be promoted, he strives with the greatest effort to bring souls to Christ.

It is a glory to Christ when multitudes are born to him. Every star adds a lustre to the sky; every convert is a member added to Christ's body and a jewel adorning his crown. Though Christ's glory cannot be increased, as he is God, yet as he is Mediator, it may. The more there are saved, the more Christ is exalted. Why else should the angels rejoice at the conversion of a sinner, but because Christ's glory now shines the more (*Luke 15:10*)?

Use 1: This excludes those who are spiritual eunuchs from the number of the godly. They do not strive to promote the salvation of others. 'The one through whom no-one else is born is himself born unworthily.'

1. If men loved Christ, they would try to draw as many as they could to him. He who loves his captain will persuade others to come under his banner. This unmasks the hypocrite. Though a hypocrite may make a show of grace himself, yet he never bothers to procure grace in others. He is without compassion. I may allude to the verse: 'that that dieth, let it die; and that that is to be cut off, let it be cut off' (*Zech. 11:9*). Let souls go to the devil, he cares not.

2. How far from being godly are those who instead of striving for grace in others, work to destroy all hopeful beginnings of grace in them! Instead of drawing them to Christ, they draw them from Christ. Their work is to poison and harm souls. This harming of souls occurs in three ways:

(i) *By bad edicts*. So Jeroboam made Israel sin (*1 Kings 16:26*). He forced them to idolatry.

(ii) *By bad examples*. Examples speak louder than precepts, but principally the examples of great men are influential. Men placed on high are like the 'pillar of cloud'. When that went, Israel went. If great men move irregularly, others will follow them.

(iii) *By bad company*. The breath of sinners is infectious. They are like the dragon which 'cast a flood out of his mouth' (*Rev. 12:15*). They cast a flood of oaths out of their mouths. Wicked tongues are set on fire by hell (*Jas. 3:6*). The sinner finds match and gunpowder, and the devil finds fire. The wicked are for ever setting snares and temptations before others, as the prophet speaks in another sense: 'I set pots full of wine, and cups, and I said unto them, Drink' (*Jer. 35:5*). So the wicked set pots of wine before others and make them drink, till reason is stupefied and lust inflamed. These who make men proselytes to the devil are prodigiously wicked. How sad will be the doom of those who, besides their own sins, have the blood of others to answer for!

3. If it is the sign of a godly man to promote grace in others, then how much more ought he to promote it in his near relations. A godly man will be careful that his children should know God. He would be sorry that any of his flesh should burn in hell. He labours to see Christ formed in those who are himself in another edition. Augustine says that his mother Monica travailed with greater care and pain for his spiritual than for his natural birth.

The time of childhood is the fittest time to be sowing seed of religion in our children. 'Whom shall he make to understand doctrine? Them that are weaned from the milk, and drawn from the breasts' (*Isa. 28:9*). The wax, while it is soft and tender, will take any impression. Children, while they are young, will fear a reproof; when they are old, they will hate it.

(i) It is pleasing to God that our children should know him early in life. When you come into a garden, you love to pluck the young bud and smell it. God loves a saint in the bud. Of all the trees which the Lord could have chosen in a prophetic vision (*Jer. 1:11*), he chose the almond tree, which is one of the first of the trees to blossom. Such an almond tree is an early convert.

(ii) By endeavouring to bring up our children in the fear of the Lord, we shall provide for God's glory when we are dead. A godly man should not only honour God while he lives, but do something that may promote God's glory when he is dead. If our children are seasoned with gracious principles, they will stand up in our place when we have gone, and will glorify God in their generation. A good piece of ground bears not only a fore-crop but an after-crop. He who is godly does not only bear God a good crop of obedience himself while he lives, but by training his child in the principles of religion, he bears God an after-crop when he is dead.

Use 2: Let all who have God's name placed on them do what in them lies to advance piety in others. A knife touched with a lodestone will attract the needle. He whose heart is divinely touched with the lodestone of God's Spirit will endeavour to attract those who are near him to Christ. The heathen could say, 'We are not born for ourselves only'. The more excellent anything is, the more communicative it is. In the body every member is diffusive: the eye conveys light; the head, spirits; the liver, blood. A Christian must not move altogether within his own circle, but seek the welfare of others. To be diffusively good makes us resemble God, whose sacred influence is universal.

And surely it will be no grief of heart when conscience can witness for us that we have brought glory to God in this matter by working to fill heaven.

Not that this is in any way meritorious, or has any causal

influence on our salvation. Christ's blood is the cause, but our promoting God's glory in the conversion of others is a signal evidence of our salvation. As the rainbow is not a cause why God will not drown the world, but is a sign that he will not drown it; or as Rahab's scarlet thread hung out of the window (*Joshua 2:18*) was not a cause why she was exempted from destruction, but was a sign of her being exempted, so our building up others in the faith is not a cause why we are saved, but it is a symbol of our piety and a presage of our felicity.

And thus I have shown the marks and characteristics of a godly man. If a person thus described is reputed a fanatic, then Abraham and Moses and David and Paul were fanatics, which I think none but atheists will dare to affirm!

5: Containing Two Conclusions

Concerning the characteristic signs aforementioned, I shall lay down two conclusions:

1. These characteristics are a Christian's box of evidences
For as an impenitent sinner has the signs of reprobation on him, by which, as by so many spots and tokens, he may know he shall die, so whoever can show these happy signs of a godly man, may see the symptoms of salvation in his soul and may know he has 'passed from death unto life' (*John 5:24*). He is as sure to go to heaven as if he were in heaven already. Such a person is undoubtedly a member of Christ and if he should perish, then something of Christ might perish.

These blessed characteristics may comfort a Christian under all worldly dejection and diabolical suggestions. Satan tempts a child of God with this, that he is a hypocrite and has no title to the land of promise. A Christian may pull out these evidences and challenge the devil to prove that any wicked man or hypocrite ever had such a good certificate to show for heaven. Satan may sooner prove himself a liar than the saint a hypocrite.

2. Whoever has one of these characteristics in truth has everything in embryo
Whoever has one link of a chain has the whole chain.

Objection: But may a child of God say, 'Either I do not have all these characteristics or else they are so faintly stamped in me that I cannot discern them'?

Answer: To satisfy this scruple you must diligently observe the distinctions which the Scripture makes between Christians. It puts them into several classes and orders. Some are little children who have only recently begun breast-feeding on the gospel; others are young men who have grown up to more maturity of grace; others are fathers who are ready to take their degree of glory (*1 John 2:12–14*). Now, you who are only in the first rank or class may still have the vitals of godliness, as well as those who have arrived at a higher stature in Christ. The Scripture speaks of the cedar and the bruised reed, the latter of which is as true a plant of the heavenly paradise as the other. So the weakest ought not to be discouraged. Not all have these characteristics of godliness written in capital letters. If they are only faintly stamped on their souls, God can read the work of his Spirit there. Though the seal is only faintly set on the wax, it ratifies the will and gives a real conveyance of an estate. If there is found just some good thing towards the Lord (as it was said of Abijah), God will accept it (*1 Kings 14:13*).

6: *An Exhortation to Godliness*

Those who are still in their natural condition, who have never yet relished any sweetness in the things of God – let me beseech them for the love of Christ to strive to get these characteristics of the godly engraved on their hearts. Though godliness is the object of the world's scorn and hatred (as in Tertullian's days, the name of a Christian was a crime), yet do not be ashamed to espouse godliness. Know that persecuted godliness is better than prosperous wickedness. What will all the world avail a man without godliness? To be learned and ungodly is like a devil transformed into an angel of light; to be beautiful and ungodly is like a lovely picture hung in an infected room; to be honourable in the world and ungodly is like an ape in purple, or like that image which had a head of gold on feet of clay (*Dan. 2:32,33*). It is godliness that ennobles and consecrates the heart, making God and angels fall in love with it.

Strive for the reality of godliness. Do not rest in the common workings of God's Spirit. Do not think that it is enough to be intelligent and discursive. A man may discourse of religion to the admiration of others, yet not feel the sweetness of those things in his own soul. The lute gives a melodious sound to others, but does not at all feel the sound itself. Judas could make an elegant discourse about Christ, but did not feel virtue from him.

Do not rest in having your affections a little stirred. A hypocrite may have affections of sorrow like Ahab, or affections of desire like Balaam. These are slight and flashy and do not amount to real godliness. Oh, strive to be like the king's daughter, 'all glorious within' (*Psa. 45:13*)!

In order that I may persuade men to become godly, I shall lay down some forcible motives and arguments, and may the Lord make them like nails fastened by his Spirit.

A. LET MEN SERIOUSLY WEIGH THEIR MISERY WHILE THEY REMAIN IN A STATE OF UNGODLINESS

It may make them run out of this Sodom. The misery of ungodly men appears in nine particulars:

1. They are in a state of death: 'dead in trespasses' (Eph. 2:1)
Dead they must surely be who are cut off from Christ, the principle of life. For as the body without the soul is dead, so is the soul without Christ. This spiritual death is visible in the effect. It bereaves men of their senses. Sinners have no sense of God in them: 'who being past feeling' (*Eph. 4:19*). All their moral endowments are only flowers strewn on a dead corpse, and what is hell but a sepulchre to bury the dead in?

2. Their offerings are polluted
Not only the ploughing but the praying of the wicked is sin: 'The sacrifice of the wicked is an abomination to the Lord' (*Prov. 15:8; 21:4*). If the water is foul in the well, it cannot be clean in the bucket. If the heart is full of sin, the duties cannot be pure. What straits every ungodly person is in if he does not come to the ordinance. He despises it if he does not come; he defiles it.

3. Those who live and die ungodly have no right to the covenant of grace
'At that time ye were without Christ, strangers from the

covenants of promise' (*Eph. 2:12*). And to be without covenant is to be like anyone in the old world without an ark. The covenant is the gospel charter, which is enriched with many glorious privileges. But who may plead the benefit of this covenant? Surely only those whose hearts are inlaid with grace. Read the charter: 'A new heart also will I give you, and a new spirit will I put within you . . . I will be your God' (*Ezek. 36:26,28*). A person dying in his ungodliness has no more to do with the new covenant than a ploughman has to do with the privileges of a city corporation.

God's writing always comes before his seal. 'Ye are declared to be the epistle of Christ, written not with ink, but with the Spirit of the living God; not in tables of stone, but in fleshy tables of the heart' (*2 Cor. 3:3*). Here is a golden epistle: the writing is the work of faith; the tablet it is written on is the heart; the finger that writes it is the Spirit. Now, after the Spirit's writing comes the Spirit's sealing: 'after that ye believed, ye were sealed with that holy Spirit' (*Eph. 1:13*). That is, you were sealed with an assurance of glory. What have ungodly men – those who have no writing – to do with the seal of the covenant?

4. The ungodly are spiritual fools

'I said unto the fools, Deal not foolishly, and to the wicked, Lift not up the horn' (*Psa. 75:4*). If a parent had a child who was very beautiful but a fool, he would take little joy in him. The Scripture has dressed the sinner in a fool's coat and let me tell you, better be a fool void of reason than a fool void of grace. This is the devil's fool (*Prov. 14:9*). Is not that man a fool who refuses a rich share? God offers Christ and salvation, but the sinner refuses this share: 'Israel would none of me' (*Psa. 81:11*). Is not that man a fool who prefers an annuity to an inheritance? Is not that man a fool who tends his mortal part and neglects his angelic part, as if a man should paint the wall of his house and let the timber rot? Is not that man a fool who will feed the devil with his soul – like that emperor who fed his lion with pheasant? Is not that man a fool who lays a snare for himself (*Prov. 1:18*); who consults his own shame (*Hab. 2:10*); who loves death (*Prov. 8:36*)?

5. The ungodly are vile persons

'I will make thy grave; for thou art vile' (*Nah. 1:14*). Sin makes men base; it blots their name; it taints their blood. 'They are all together become filthy' (*Psa. 14:3*). In the Hebrew it is 'they have become stinking'. If you call wicked men never so bad, you cannot call them worse than their name deserves: they are swine (*Matt. 7:6*); vipers (*Matt. 3:7*); devils (*John 6:70*). The wicked are dross and refuse (*Psa. 119:119*), and heaven is too pure to have any dross mingled with it.

6. Their temporal mercies are continued in judgment

The wicked may have health and estate, yes, more than heart can wish (*Psa. 73:7*), but 'their table is a snare' (*Psa. 69:22*). Sinners have their mercies with God's leave but not with his love. The people of Israel would have been better without their quails than to have had such sour sauce. The ungodly are usurpers; they lack a spiritual title to what they possess. Their good things are like cloth picked up at the draper's which is not paid for. Death will bring a sad reckoning at last.

7. Their temporal judgments are not removed in mercy

Pharaoh had ten arrows shot at him (ten plagues) and all those plagues were removed; but as his heart remained hard, those plagues were not removed in mercy. It was not a preservation, but a reservation. God reserved him as a signal monument of his justice when he was drowned in the depths of the sea. God may reprieve men's persons when he does not remit their sins. The wicked may have sparing mercy but not saving mercy.

8. The ungodly, while they live, are exposed to the wrath of God

'He that believeth not, the wrath of God abideth on him' (*John 3:36*). Whoever lacks grace is like someone who lacks a pardon; every hour he is in fear of execution. How can a wicked man rejoice? Over his head hangs the sword of God's justice and under him hell-fire burns.

9. The ungodly at death must undergo God's fury and indignation

'The wicked shall be turned into hell' (*Psa. 9:17*). I have read of a lodestone in Ethiopia which has two corners. With one it attracts iron and with the other it repels it. So God has two hands: one of mercy and one of justice. With the one, he will draw the godly to heaven; with the other, he will thrust the sinner to hell. And oh, how dreadful is that place! It is called a fiery lake (*Rev. 20:15*): a lake to denote the many torments in hell, a fiery lake to show their fierceness. Fire is the most torturing element. Strabo in his 'Geography' mentions a lake in Galilee of such a pestiferous nature that it scalds off the skin of whatever is thrown into it. But alas, that lake is cool compared with this fiery lake into which the damned are thrown. To demonstrate that this fire is terrible, there are two most pernicious qualities in it:

(i) It is sulphurous; it is mixed with brimstone (*Rev. 21:8*), which is unsavoury and suffocating.

(ii) It is inextinguishable: the wicked shall be choked in the flames, though not consumed: 'And the devil was cast into the lake of fire and brimstone, where the beast and the false prophet are, and shall be tormented day and night for ever and ever' (*Rev. 20:10*). See the deplorable condition of all ungodly people! In the other world, they shall have a life that always dies and a death that always lives. May this not frighten men off their sins and make them become godly, unless they are resolved to try how hot hell-fire is?

B. WHAT RARE PERSONS THE GODLY ARE

'The righteous is more excellent than his neighbour' (*Prov. 12:26*). Like the flower of the sun, like the wine of Lebanon, like the sparkling on Aaron's breastplate, such is the oriental splendour of a person embellished with godliness. The excellence of the persons of the godly appears in seven particulars:

1. *They are precious*
Therefore they are set apart for God: 'know that the Lord hath set apart him that is godly for himself' (*Psa. 4:3*). We set apart things that are precious. The godly are set apart as God's peculiar treasure (*Psa. 135:4*); as his garden of delight (*Song 4:12*); as his royal diadem (*Isa. 62:3*). The godly are the excellent of the earth (*Psa. 16:3*), comparable to fine gold (*Lam. 4:2*); doubly refined (*Zech. 13:9*); they are the glory of creation (*Isa. 46:13*. Origen compares the saints to sapphires and crystal. God calls them jewels (*Mal. 3:17*). They are jewels:

(i) For their *value*. Diamonds (says Pliny) were not known for a long time except among princes and were hung on their diadems. God so values his people that he will give kingdoms for their ransom (*Isa. 43:3*);. He put his best Jewel in pawn for them (*John 3:16*).

(ii) For their *lustre*. If one pearl of grace shines so brightly that it delights Christ's heart – 'Thou hast ravished my heart with one of thine eyes' (*Song 4:9*), that is, one of thy graces – then how illustrious are all the graces together in a constellation!

2. The godly are honourable

'Thou hast been honourable' (*Isa. 43:4*). The godly are 'a crown of glory in the hand of the Lord' (*Isa. 62:3*). They are 'plants of renown' (*Ezek. 16:14*). They are not only vessels of mercy but vessels of honour (*2 Tim. 2:21*). Aristotle calls honour the chief good thing. The godly are near akin to the blessed Trinity: they have the tutelage and guardianship of angels; they have 'God's name written upon them' (*Rev. 3:12*) and 'the Holy Ghost dwelling in them' (*2 Tim. 1:14*).

The godly are a sacred priesthood. The priesthood under the law was honourable. The king's daughter was wife to Jehoiada the priest (*2 Chron. 22:11*). It was a custom among the Egyptians to have their kings chosen from their priests. The saints are a divine priesthood to offer up spiritual sacrifices (*1 Pet 2:9*). They are co-heirs with Christ (*Rom. 8:17*). They are kings (*Rev. 1:6*). Novarinus tells of an ancient king who invited a company of poor Christians and made them a great feast. On being asked why he showed so much respect to persons of such mean birth and extraction, he told them, 'These I must honour as the children of the most high God. They will be kings and princes with me in another world.' The godly are in some sense higher than the angels. The angels are Christ's friends; these are his spouse. The angels are called morning stars (*Job 38:7*), but the saints are clothed with the Sun of righteousness (*Rev. 12:1*). All men, says Chrysostom, are ambitious of honour. See, then, the honour of the godly! 'Wisdom is the principal thing; therefore get wisdom: exalt her, and she shall promote thee: she shall bring thee to honour, when thou dost embrace her' (*Prov. 4:7,8*). The trophies of the saints' renown will be erected in another world.

3. The godly are beloved by God

'The excellency of Jacob whom he loved' (*Psa. 47:4*). A holy heart is the garden where God plants the flower of his love. God's love to his people is an ancient love, it dates from eternity (*Eph. 1:4*). He loves them with a choice, distinguishing love; they are the 'dearly beloved of his soul' (*Jer. 12:7*). The men of the world have bounty dropping from God's fingers, but the godly have love dropping from God's heart. He gives to one a golden cup, to the other a golden kiss. He loves the godly as he loves Christ (*John 17:26*). It is the same love in kind, though not in degree. Here the saints merely sip God's love; in heaven they shall drink of rivers of pleasure (*Psa. 36:8*). And this love of God is permanent. Death may take their life away from them, but not God's love: 'I have loved thee with a love of perpetuity' (*Jer. 31:3*).

4. The godly are prudent persons

They have good insight and foresight:

(i) They have *good insight*: 'he that is spiritual judgeth all things' (*1 Cor. 2:15*). The godly have insight into persons and things. They have insight into persons because they have the anointing of God, and by a spirit of discerning they can see some differences between the precious and the vile (*Jer. 15:19*). God's people are not censorious, but they are judicious. They can see a wanton heart through a naked breast and a spotted face. They can see a revengeful spirit through a bitter tongue. They can guess at the tree by the fruit (*Matt. 12:33*). They can see the plague tokens of sin appearing in the wicked, which makes them leave the tents of those sinners (*Numb. 16:26*).

The godly have insight into things mysterious. They can see much of the mystery of their own hearts. Take the greatest politician who understands the mysteries of state – he still does not understand the mystery of his own heart.

You will sometimes hear him swear that his heart is good, but a child of God sees much heart corruption (*1 Kings 8:38*). Though some flowers of grace grow there, he still sees how fast the weeds of sin grow and is therefore continually weeding his heart by repentance and mortification.

The godly can discern the mystery of the times: 'The children of Issachar were men that had understanding of the times' (*1 Chron. 12:32*). The godly can see when an age runs to seed – when God's name is dishonoured, his messengers despised, his gospel eclipsed. The people of God strive to keep their garments pure (*Rev. 16:15*). Their care is that the times may not be the worse for them, nor they the worse for the times.

The godly understand the mystery of living by faith: 'The just shall live by faith' (*Heb. 10:38*). They can trust God where they cannot trace him. They can get comfort out of a promise, as Moses got water out of the rock (*Exod. 17:6*). 'Though the fig tree doth not blossom, yet I will rejoice in the Lord' (*Hab. 3:17,18*).

(ii) They have *good foresight*. They foresee the evil of a temptation: 'we are not ignorant of his devices' (*2 Cor. 2:11*). The wicked swallow temptations like pills, and when it is too late, feel these pills afflict their conscience. But the godly foresee a temptation and will not come near. They see a snake under the green grass; they know Satan's kindness is craftiness. He does what Jephthah's daughter did: he brings out the tambourine and dances before men with a temptation and then brings them very low (*Judges 11:35*).

The godly foresee temporal dangers: 'A prudent man foreseeth the evil, and hideth himself' (*Prov. 22:3*). The people of God see when the cloud of wrath is ready to drop on a nation, and they get into their rooms (*Isa. 26:20*) – the attributes and promises of God – and into the clefts of the rocks – the bleeding wounds of Christ – and hide themselves. Well therefore may they be baptized with the name of wise virgins.

5. *The godly are the bulwark of a nation*

'My father, the chariot of Israel, and the horsemen thereof' (*2 Kings 2:12*). The godly are the pillars to keep a city and nation from falling; they stave off judgment from a land. It was said of old that so long as Hector lived, Troy could not be demolished. God could do nothing to Sodom till Lot had gone out of it (*Gen. 19:22*). Golden Christians are brazen walls. The Lord would soon execute judgment in the world were it not for the sake of a few religious people. Would God (we think) preserve the world only for drunkards and swearers? He would soon sink the ship of church and state but for the fact that some of his elect are in it. Yet such is the indiscretion of men that they injure the saints and count as burdens those who are the chief blessings (*Isa. 19:24*).

6. *The godly are of a brave, heroic spirit*

'My servant Caleb, because he had another spirit' (*Numb. 14:24*). An excellent spirit was found in Daniel (*Dan. 5:12*). The godly hate that which is base and sordid. They will not enrich their purses by enslaving their consciences. They are noble and courageous in God's cause: 'the righteous are bold as a lion' (*Prov. 28.1*). The saints live in accordance with their high birth: they yearn for God's love; they aspire to glory; they set their feet where worldly men set their heart; they display the banner of the gospel, lifting up Christ's name and interest in the world.

7. *The godly are happy people*

King Balak sent to curse the people of God, but the Lord would not allow it. 'God said unto Balaam, Thou shalt not curse the people: for they are blessed' (*Numb. 22:12*). And Moses afterwards records it as a memorable thing that God turned the king's intended curse into a blessing: 'the Lord thy God turned the curse into a blessing unto thee' (*Deut. 23:5*). Those who are always on the strongest side must of necessity be happy: 'The Lord is on my side' (*Psa. 118:6*). They are happy who have all conditions sanctified to them (*Rom. 8:28*), who are crowned with peace while they live (*Psa. 119:165*) and with glory when they die (*Psa. 73:24*). And may this not tempt everyone to become godly? 'Happy art thou, O Israel: a people saved by the Lord' (*Deut. 33:29*).

C. TO STRIVE FOR GODLINESS IS MOST RATIONAL

1. It is the highest act of reason for a man to become another man

If, while he remains in nature's soil, he is poisoned with sin – no more actually fit for communion with God than a toad is fit to be made an angel – then it is very consonant to reason that he should strive for a change.

2. It is rational because this change is for the better

'Now are ye light in the Lord' (*Eph. 5:8*). Will not anyone be willing to exchange a dark prison for a king's palace? Will he not exchange his brass for gold? You who become godly change for the better: you change your pride for humility, your uncleanness for holiness. You change a lust that will damn you for a Christ who will save you. If men were not besotted, if their fall had not knocked their brains out, they would see that it is the most rational thing in the world to become godly.

D. THE EXCELLENCE OF GODLINESS

'What is better than gold? Jasper. And what is better than jasper? Virtue.'

The excellence of godliness appears in several ways:

1. Godliness is our spiritual beauty
'The beauties of holiness' (*Psa. 110:3*). Godliness is to the soul what the light is to the world: to illustrate and adorn it. It is not greatness which sets us off in God's eye but goodness. What is the beauty of the angels but their sanctity? Godliness is the intricate embroidery and workmanship of the Holy Ghost. A soul furnished with godliness is damasked with beauty, it is enamelled with purity. This is the clothing of wrought gold which makes the King of heaven fall in love with us. Were there no excellence in holiness, the hypocrite would never try to paint it. Godliness sheds a glory and lustre on the saints. What are the graces but the golden feathers in which Christ's dove shines (*Psa. 68:13*)?

2. Godliness is our defence
Grace is called 'the armour of light' (*Rom. 13:12*). It is light for beauty and armour for defence. A Christian has armour of God's making which cannot be shot through. He has the shield of faith, the helmet of hope, the breastplate of righteousness. This is proof armour, which defends against the assaults of temptation and the terror of hell.

3. Godliness breeds solid peace
'Great peace have they which love thy law' (*Psa. 119:165*). Godliness composes the heart, making it quiet and calm like the upper region, where there are no winds and tempests. How can that heart be unquiet where the Prince of Peace dwells? 'Christ in you' (*Col. 1:27*). A holy heart may be compared to the doors of Solomon's temple, which were made of olive tree, carved with open flowers (*1 Kings 6:32*). The olive of peace and the open flowers of joy are in that heart. Godliness does not destroy a Christian's mirth,

but refines it. His rose is without prickles, his wine without froth. He who is a favourite of heaven must of necessity be full of joy and peace. He may truly sing a requiem to his soul and say, 'Soul, take thine ease' (*Luke 12:19*). King Ptolemy asked someone how he might be at rest when he dreamed. He replied, 'Let piety be the scope of all your actions.' If anyone should ask me how he should be at rest when he is awake, I would return a similar answer: 'Let his soul be inlaid with godliness.'

4. Godliness is the best trade we can engage in: it brings profit
Wicked men say, 'It is vain to serve God; and what profit is it?' (*Mal. 3:14*). To be sure, there is no profit in sin: 'Treasures of wickedness profit nothing' (*Prov. 10:2*). But godliness is profitable (*1 Tim. 4:8*). It is like digging in a gold mine, where there is gain as well as toil. Godliness makes God himself our portion: 'The Lord is the portion of mine inheritance' (*Psa. 16:5*). If God is our portion, all our estate lies in jewels. Where God gives himself, he gives everything else. Whoever has the manor has all the royalties belonging to it. God is a portion that can be neither spent nor lost (*Psa. 73:26*). Thus we see that godliness is a thriving trade.

And as godliness brings profit with it, so it is profitable 'for all things' (*1 Tim. 4:8*). What else is, besides godliness? Food will not give a man wisdom; gold will not give him health; honour will not give him beauty. But godliness is useful for all things: it fences off all troubles; it supplies all wants; it makes soul and body completely happy.

5. Godliness is an enduring substance; it knows no fall of the leaf
All worldly delights have a death's-head set on them. They are only shadows and they are fleeting. Earthly comforts are like Paul's friends, who took him to the ship and left him

there (*Acts 20:38*). So these will bring a man to his grave and then take their farewell. But godliness is a possession we cannot be robbed of. It runs parallel with eternity. Force cannot weaken it; age cannot wither it. It outbraves sufferings; it outlives death (*Prov. 10:2*). Death may pluck the stalk of the body but the flower of grace is not hurt.

6. Godliness is so excellent that the worst men would like to have it when they are going hence

Though at present godliness is despised and under a cloud, yet at death all would like to be godly. A philosopher asked a young man whether he would like to be rich Croesus or virtuous Socrates. He answered that he would like to live with Croesus and die with Socrates. So men would like to live with the wicked in pleasure but die with the godly: 'Let me die the death of the righteous, and let my last end be like his!' (*Numb. 23:10*). If, then, godliness is so desirable at death, why should we not pursue it now? Godliness is as needful now and would be more feasible.

E. THERE ARE ONLY A FEW GODLY

They are like the gleanings after vintage. Most receive the mark of the beast (*Rev. 13:17*). The devil keeps open house for all comers, and he is never without guests. This may prevail with us to be godly. If the number of the saints is so small, how we should strive to be found among these pearls! 'But a remnant shall be saved' (*Rom. 9:27*). It is better to go to heaven with a few than to hell in the crowd.

F. CONSIDER HOW VAIN AND CONTEMPTIBLE OTHER THINGS ARE, ABOUT WHICH PERSONS VOID OF GODLINESS BUSY THEMSELVES

Men are taken up with the things of this life, and 'what

profit hath he that hath laboured for the wind?' (*Eccles. 5:16*). Can the wind fill? What is gold but dust (*Amos 2:7*), which will sooner choke than satisfy? Pull off the mask of the most beautiful thing under the sun and look what is inside. There is care and vexation. And the greatest care is still to come – and that is to give account to God. The things of the world are just like a bubble in the water or a meteor in the air.

But godliness has real worth in it. If you speak of true honour, it is to be born of God; if of true valour, it is to fight the good fight of faith; if of true delight, it is to have joy in the Holy Ghost. Oh, then, espouse godliness! Here reality is to be had. Of other things we may say, 'They comfort in vain' (*Zech. 10:2*).

7: *Prescribing Some Helps to Godliness*

Question: But what shall we do that we may be godly?

Answer: I shall briefly lay down some rules or helps to godliness:

1. *Be diligent in the use of all means that may promote godliness*: 'Strive to enter in at the strait gate' (*Luke 13:24*). What is purpose without pursuit? When you have made your estimate of godliness, pursue those means which are most expedient for obtaining it.

2. *Take heed of the world.* It is hard for a clod of dust to become a star. 'Love not the world' (*1 John 2:15*). Many would like to be godly, but the honours and profits of the world divert them. Where the world fills both head and heart, there is no room for Christ. He whose mind is rooted in the earth is likely enough to deride godliness. When our Saviour was preaching against sin, 'the Pharisees, who were covetous, derided him' (*Luke 16:14*). The world eats the heart out of godliness, as the ivy eats the heart out of the oak. The world kills with her silver darts.

3. *Accustom yourselves to holy thoughts.* Serious meditation represents everything in its native colour. It shows an evil in sin and a lustre in grace. By holy thoughts, the head grows clearer and the heart better: 'I thought on my ways,

and turned my feet unto thy testimonies' (*Psa. 119:59*). If men would step aside a little out of the noise and hurry of business, and spend only half-an-hour every day thinking about their souls and eternity, it would produce a wonderful alteration in them and tend very much to a real and blessed conversion.

4. Watch your hearts. This was Christ's watchword to his disciples: 'Watch, therefore' (*Matt. 24:42*). The heart will precipitate us to sin before we are aware. A subtle heart needs a watchful eye. Watch your thoughts, your affections. The heart has a thousand doors to run out from. Oh, keep close watch on your souls! Stand continually on your watch-towers (*Hab. 2:1*). When you have prayed against sin, watch against temptation. Most wickedness in the world is committed for want of watchfulness. Watchfulness maintains godliness. It is the edging which keeps religion from fraying.

5. Make spending your time a matter of conscience: 're-deeming the time' (*Eph. 5:16*). Many people fool away their time, some in idle visits, others in recreations and pleasures which secretly bewitch the heart and take it away from better things. What are our golden hours for but to attend to our souls? Time misspent is not time lived but time lost. Time is a precious commodity. A piece of wax in itself is not worth much, but when it is affixed to the label of a will and conveys an estate, it is of great value. Thus, time simply in itself is not so considerable, but as salvation is to be worked out in it, and a conveyance of heaven depends on using it well, it is of infinite concern.

6. Think of your short stay in the world: 'our days on the earth are as a shadow, and there is none abiding' (*1 Chron. 29:15*). There is only a span between the cradle and the grave. Solomon says there is a time to be born and a time to die (*Eccles. 3:2*), but mentions no time of living, as if that were so short it was not worth naming. And time, when it has once gone, cannot be recalled. The Scripture compares time to a flying eagle (*Job 9:26*). Yet time differs from the eagle in this: the eagle flies forward and then back again, but time has wings only to fly forward – it never returns. 'Time flies irrevocably.'

The serious thoughts of our short stay here would be a great means of promoting godliness. What if death should come before we are ready? What if our life should breathe out before God's Spirit has breathed in? Whoever considers how flitting and winged his life is, will hasten his repentance. When God is about to do a short work, he will not do a long work.

7. *Make this maxim your own, that godliness is the purpose of your creation.*   God never sent men into the world only to eat and drink and put on fine clothes, but that they might 'serve him in holiness and righteousness' (*Luke 1:74,75*). God made the world only as a dressing room to dress our souls in. He sent us here on the grand errand of godliness. Should nothing but the body (the brutish part) be looked after, this would be basely to degenerate, yes, to invert and frustrate the very purpose of our being.

8. *Be often among the godly.*   They are the salt of the earth, and will help to season you. Their counsel may direct, their prayers may enliven you. Such holy sparks may be thrown into your breasts as may kindle devotion in you. It is good to be among the saints to learn the trade of godliness: 'He that walketh with wise men shall be wise' (*Prov. 13:20*).

8: *An Exhortation to Persevere in Godliness*

Those who wear the mantle of godliness – and in the judgment of others are looked upon as godly – let me exhort thee to perservere: 'Let us hold fast the profession of our faith' (*Heb. 10:23*). This is a seasonable exhortation in these times when the devil's agents are abroad, whose whole work is to unsettle people and make them fall away from that former strictness in religion which they have professed. It is much to be lamented to see Christians:

1. Wavering in religion

How many we see unresolved and unsteady, like Reuben, unstable as water (*Gen. 49:4*). These the apostle rightly compares to 'waves of the sea . . . and wandering stars' (*Jude 13*). They are not fixed in the principles of godliness. Beza writes of one Bolsechus, 'his religion changed like the moon'. Such were the Ebionites, who kept both the Jewish and the Christian Sabbath. Many professing Christians are like the river Euripus, ebbing and flowing in matters of religion. They are like reeds bending every way, either to the mass or to the Koran. They are like the planet Mercury, which varies and is seldom constant in its motion. When men think of heaven and the recompense of reward, then they want to be godly, but when they think of persecution, then they are like the Jews who deserted Christ and 'walked no more with him' (*John 6:66*). If men's faces altered as fast as their opinions, we should not recognize them. To be thus vacillating and wavering in religion argues lightness. Feathers are blown in every direction, and so are feathery Christians.

2. Falling from that godliness which once they seemed to have
They have turned to worldliness and wantonness. The very mantle of their profession has fallen off, and indeed, if they were not fixed stars, it is no wonder to see them as falling stars. This spiritual epilepsy, or falling sickness, was never more rife. It is a dreadful sin for men to fall from that godliness which they once seemed to have. Chrysostom says, 'Apostates are worse than those who are openly wicked. They give godliness a bad name.' 'The apostate', says Tertullian, 'seems to put God and Satan in the balance, and having weighed both their services, prefers the devil's service and proclaims him to be the best master.' In that respect the apostate is said to put Christ to open shame (*Heb. 6:6*).

This will be bitter in the end (*Heb. 10:38*). What a worm Spira felt in his conscience! In what horror of mind did Stephen Gardiner cry out upon his death-bed that he had denied his Master with Peter! But he had not repented with Peter!

That we may be steadfast in godliness and persevere, let us do two things:

1. Let us take heed of those things which will make us by degrees fall away from our profession
Let us:

(i) *Beware of covetousness*: 'men shall be covetous . . . having a form of godliness, but denying the power' (*2 Tim. 3:2,5*). One of Christ's own apostles was caught with a silver bait. Covetousness will make a man betray a good cause and make shipwreck of a good conscience. I have read of some in the time of the Emperor Valens who denied the Christian faith to prevent the confiscation of their goods.

(ii) *Beware of unbelief*: 'Take heed, brethren, lest there be in any of you an evil heart of unbelief, in departing from the living God' (*Heb. 3:12*). There is no evil like an evil heart; no evil heart like an unbelieving heart. Why so? It makes men depart from the blessed God. He who does not believe God's mercy will not dread his justice. Infidelity is the nurse of apostasy, therefore unbelieving and unstable go together: 'they believed not in God . . . they turned back and tempted God' (*Psa. 78:22,41*).

(iii) *Take heed of cowardice*. He who is afraid to be good must surely be evil: 'The fear of man bringeth a snare' (*Prov. 29:25*). They who fear danger more than sin will commit sin to avoid danger. Origen, out of a spirit of fear, offered incense to the idol. Aristotle says, 'The reason why the chameleon turns so many colours is through excessive fear'. Fear will make men change their religion as often as the chameleon does her colour. Christian, you who have made a profession of godliness so long and others have noted you for a saint in their calendar, why do you fear and begin to shrink back? The cause which you have embarked on is good; you are fighting against sin; you have a good Captain who is marching before you: Christ, 'the captain of your salvation' (*Heb. 2:10*). What is it that you fear? Is it loss of liberty? What is liberty worth when conscience is in bonds? It is better to lose your liberty and keep your peace than to lose your peace and keep your liberty. Is it loss of estate? Do you say, like Amaziah, 'What shall we do for the hundred talents?' (*2 Chron. 25:9*)? I would answer with the prophet, 'The Lord can give thee much more than this' (*v.10*). He has promised you 'an hundredfold' in this life, and if that is nothing, he will give you life everlasting (*Matt. 19:29*).

2. Let us use all means for perseverance
(i) Strive for a real work of grace in your soul. Grace is the
best fortification: 'it is a good thing that the heart be
stablished with grace' (*Heb. 13:9*).

Question: What is this real work of grace?

Answer: It consists in two things:
1. Grace lies in *a heart-humbling work*. The thorn of sin
pricked Paul's conscience: 'sin revived, and I died' (*Rom.
7:9*). Though some are less humbled than others, as some
bring forth children with less pangs, yet all have pangs.
2. Grace lies in *a heart-changing work*: 'but ye are washed,
but ye are sanctified' (*1 Cor. 6:11*). A man is so changed as if
another soul lived in the same body. If ever you would hold
out in the ways of God, get this vital principle of grace. Why
do men change their religion but because their hearts were
never changed? They do not fall away *from* grace, but for
lack of grace.

(ii) Be deliberate and judicious. Weigh things well in the
balance: 'Which of you, intending to build a tower, sitteth
not down first, and counteth the cost?' (*Luke 14:28*). Think
to yourselves what it will cost you to be godly. You must
expect the hatred of the world (*John 15:19*). The wicked
hate the godly for their piety. It is strange that they should
do so. Do we hate a flower because it is sweet? The godly are
hated for the perfume of their graces. Is a virgin hated for
her beauty? The wicked hate the godly for the beauty of
holiness which shines in them. Secret hatred will break
forth into open violence (*2 Tim. 3:12*). Christians must
count the cost before they build. Why are people so hasty in
abandoning religion if not because they were so hasty in
taking it up?

(iii) Get a clear, distinct knowledge of God. Know the love

of the Father, the merit of the Son, the efficacy of the Holy Ghost. Those who do not know God aright will by degrees renounce their profession. The Samaritans sometimes sided with the Jews, when they were in favour. Afterwards they disclaimed all kindred with the Jews, when they were persecuted by Antiochus. And no wonder they shuffled so in their religion, if you consider what Christ said of the Samaritans, 'Ye worship ye know not what' (*John 4:22*). They were enveloped by ignorance. Blind men are apt to fall, and so are they who are blinded in their minds.

(*iv*) *Enter on it purely out of choice*: 'I have chosen the way of truth' (*Psa. 119:30*). Espouse godliness for its own worth. Whoever wishes to persevere must rather choose godliness with reproach than sin with all its worldly pomp. Whoever takes up religion for fear will lay it down again for fear. Whoever embraces godliness for gain will desert it when the jewels of promotion are pulled off. Do not be godly from worldly design but from religious choice.

(*v*) *Strive for integrity*. This will be a golden pillar to support you. A tree that is hollow must of necessity be blown down. The hypocrite sets up in the trade of religion, but he will soon break: 'their heart was not right with him, neither were they steadfast' (*Psa. 78:37*). Judas was first a sly hypocrite and then a traitor. If a piece of copper is gilded, the gilding will wash off. Nothing will hold out but sincerity: 'Let integrity preserve me' (*Psa. 25:21*). How many storms Job was in! Not only Satan, but God himself set on him (*Job 7:20*), which was enough to have made him desist from being godly. Yet Job stood fast because he stood upright: 'My righteousness I hold fast, and will not let it go; my heart shall not reproach me as long as I live' (*Job 27:6*). Those colours hold best which are fixed in oils. If we wish to have our profession hold its colour, it must be fixed in the oil of sincerity.

(*vi*) *Hold up the life and fervour of duty*: 'fervent in spirit, serving the Lord' (*Rom. 12:11*). We put coals on the fire to keep it from going out. When Christians grow into a dull formality, they begin to be dispirited and by degrees abate in their godliness. No-one is so fit to make an apostate as a lukewarm professing Christian.

(*vii*) *Exercise great self-denial*: 'Let him deny himself' (*Matt. 16:24*). Self-ease, self-ends, whatever comes in competition with (or stands in opposition to) Christ's glory and interest must be denied. Self is the great snare; self-love undermines the power of godliness. The young man in the Gospel might have followed Christ, but something of self hindered (*Matt. 19:20–22*). Self-love is self-hatred. The man who cannot get beyond himself will never get to heaven.

(*viii*) *Preserve a holy jealousy over your hearts*: 'Be not high-minded, but fear' (*Rom. 11:20*). The man who has gunpowder in his house fears lest it should catch fire. Sin in the heart is like gunpowder; it may make us fear lest a spark of temptation should fall on us and blow us up. There are two things which may make us always jealous of our hearts: the deceits of our hearts and the lusts of our hearts. When Peter was afraid that he should sink and cried to Christ, 'Lord, save me', then Christ took him by the hand and helped him (*Matt. 14:30,31*); but when Peter grew confident and thought he could stand alone, then Christ allowed him to fall. Oh, let us be suspicious of ourselves and in a holy sense 'clothe ourselves with trembling' (*Ezek. 26:16*).

(ix) Strive for assurance: 'give diligence to make your calling and election sure' (*2 Pet. 1:10*). The man who is sure that God is his God is like a castle built on a rock – all the powers of hell cannot shake him. How can that man be constant in religion who is at a loss about his spiritual estate, and does not know whether he has grace or not? It will be a difficult matter for a man to die for Christ, if he does not know that Christ has died for him. Assurance establishes a Christian in shaking times. He who has the Spirit of God bearing witness to his heart is the most likely to bear witness to the truth (*Rom. 8:16*). Oh, give diligence! Be much in prayer, reading, holy conversation. These things are the oil without which the lamp of assurance will not shine.

(x) Lay hold of God's strength.   God is called the Strength of Israel (*1 Sam. 15:29*). It is in his strength that we stand, more than our own. The child is safest in the nurse's hands. It is not our holding God, but his holding us that preserves us. A little boat tied fast to a rock is safe, and so are we, when we are tied to the 'rock of ages'.

9: *Motives to Persevere in Godliness*

So that I may encourage Christians to persevere in the profession of godliness, I shall propose these four considerations:

1. It is the glory and crown of a Christian to be grey-headed in godliness
'Mnason of Cyprus, an old disciple' (*Acts 21: 16*). What an honour it is to see a Christian's garments red with blood, yet his conscience pure white and his graces green and flourishing!

2. How sinners persevere in their sins!
They are settled on their lees (*Zeph. 1:12*). The judgments of God will not deter or remove them. They say to their sin, as Ruth said to Naomi, 'Where thou goest, I will go . . . the Lord do so to me, and more also, if ought but death part thee and me' (*Ruth 1:16,17*). So nothing shall part men from their sins. Oh, what a shame it is that the wicked should be fixed in evil and we unfixed in good, that they should be more constant in the devil's service than we are in Christ's!

3. Our perseverance in godliness may be a means of confirming others
Cyprian's hearers followed him to the place of his suffering, and when they saw his steadfastness in the faith, they cried

out, 'Let us also die with our holy pastor'. 'Many of the brethren, waxing confident by my bonds, are much more bold to speak the word' (*Phil. 1:14*). St Paul's zeal and constancy animated the onlookers. His prison chains made converts in Nero's court, and two of those converts were afterwards martyrs, as history relates.

4. We shall lose nothing by our perseverance in godliness
There are eight glorious promises which God has entailed on the persevering saints:

(i) 'Be thou faithful unto death, and I will give thee a crown of life' (*Rev. 2:10*). Christian, you may lose the breath of life but not the crown of life.

(ii) 'To him that overcometh will I give to eat of the tree of life' (*Rev. 2:7*). This tree of life is the Lord Jesus. This tree infuses life and prevents death. The day we eat of this tree, our eyes shall indeed be opened to see God.

(iii) 'To him that overcometh will I give to eat of the hidden manna, and will give him a white stone, and in the stone a new name written, which no man knoweth saving he that receiveth it' (*Rev. 2:17*). This promise consists of three branches:

(a) 'I will give to eat of the hidden manna.' This is mysterious. It signifies the love of God which is manna for sweetness and hidden for its rarity.

(b) 'I will give him a white stone', that is, absolution. It may be called a precious stone, says Jerome.

(c) 'And in the stone a new name', that is, adoption. He shall be reputed an heir of heaven, and no-one can know it, except the one who has the privy seal of the Spirit to assure him of it.

(iv) 'He that overcometh, the same shall be clothed in white raiment, and I will not blot his name out of the book of life, but I will confess his name before my Father, and before his angels' (*Rev. 3:5*). The persevering saint shall be clothed in white. This is an emblem of joy (*Eccles. 9:8*). He shall put off his mourning and be clothed in the white robe of glory. 'And I will not blot his name out of the book of life.' God will blot a believer's sins out, but he will not blot his name out. The book of God's decree has no errata in it. 'But I will confess his name.' If anyone has owned Christ on earth and worn his colours when it was death to wear them, Christ will not be ashamed of him, but will confess his name before his Father and the holy angels. Oh, what a comfort and honour it will be to have a good look from Christ, at the last day, no, to have Christ own us by name and say, 'These were they who stood up for my truth and kept their garments pure in a defiling age. These shall walk with me in white, for they are worthy.'

(v) 'Him that overcometh will I make a pillar in the temple of my God, and he shall go no more out; and I will write upon him the name of my God, and the name of the city of my God' (*Rev. 3:12*). There are many excellent things couched in this promise: 'I will make him a pillar in the temple of my God'. The hypocrite is a reed shaken by the wind, but the conquering saint shall be a glorious pillar, a pillar of strength and a pillar in the temple for sanctity. 'And he shall go no more out.' I understand this of a glorified state. 'He shall go no more out,' that is, after he has overcome, he shall not go out to the wars any more. He shall never have any more sin or temptation to conflict with. No more noise of drum or cannon shall be heard, but having won the field, the believer shall now stay at home and divide the spoil. 'And I will write upon him the name of my God', that is, he shall be openly acknowledged as my child, just as the Son bears his Father's name. How honourable that saint must be who has God's own name written on him! 'And I will write upon him the name of the city of my God', that is, he shall be enrolled as a denizen or citizen of the Jerusalem above. He shall be made free in the angelic society.

(vi) 'He that overcometh, and keepeth my works unto the end, to him will I give power over the nations' (*Rev. 2:26*). This may have a double mystery. Either it may be understood of the saints living on earth: they shall have power over the nations; their zeal and patience shall overpower the adversaries of truth (*Acts 6:10*); or, principally, it may be understood of the saints triumphing in heaven. They shall have power over the nations: they shall share with Christ in some of his power; they shall join with him in judging the world in the last days: 'Know ye not that the saints shall judge the world?' (*1 Cor. 6:2*).

(vii) 'To him that overcometh will I grant to sit with me in my throne' (*Rev. 3:21*):

(a) Here is, first, the saints' dignity: they shall sit upon the throne.

(b) Their safety: they shall sit with Christ. Christ holds them fast and no-one shall pluck them off his throne. The saints may be turned out of their houses, but they cannot be turned out of Christ's throne. Men may as well pluck a star out of the sky as a saint out of the throne.

(viii) 'I will give him the morning star' (*Rev. 2:28*). Though the saints may be sullied with reproach in this life, though they may be termed factious and disloyal – St Paul himself suffered trouble, in the opinion of some, as an evildoer (*2 Tim. 2:9*) – yet God will bring forth the saints' righteousness as the light, and they shall shine like the morning star, which is brighter than the rest. 'I will give him the morning star.' This morning star is meant of Christ, as if Christ had said, 'I will give the persevering saint some of my beauty; I will put some of my splendid rays on him; he shall have the nearest degree of glory to me, as the morning star is nearest the sun.

Oh, what soul-ravishing promises there are here! Who would not persevere in godliness! Whoever is not affected by these promises is either a stone or a brute.

10: *Counsel for the Godly*

Let me, in the next place, direct myself to those who have a real work of godliness in their hearts, and I would speak to them by way of:

1. Caution.
2. Counsel.
3. Comfort.

1. *By way of caution*

Do not blur these characteristics of grace in your souls. Though God's children cannot quite deface their graces, yet they may disfigure them. Too much carnal liberty may weaken their evidences, and so dim their lustre that they cannot be read. These characteristics of the godly are precious things. Gold and crystal cannot be compared with them. Oh, keep them well written in your hearts and they will be so many living comforts in a dying hour. It will not frighten a Christian to have all the signs of death in his body, when he can see all the signs of grace in his soul. He will say with Simeon, 'Lord, now lettest thou thy servant depart in peace' (*Luke 2:29*).

2. *By way of counsel*

You who are enriched with the treasures of godliness, bless God for it. This flower does not grow in nature's garden. You had enlisted yourselves under the devil and taken pay on his side, fighting against your own happiness, and then

God came with converting grace and put forth a loving and gentle violence, causing you to espouse his quarrel against Satan! You had lain many years soaking in wickedness, as if you had been parboiled for hell, and then God laid you steeping in Christ's blood and breathed holiness into your heart! Oh, what cause you have to write yourselves as eternal debtors to free grace! He who does not give God the praise for his grace denies that God is its author. Oh, acknowledge the love of God; admire distinguishing mercy; set the crown of your praise on the head of free grace! If we are to be thankful for the fruits of the earth, how much more for the fruits of the Spirit. It is good that there is an eternity coming, when the saints shall triumph in God and make his praise glorious.

3. By way of comfort

You who have only the least dram of godliness in sincerity, let me give you rich consolation: Jesus Christ will not discourage the weakest grace but will cherish and preserve it to eternity. Grace which has only newly budded shall, by the beams of the Sun of righteousness, be prepared and ripened for glory. This I shall speak about more fully in the next chapter.

11: *Comfort to the Godly*

'A BRUISED REED SHALL HE NOT BREAK AND SMOKING FLAX SHALL HE NOT QUENCH, TILL HE SEND FORTH JUDGMENT UNTO VICTORY' (*Matt.* 12:20)

This text is spoken prophetically of Christ. He will not crow over the infirmities of his people; he will not crush grace in its infancy. I begin with the first, 'the bruised reed'.

Question: What is to be understood here by a reed?

Answer: It is not to be taken literally, but mystically. It is a rational reed, the spiritual part of man, the soul, which may well be compared to a reed because it is subject to imbecility and shaking in this life, till it grows up unto a firm cedar in heven.

Question: What is meant by a bruised reed?

Answer: It is a soul humbled and bruised by the sense of sin. It weeps, but does not despair; it is tossed upon the waves of fear, yet not without the anchor of hope.

Question: What is meant by Christ's not breaking this reed?

Answer: The sense is that Christ will not discourage any mournful spirit who is in the pangs of the new birth. If the

[222]

bruise of sin is felt, it shall not be mortal: 'A bruised reed shall he not break'. In the words there is an understatement; he will not break, that is, he will bind up the bruised reed, he will comfort it.

The result of the whole is to show Christ's compassion to a poor dejected sinner who smites on his breast and dare hardly lift up his eye for mercy. The heart of the Lord Jesus yearns for him; this bruised reed he will not break.

In the text there are two parts: (i) A supposition: a soul penitentially bruised. (ii) A proposition: it shall not be broken.

Doctrine: The bruised soul shall not be broken: 'He bindeth up their wounds' (*Psa. 147:3*). For this purpose Christ received both his mission and his unction, that he might bind up the bruised soul: 'the Lord hath anointed me to bind up the broken-hearted' (*Isa. 61:1*). But why will Christ not break a bruised reed?

1. Out of the sweetness of his nature: 'the Lord is very pitiful [compassionate]' (*James 5:11*). He begets compassion in other creatures and is therefore called 'the Father of mercies' (*2 Cor. 1:3*). And surely he himself is not without compassion. When a poor soul is afflicted in spirit, God will not exercise hardness towards it, lest he should be thought to lay aside his own tender disposition.

Hence it is that the Lord has always been most solicitous for his bruised ones. As the mother is most careful of her children who are weak and sickly, 'He shall gather the lambs with his arm, and carry them in his bosom' (*Isa. 40:11*). Those who have been spiritually bruised, who like lambs are weakly and tender, Christ will carry in the arms of free grace.

2. Because a contrite heart is his sacrifice (Psa. 51:17). A bruised spirit sends forth tears which are like precious wine

(*Psa. 56:8*). A bruised soul is big with holy desires, yes, is love-sick. Therefore, if a bruised reed has such virtue in it, Christ will not break it. No spices, when they are bruised, are so fragrant to us as a contrite spirit is to God.

3. Because it so closely resembles Christ. Jesus Christ was once bruised on the cross: 'it pleased the Lord to bruise him' (*Isa. 53:10*). His hands and feet were bruised with the nails; his side was bruised with the spear. A bruised reed resembles a bruised Saviour. No, a bruised reed is a member of Christ; and though it is weak, Christ will not cut it off, but will cherish it so much the more.

(i) Will Christ not break the bruised reed? This tacitly implies that he will break unbruised reeds. Those who were never touched with trouble of spirit, but live and die in impenitence, are hard reeds or, rather, rocks. Christ will not break a bruised reed, but he will break a hard reed. Many do not know what it is to be bruised reeds. They are bruised outwardly by affliction, but they are not bruised for sin. They never knew what the pangs of the new birth meant. You will hear some thank God that they were always quiet, they never had any anxiety of spirit. These bless God for the greatest curse. Those who are not bruised penitentially shall be broken judicially. Those whose hearts would not break for sin shall break with despair. In hell there is nothing to be seen but a heap of stones and a hammer. A heap of stones – that is hard hearts; a hammer – that is God's power and justice, breaking them in pieces.

(ii) Will Christ not break a bruised reed? See, then, the gracious disposition of Jesus Christ – he is full of clemency and sympathy. Though he may bruise the soul for sin, he will not break it. The surgeon may lance the body and make it bleed, but he will bind up the wound. As Christ has beams of majesty, so he has a heart of mercy. Christ has both the lion and the lamb in his escutcheon: the lion, in respect of his fierceness to the wicked (*Psa. 50:22*), and the lamb, in respect of his mildness to his people. His name is Jesus, a Saviour, and his office is a healer (*Mal. 4:2*). Christ made a plaster of his own blood to heal a broken heart. Christ is the quintessence of love. Someone says, 'If the sweetness of all flowers were in one flower, how sweet that flower would be!' How full of mercy is Christ, in whom all mercy meets! Christ has a skilful hand and a tender heart. 'He will not break a bruised reed.'

Some are so full of ostracism and cruelty as to add affliction to affliction, which is to lay a greater burden on a dying man. But our Lord Jesus is a compassionate High Priest (*Heb. 2:17*). He is touched with the feeling of our infirmity. Every bruise of the soul goes to his heart. None refuse Christ, but such as do not know him. He is nothing but love incarnate. He himself was bruised to heal those who are bruised.

(iii) See, then, what encouragement there is here for faith! Had Christ said that he would break the bruised reed, then indeed there would be ground for despair. But when Christ said that he will not break a bruised reed, this opens a door of hope for humble, bruised souls. If we can say that we have been bruised for sin, why do we not believe? Why do we droop under our fears and discouragements, as if there were no mercy for us? Christ says, 'He healeth the broken in heart' (*Psa. 147:3*). 'No,' says unbelief, 'he will not heal me.' Christ says that he will cure the bruised soul. 'No,' says unbelief, 'he will kill it.' As unbelief makes our comforts void, so it tries to make the Word void, as if all God's promises were but forgeries or like blanks in a lottery. Has the Lord said that he will not break a bruised reed? Can truth lie? Oh, what a sin unbelief is! Some think it dreadful to be among the number of drunkards, swearers and whoremongers. Let me tell you, it is no less dreadful to be among the number of unbelievers (*Rev. 21:8*). Unbelief is worse than any other sin, because it brings God into suspicion with the creature. It robs him of the richest jewel in his crown, which is his truth: 'He that believeth not God hath made him a liar' (*1 John 5:10*).

Oh then, let all humbled sinners go to Jesus Christ. Christ was bruised with desertion to heal those who are bruised with sin. If you can show Christ your sores and touch him by faith, you shall be healed of all your soul bruises. Will Christ not break you? Then do not undo yourself by despair.

Use 1: Will Jesus Christ not break a bruised reed? Then it reproves those who do what they can to break the bruised reed. And they are such as try to hinder the work of conversion in others. When they see them wounded and troubled for sin, they dishearten them, telling them that religion is a sour, melancholy thing and they had better return to their former pleasures. When an arrow of conviction is shot into their conscience, these pull it out again, and will not allow the work of conviction to go forward. Thus, when the soul is almost bruised, they hinder it from a thorough bruise. This is for men to be devils to others. If to shed the blood of another makes a man guilty, what is it to damn another's soul?

Use 2: This text is a spiritual honeycomb, dropping consolation into all bruised hearts. As we give stimulants to a body suffering from a lipothymy, or fainting fit, so when sinners are bruised for their sins, I shall give some stimulant to revive them. This text is comforting to a poor soul who sits with Job among the ashes and is dejected at the sense of its unworthiness. 'Ah!' says the soul, 'I am unworthy of mercy; what am I, that ever God should look on me? Those who have greater gifts and graces perhaps may obtain a look from God, but alas! I am unworthy.' Does your unworthiness trouble you? What more unworthy than a bruised reed? Yet there is a promise made to that condition: 'a bruised reed he will not break'. The promise is not made to the fig-tree or olive, which are fertile plants, but to the bruised reed. Though you are despicable in your own eyes, a poor shattered reed, yet you may be glorious in the eyes of the Lord. Do not let your unworthiness discourage you. If you see yourself as vile and Christ as precious, this promise is yours. Christ will not break you, but will bind up your wounds.

Question: But how shall I know that I am savingly bruised?

Answer: Did God ever bring you to your knees? Has your proud heart been humbled? Did you ever see yourself as a sinner and nothing but a sinner? Did you ever, with a weeping eye, look on Christ (*Zech. 12:10*)? And did those tears drop from the eye of faith (*Mark 9:24*)? This is gospel bruising. Can you say, 'Lord, though I do not see thee, yet I love thee; though I am in the dark, yet I cast anchor'? This is to be a bruised reed.

Objection 1: But I fear I am not bruised enough.

Answer: It is hard to prescribe a just measure of humiliation. It is the same in the new birth as in the natural. Some give birth with more pangs, and some with fewer. But would you like to know when you are bruised enough? When your spirit is so troubled that you are willing to let go those lusts which brought in the greatest income of pleasure and delight. When not only is sin discarded but you are disgusted with it, then you have been bruised enough. The medicine is strong enough when it has purged out the disease. The soul is bruised enough when the love of sin is purged out.

Objection 2: But I fear I am not bruised as I should be. I find my heart so hard.

Answer 1: We must distinguish between hardness of heart and a hard heart. The best heart may have some hardness, but though there is some hardness in it, it is not a hard heart. Names are given according to the better part. If we come into a field that has tares and wheat in it, we do not call it a field of tares but a wheat field. So though there is hardness in the heart as well as softness, yet God, who judges by that part which is more excellent, looks on it as a soft heart.

Answer 2: There is a great difference between the hardness in the wicked and that in the godly. The one is natural, the other is only accidental. The hardness in a wicked man is like the hardness of a stone, which is an innate continued hardness. The hardness in a child of God is like the hardness of ice, which is soon melted by the sunbeams. Perhaps God has at present withdrawn his Spirit, so the heart is congealed like ice. But let God's Spirit, like the sun, return and shine on the heart, and now it has a gracious thaw on it and it melts in love.

Answer 3: Do you not grieve under your hardness? You sigh for lack of groans, you weep for lack of tears. The hard reed cannot weep. If you were not a bruised reed, all this weeping could not come from you.

Objection 3: But I am a barren reed; I bear no fruit; therefore I fear I shall be broken.

Answer: Gracious hearts are apt to overlook the good that is in them. They can spy the worm in the leaf but not the fruit. Why do you say you are barren? If you are a bruised reed, you are not barren. The spiritual reed ingrafted into the true vine is fruitful. There is so much sap in Christ that it makes all who are inoculated into him bear fruit. Christ distils grace like drops of dew on the soul: 'I will be as the dew unto Israel; he shall grow as the lily; his branches shall spread, and his beauty shall be as the olive tree' (*Hos. 14:5,6*). The God who made the dry rod blossom will make the dry reed flourish.

So much for the first expression in the text. I proceed to the second: 'the smoking flax shall he not quench'.

Question: What is meant by smoking?

Answer: By smoke is meant corruption. Smoke is offensive to the eye, so sin offends the pure eye of God.

Question: What is meant by smoking flax?

Answer: It means grace mingled with corruption. As with a little fire there may be much smoke, so with a little grace there may be much corruption.

Question: What is meant by Christ's not quenching the smoking flax?

Answer: The meaning is that though there is only a spark of grace with much sin, Christ will not put out this spark. In the words there is a figure; 'he will not quench', that is, he will increase. Nothing is easier than to quench smoking flax; the least touch does it. But Christ will not quench it. He will not blow the spark of grace out, but will blow it up. He will increase it into flame, he will make this smoking flax a burning taper.

Doctrine: That a little grace mixed with much corruption shall not be quenched. For the illustrating of this I shall show you:

1. That a little grace is often mixed with much corruption.
2. That this little grace mixed with corruption shall not be quenched.
3. The reasons for the proposition.

1. Often in the godly a little grace is mingled with much corruption

'Lord, I believe' – there was some faith; 'help thou mine unbelief' (*Mark 9:24*) – there was corruption mixed with it. There are, in the best saints, interweavings of sin and grace: a dark side with the light; much pride mixed with humility; much earthliness with heavenliness. Grace in the godly smacks of an old crabtree stock.

No, in many of the regenerate there is more corruption than grace. So much smoke that you can scarcely discern any fire; so much distrust that you can hardly see any faith (*1 Sam. 27:1*); so much passion that you can hardly see any meekness. Jonah, a peevish prophet, quarrels with God, no, he justifies his passion: 'I do well to be angry, even unto death' (*Jonah 4:9*). Here there was so much passion that it was hard to see any grace. A Christian in this life is like a glass that has more froth than wine, or like a diseased body that has more fluids than vigour. It may humble the best to consider how much corruption is interlarded with their grace.

2. This little grace mixed with much corruption shall not be quenched

'The smoking flax he will not quench.' The disciples' faith was at first only small: 'they forsook Christ, and fled' (*Matt. 26:56*). Here there was smoking flax, but Christ did not quench that little grace but cherished and animated it. Their faith afterwards grew stronger and they openly confessed Christ (*Acts 4:29,30*). Here the flax was flaming.

3. The reasons why Christ will not quench the smoking flax

(i) Because this scintilla, this little spark which is in the smoking flax, is of divine production. It comes from the Father of lights, and the Lord will not quench the work of his own grace. Everything by the instinct of nature will preserve its own. The hen that hatches her young will preserve and cherish them; she will not destroy them as soon as they are hatched. God, who has put this tenderness into the creature to preserve its young, will much more cherish the work of his own Spirit in the heart. Will he light up the lamp of grace in the soul and then put it out? This would be neither for his interest nor for his honour.

(ii) Christ will not quench the beginnings of grace, because a little grace is precious as well as more grace. A small pearl is of value. Though the pearl of faith is little, yet if it is a true pearl, it shines gloriously in God's eyes. A goldsmith takes account of the least filings of gold and will not throw them away. The apple of the eye is only little, yet it is of great use; it can at once view a huge part of the heavens. A little faith can justify; a weak hand can tie the nuptial knot; a weak faith can unite to Christ as well as a strong; a little grace makes us like God; a silver penny bears the king's image on it as well as a larger coin. The least dram of grace bears God's image on it, and will God destroy his own image? When the temples in Greece were demolished, Xerxes caused the temple of Diana to be preserved for the beauty of its structure. When God destroys all the glory of the world and sets it on fire, yet he will not destroy the least grace, because it bears a print of his own likeness on it. That little spark in the smoking flax is a ray and beam of God's own glory.

(iii) Christ will not quench the smoking flax, because this little light in the flax may grow bigger. Grace is compared to a grain of mustard seed; it is the smallest of all seeds, but when it has grown, it is the largest of herbs, and becomes a tree (*Matt. 13:31,32*). The greatest grace was once little. The oak was once an acorn. The most renowned faith in the world was once in its spiritual infancy; the greatest flame of zeal was once only smoking flax. Grace, like the waters of the sanctuary, rises higher (*Ezek. 47:1–5*). If, then, the smallest embryo and seed of holiness has a ripening and growing nature, the Lord will not allow it to be abortive.

(iv) Christ will not quench the smoking flax, because when he preserves a little light in a great deal of smoke, here the glory of his power shines forth. The trembling soul thinks it will be swallowed up by sin. But God preserves a little quantity of grace in the heart – no, he makes that spark prevail over corruption, as the fire from heaven 'licked up the water in the trench' (*1 Kings 18:38*). So God gets himself a glorious name and carries away the trophies of honour: 'My strength is made perfect in weakness' (*2 Cor. 12:9*).

1. See the different dealings of God and men. Men, for a little smoke, will quench a great deal of light; God, for a great deal of smoke, will not quench a little light. It is the manner of the world, if they see a little failure in another, to pass by and quench a great deal of worth because of that failure. This is our nature, to aggravate a little fault and diminish a great deal of virtue; to see the infirmities and darken the excellences of others – as we take more notice of the twinkling of a star than the shining of a star. We censure others for their passion, but do not admire them for their piety. Thus, because of a little smoke that we see in others, we quench much light.

God does not act like that. For a great deal of smoke, he will not quench a little light. He sees the sincerity and overlooks many infirmities. The least sparks of grace he cherishes, and blows them gently with the breath of his Spirit till they break forth into a flame.

2. If Christ will not quench the smoking flax, then we must not quench the smoking flax in ourselves. If grace does not increase into so great a flame as we see in others and we therefore conclude that we have no fire of the Spirit in us – that is to quench the smoking flax and to bear false witness against ourselves. As we must not credit false evidence, so neither must we deny true. As fire may be hidden in the

embers, so grace may be hidden under many disorders of soul. Some Christians are so skilful at this – accusing themselves for lack of grace, as if they had received a fee from Satan to plead for him against themselves.

It is a great mistake to argue from the weakness of grace to its absence. It is one thing to be weak in faith and another to lack faith. He whose eyesight is dim has defective sight, but he is not without sight. A little grace is grace, though it is smothered under much corruption.

3. If the least spark of grace shall not be quenched, then it follows as a great truth that there is no falling from grace. If the least dram of grace should perish, then the smoking flax would be quenched. Grace may be shaken by fears and doubts, but not blown up by the roots. I grant that seeming grace may be lost; this wildfire may be blown out, but not the fire of the Spirit's kindling. Grace may be dormant in the soul, but not dead. As a man in an apoplexy does not exert vital energy, grace may be eclipsed, not extinct. A Christian may lose his comfort, like a tree in autumn that has shed its fruit, but there is still sap in the vine and 'the seed of God remaineth in him' (*1 John 3:9*). Grace is a flower of eternity.

This smoking flax cannot be quenched by affliction, but is like those trees of which Pliny writes – trees growing in the Red Sea, which though beaten by the waves, stand immovable, and though sometimes covered with water, flourish the more. Grace is like a true oriental diamond that sparkles and cannot be broken.

I confess it is a matter of wonder that grace should not be wholly annihilated, especially if we consider two things:

(i) The malice of Satan. He is a malignant spirit and lays barriers in our way to heaven. The devil, with the wind of temptation, tries to blow out the spark of grace in our hearts. If this will not do, he stirs up wicked men and raises the militia of hell against us. What a wonder it is that this bright star of grace should not be swept down by the tail of the dragon!

(ii) *The world of corruption in our hearts.* Sin makes up the major part in a Christian. There are more dregs than spirit in the best heart. The heart swarms with sin. What a deal of pride and atheism there is in the soul! Now is it not admirable that this lily of grace should be able to grow among so many thorns? It is as great a wonder that a little grace should be preserved in the midst of so much corruption as to see a taper burning in the sea and not extinguished.

But though grace lives with so much difficulty, like the infant that struggles for breath, yet being born of God, it is immortal. Grace conflicting with corruption is like a ship tossed and beaten by the waves, yet it weathers the storm and at last gets to the desired haven. If grace should expire, how could this text be verified, 'The smoking flax he will not quench'?

Question: But how is it that grace, even the least degree of it, should not be quenched?

Answer: It is from the mighty operation of the Holy Ghost. The Spirit of God, who is the source, continually excites and awakens grace in the heart. He is at work in a believer every day. He pours in oil and keeps the lamp of grace burning. Grace is compared to a river of life (*John 7:38*). The river of grace can never be dried up, for the Spirit of God is the spring which feeds it.

Now it is evident from the covenant of grace that the smoking flax cannot be quenched. 'The mountains shall depart, and the hills be removed; but the covenant of my peace shall not be removed, saith the Lord' (*Isa. 54:10*). If there is falling from grace, how is it an immovable covenant? If grace dies and the smoking flax is quenched, how is our state in Christ better than it was in Adam? The

[234]

covenant of grace is called 'a better covenant' (*Heb. 7:22*). How is it a better covenant than that which was made with Adam? Not only because it has a better Surety and contains better privileges, but because it has better conditions annexed to it: 'It is ordered in all things, and sure' (*2 Sam. 23:5*). Those who are taken into the covenant shall be like stars fixed in their orbit and shall never fall away. If grace might die and be quenched, then it would not be a better covenant.

Objection: But we are bidden not to quench the Spirit (*1 Thess. 5:19*), which implies that the grace of the Spirit may be lost and the smoking flax quenched.

Answer: We must distinguish between the common work of the Spirit and the sanctifying work. The one may be quenched but not the other. The common work of the Spirit is like a picture drawn on the ice, which is soon defaced; the sanctifying work is like a statue carved in gold, which endures. The gifts of the Spirit may be quenched but not the grace. There is the enlightening of the Spirit and the anointing. The enlightening of the Spirit may fail, but the anointing of the Spirit abides: 'the anointing which ye have received of him abideth in you' (*1 John 2:27*). The hypocrite's blaze goes out, the true believer's spark lives and flourishes. The one is the light of a comet which wastes and evaporates (*Matt. 25:8*); the other is the light of a star which retains its lustre.

From all that has been said, let a saint of the Lord be persuaded to do these two things:
1. To believe his privilege.
2. To pursue his duty.

1. To believe his privilege
It is the incomparable and unparalleled happiness of a saint that his coal shall not be quenched (*2 Sam. 14:7*). That

grace in his soul which is minute and languid shall not give up the ghost but recover its strength and increase with the increase of God. The Lord will make the smoking flax a burning lamp. It would be very sad for a Christian to be continually chopping and changing: one day a member of Christ and the next day a limb of Satan; one day to have grace shine in his soul and the next day his light be put out in obscurity. This would spoil a Christian's comfort and break asunder the golden chain of salvation. But be assured, O Christian, that he who has begun a good work will ripen it to perfection (*Phil. 1:6*). Christ will send forth judgment unto victory. He will make grace victorious over all opposing corruption. If grace should finally perish, what would become of the smoking flax? And how would that title properly be given to Christ, 'Finisher of the faith' (*Heb. 12:2*)?

Objection: There is no question that this is an undoubted privilege to those who are smoking flax and have the least beginnings of grace, but I fear I am not smoking flax; I cannot see the light of grace in myself.

Answer: So that I may comfort the smoking flax, why do you thus dispute against yourself? What makes you think you have no grace? I believe you have more than you would be willing to part with. You value grace above the gold of Ophir. How could you see the worth and lustre of this jewel, if God's Spirit had not opened your eyes? You desire to believe and mourn that you cannot believe. Are these tears not the beginnings of faith? You desire Christ and cannot be satisfied without him. This beating of the pulse evidences life. The iron could not move upwards if the lodestone did not draw it. The heart could not ascend in holy desires for God, if some heavenly lodestone had not been drawing it. Christian, can you say that sin is your burden, Christ is your delight and, as Peter once said, 'Lord, thou knowest that I love thee' (*John 21:17*)? This is smoking flax and the Lord will not quench it. Your grace shall flourish into glory. God will sooner extinguish the light of the sun than extinguish the dawning light of his Spirit in your heart.

2. *To pursue his duty*

There are two duties required of believers:

(*i*) *Love.* Will the Lord not quench the smoking flax, but make it at last victorious over all opposition? How the smoking flax should flame in love to God! 'Oh, love the Lord, all ye his saints' (*Psa. 31:23*). The saints owe much to God, and when they have nothing to pay, it is hard if they cannot love him. O you saints, it is God who carries on grace progressively in your souls. He is like a father who gives his son a small stock of money to begin with, and when he has traded a little, he adds more to the stock. So God adds continually to your stock. He drops oil into the lamp of your grace every day and so keeps the lamp burning. This may inflame your love to God, who will not let the work of grace fail but will bring it to perfection: 'the smoking flax he will not quench.' How God's people should long for heaven, when it will be their constant work to breathe out love and sound out praise!

(*ii*) *Labour.* Some may think that if Christ will not quench the smoking flax, but make it burn brighter to the meridian of glory, then we need take no pains but leave God to do his own work. Take heed of drawing so bad a conclusion from such good premises. What I have spoken is to encourage faith, not to indulge sloth. Do not think God will do our work for us while we sit still. As God will blow up the spark of grace by his Spirit, so we must be blowing it up by holy efforts. God will not bring us to heaven sleeping, but praying. The Lord told Paul that all in the ship should come safely to shore, but it must be by the use of means: 'Except these abide in the ship, ye cannot be saved' (*Acts 27:31*). So the saints shall certainly arrive at salvation. They shall come to shore at last, but they must stay in the ship, in the use of ordinances, else they cannot be saved. Christ assures his disciples: 'None shall pluck them out of my hand' (*John 10:28*). But he still gives that counsel, 'Watch and pray, that ye enter not into temptation' (*Matt. 26:41*). The seed of God shall not die, but we must water it with our tears. The smoking flax shall not be quenched, but we must blow it up with the breath of our effort.

The second comfort to the godly is that godliness promotes them to a close and glorious union with Jesus Christ. But I reserve this for the next chapter.

12: *Showing the Mystic Union between Christ and the Saints*

'MY BELOVED IS MINE, AND I AM HIS' (*SONG 2:16*)

In this Song of Songs we see the love of Christ and his church running towards each other in a full torrent.

The text contains three general parts:

1. *A symbol of affection: 'My beloved'*.
2. *A term of appropriation: 'is mine'*.
3. *A holy resignation: 'I am his'*.

Doctrine: That there is a conjugal union between Christ and believers. The apostle, having treated at large of marriage, winds up the whole chapter thus: 'This is a great mystery, but I speak concerning Christ and the church' (*Eph. 5:32*). What is closer than union? What sweeter? There is a twofold union with Christ:

1. A natural union. This all men have, Christ having taken their nature on him and not that of the angels (*Heb. 2:16*). But if there is no more than this natural union, it will give little comfort. Thousands are damned though Christ is united to their nature.

2. A sacred union. By this we are mystically united to Christ. The union with Christ is not personal. If Christ's essence were transfused into the person of a believer, then it would follow that all that a believer does should be meritorious.

But the union between Christ and a saint is:

(i) *Federal*: 'My beloved is mine.' God the Father gives the bride; God the Son receives the bride; God the Holy Ghost ties the knot in marriage – he knits our wills to Christ and Christ's love to us.

(ii) *Effectual*. Christ unites himself to his spouse by his graces and influences: 'of his fulness have all we received, and grace for grace' (*John 1:16*). Christ makes himself one with the spouse by conveying his image and stamping the impress of his own holiness upon her.

This union with Christ may well be called mystic. It is hard to describe the manner of it. It is hard to show how the soul is united to the body, and how Christ is united to the soul. But though this union is spiritual, it is real. Things in nature often work insensibly, yet really (*Eccles. 11:5*). We do not see the hand move on the dial, yet it moves. The sun exhales and draws up the vapours of the earth insensibly yet really. So the union between Christ and the soul, though it is imperceptible to the eye of reason, is still real (*1 Cor. 6:17*).

Before this union with Christ there must be a separation. The heart must be separated from all other lovers, as in marriage there is a leaving of father and mother: 'forget also thine own people, and thy father's house' (*Psa. 45:10*). So there must be a leaving of our former sins, a breaking off the old league with hell before we can be united to Christ. 'Ephraim shall say, What have I to do any more with idols?' (*Hos. 14:8*), or as it is in the Hebrew, 'with sorrows'. Those sins which were looked on before as lovers, are now sorrows. There must be a divorce before a union.

The purpose of our conjugal union with Christ is twofold:

1. *Co-habitation*. This is one purpose of marriage, to live together: 'that Christ may dwell in your hearts' (*Eph. 3:17*).

It is not enough to pay Christ a few complimentary visits in his ordinances – hypocrites may do so – but there must be a mutual associating. We must dwell upon the thoughts of Christ: 'he that dwelleth in God' (*1 John 3:24*). Married persons should not live apart.

2. *Fructification*: 'that ye should be married to another, even to him who is raised from the dead, that we should bring forth fruit unto God' (*Rom. 7:4*). The spouse bears the fruits of the Spirit: love, joy, peace, long-suffering, gentleness (*Gal. 5:22*). Barrenness is a shame in Christ's spouse.

This marriage union with Christ is the most noble and excellent union:

(i) Christ unites himself to many. In other marriages only one person is taken, but here millions are taken. Otherwise, poor souls might cry out, 'Alas! Christ has married So-and-so, but what is that to me? I am left out.' No, Christ marries thousands. It is a holy and chaste polygamy. Multitudes of people do not defile this marriage bed. Any poor sinner who brings a humble, believing heart may be married to Christ.

(ii) There is a closer union in this holy marriage than there can be in any other. In other marriages, two make one flesh, but Christ and the believer make one spirit: 'he that is joined unto the Lord is one spirit' (*1 Cor. 6:17*). Now as the soul is more excellent than the body, and admits of far greater joy, so this spiritual union brings in more astonishing delights and ravishments than any other marriage relationship is capable of. The joy that flows from the mystic union is unspeakable and full of glory (*1 Peter 1:8*).

(iii) This union with Christ never ceases. 'Thrice happy they whom an unbroken bond unites' (*Horace*). Other marriages are soon at an end. Death cuts asunder the marriage knot, but this conjugal union is eternal. You who are once Christ's spouse shall never again be a widow: 'I will betroth thee unto me for ever' (*Hos. 2:19*). To speak properly, our marriage with Christ begins where other marriages end, at death.

In this life there is only the contract. The Jews had a time set between their engagement and marriage, sometimes a year or more. In this life there is only the engagement and contract; promises are made on both sides, and love passes secretly between Christ and the soul. He gives some smiles of his face, and the soul sends up her sighs and drops tears of love. But all this is only a preliminary work, and something leading up to the marriage. The glorious completing and solemnizing of the marriage is reserved for heaven. There is the marriage supper of the Lamb (*Rev. 19:9*) and the bed of glory perfumed with love where the souls of the elect shall be perpetually consoling themselves. 'Then shall we ever be with the Lord' (*1 Thess. 4:17*). So death merely begins our marriage with Christ.

Use 1: If Christ is the head of the mystic body (*Eph. 1:22*), then this doctrine beheads the Pope, that man of sin who usurps this prerogative of being the head of the church, and so would defile Christ's marriage bed. What blasphemy this is! Two heads are monstrous. Christ is Head, as he is Husband. There is no vice-husband, no deputy in his place. The Pope is the beast in Revelation (*Rev. 13:11*). To make him head of the church, what would this be but to set the head of a beast upon the body of a man?

Use 2: If there is such a conjugal union, let us test whether we are united to Christ:

1. Have we chosen Christ to set our love upon, and is this choice founded on knowledge?

2. Have we consented to the match? It is not enough that Christ is willing to have us, but are we willing to have him? God does not so force salvation upon us that we shall

have Christ whether we want to or not. We must consent to have him. Many approve of Christ, but do not give their consent. And this consent must be:

(i) Pure and genuine. We consent to have him for his own worth and excellence: 'Thou art fairer than the children of men' (*Psa. 45:2*).

(ii) A present consent: 'now is the accepted time' (*2 Cor. 6:2*). If we put Christ off with delays and excuses, perhaps he will stop coming. He will leave off wooing. 'His spirit shall no longer strive', and then, poor sinner, what will you do? When God's wooing ends, your woes begin.

3. Have we taken Christ? Faith is the bond of the union. Christ is joined to us by his Spirit, and we are joined to him by faith. Faith ties the marriage knot.

4. Have we given ourselves up to Christ? Thus the spouse in the text says, 'I am his', as if she had said, 'All I have is for the use and service of Christ.' Have we made a surrender? Have we given up our name and will to Christ? When the devil solicits by a temptation, do we say, 'We are not our own, we are Christ's; our tongues are his, we must not defile them with oaths; our bodies are his temple, we must not pollute them with sin'? If it is so, it is a sign that the Holy Ghost has produced this blessed union between Christ and us.

Use 3: Is there this mystic union? Then from that we may draw many inferences:

1. See the dignity of all true believers. They are joined in marriage with Christ. There is not only assimilation but union; they are not only like Christ but one with Christ. All the saints have this honour. When a king marries a beggar, by virtue of the union she is ennobled and made of the blood royal. As wicked men are united to the prince of darkness, and he settles hell upon them as their inheritance, so the godly are divinely united to Christ, who is King of kings, and Lord of lords (*Rev. 19:16*). By virtue of this sacred union the saints are dignified above the angels. Christ is the Lord of the angels, but not their husband.

2. *See how happily all the saints are married.* They are united to Christ, who is the best Husband, 'the chiefest among ten thousand' (*Song 5:10*). Christ is a Husband that cannot be paralleled:

(i) For *tender care*. The spouse cannot be as considerate of her own soul and credit as Christ is considerate of her: 'He careth for you' (*1 Pet. 5:7*). Christ has a debate with himself, consulting and projecting how to carry on the work of our salvation. He transacts all our affairs, he attends to our business as his own. Indeed, he himself is concerned in it. He brings fresh supplies to his spouse. If she wanders out of the way, he guides her. If she stumbles, he holds her by the hand. If she falls, he raises her. If she is dull, he quickens her by his Spirit. If she is perverse, he draws her with cords of love. If she is sad, he comforts her with promises.

(ii) For *ardent affection*. No husband loves like Christ. The Lord says to the people, 'I have loved you', and they say, 'Wherein hast thou loved us?' (*Mal. 1:2*). But we cannot say to Christ, 'Wherein hast thou loved us?' Christ has given real demonstrations of his love to his spouse. He has sent her his Word, which is a love-letter, and he has given her his Spirit, which is a love-token. Christ loves more than any other husband:

(a) Christ puts a richer robe on his bride: 'He hath clothed me with the garments of salvation, he hath covered me with the robe of righteousness' (*Isa. 61:10*). In this robe, God looks on us as if we had not sinned. This robe is as truly ours to justify us, as it is Christ's to bestow on us. This robe not only covers but adorns. Having on this robe, we are reputed righteous, not only as righteous as angels, but as righteous as Christ: 'that we might be made the righteousness of God in him' (*2 Cor. 5:21*).

(b) Christ gives his bride not only his golden garments but his image. He loves her into his own likeness. A husband may have a dear affection for his wife, but he cannot stamp his own image on her. If she is deformed, he may give her a veil to hide it, but he cannot put his beauty on her. But Christ imparts 'the beauty of holiness' to his spouse: 'thy beauty was perfect through my comeliness' (*Ezek. 16:14*). When Christ marries a soul, he makes it fair: 'Thou art all fair, my love' (*Song 4:7*). Christ never thinks he has loved his spouse enough till he can see his own face in her.

(c) Christ discharges those debts which no other husband can. Our sins are the worst debts we owe. If all the angels should contribute money, they could not pay one of these debts, but Christ frees us from these. He is both a Husband and a Surety. He says to justice what Paul said concerning Onesimus, 'If he oweth thee ought, put that to mine account. I will repay it' (*Philem. 18*).

(d) Christ has suffered more for his spouse than ever any husband did for a wife. He suffered poverty and ignominy. He who crowned the heavens with stars was himself crowned with thorns. He was called a companion of sinners, so that we might be made companions of angels. He was regardless of his life; he leaped into the sea of his Father's wrath to save his spouse from drowning.

(e) Christ's love does not end with his life. He loves his spouse for ever: 'I will betroth thee unto me for ever' (*Hos. 2:19*). Well may the apostle call it 'a love which passeth knowledge' (*Eph. 3:19*).

3. See how rich believers are. They have married into the crown of heaven, and by virtue of the conjugal union all Christ's riches go to believers: 'communion is founded in union'. Christ communicates his graces (*John 1:16*). As long as Christ has them, believers shall not be in want. And he communicates his privileges – justification, glorification. He settles a kingdom on his spouse as her inheritance (*Heb. 12:28*). This is a key to the apostle's riddle, 'as having nothing, and yet possessing all things' (*2 Cor. 6:10*). By virtue of the marriage union, the saints have an interest in all Christ's riches.

4. See how fearful a sin it is to abuse the saints. It is an injury done to Christ, for believers are mystically one with him: 'Saul, Saul, why persecutest thou me?' (*Acts 9:4*). When the body was wounded, the Head, being in heaven, cried out. In this sense, men crucify Christ afresh (*Heb. 6:6*), because what is done to his members is done to him. If Gideon was avenged upon those who slew his brethren, will not Christ much more be avenged on those that wrong his spouse (*Judges 8:21*)? Will a king tolerate having his treasure rifled, his crown thrown in the dust, his queen beheaded? Will Christ bear with the affronts and injuries done to his bride? The saints are the apple of Christ's eye (*Zech. 2:8*), and let those who strike at his eye answer for it. 'I will feed them that oppress thee with their own flesh; and they shall be drunk with their own blood, as with sweet wine' (*Isa. 49:26*).

5. See the reason why the saints so rejoice in the Word and sacrament, because here they meet with their Husband, Christ. The wife desires to be in the presence of her husband. The ordinances are the chariot in which Christ rides, the lattice through which he looks forth and shows his smiling face. Here Christ displays the banner of love (*Song 2:4*). The Lord's Supper is nothing other than a pledge and earnest of that eternal communion which the saints shall have with Christ in heaven. Then he will take the spouse into his bosom. If Christ is so sweet in an ordinance, when we have only short glances and dark glimpses of him by faith, oh then, how delightful and ravishing will his presence be in heaven when we see him face to face and are for ever in his loving embraces!

Use 4: This mystic union affords much comfort to believers in several cases:

1. In the case of the disrespect and unkindness of the world: 'in wrath they hate me' (*Psa. 55:3*). But though we live in an unkind world, we have a kind Husband: 'As the Father hath loved me, so have I loved you' (*John 15:9*). What angel can tell how God the Father loves Christ? Yet the Father's love to Christ is made the copy and pattern of Christ's love to his spouse. This love of Christ as far exceeds all created love as the sun outshines the light of a torch. And is not this a matter of comfort? Though the world hates me, Christ still loves me.

2. In the case of weakness of grace. The believer cannot lay hold on Christ, except with a trembling hand. There is a 'spirit of infirmity' on him, but oh, weak Christian, here is strong consolation: there is a conjugal union. You are the spouse of Christ, and he will bear with you as the weaker vessel. Will a husband divorce his wife because she is weak and sickly? No, he will be the more tender with her. Christ hates treachery, but he will pity infirmity. When the spouse is faint and ready to be discouraged, Christ puts his left hand under her head (*Song 2:6*). This is the spouse's comfort when she is weak. Her Husband can infuse strength into her: 'My God shall be my strength' (*Isa. 49:5*).

3. In the case of death. When believers die, they go to their Husband. Who would not be willing to shoot the gulf of death that they might meet with their Husband, Christ? 'I desire to loosen anchor' (*Phil. 1:23*), and be with Christ. What though the way is dirty? We are going to our friend. When a woman is engaged, she longs for the day of marriage. After the saints' funeral, their marriage begins. The body is a prison to the soul. Who would not desire to exchange a prison for a marriage bed? How glad Joseph was to go out of prison to the king's court! God is wise; he lets us meet with changes and troubles here, so that he may wean us from the world and make us long for death. When the soul is divorced from the body, it is married to Christ.

4. *In the case of passing sentence at the day of judgment.* There is a marriage union and, oh Christian, your Husband shall be your judge. A wife would not fear appearing at the bar if her husband was sitting as judge. What though the devil should bring in many indictments against you? Christ will expunge your sins in his blood. He will say, 'Shall I condemn my spouse?' Oh, what a comfort this is! The Husband is judge. Christ cannot pass sentence against his spouse without passing it against himself. For Christ and believers are one.

5. *In the case of the saints' suffering.* The church of God is exposed in this life to many injuries, but she has a Husband in heaven who is mindful of her and will 'turn water into wine' for her. Now it is a time of mourning with the spouse because the Bridegroom is absent (*Matt. 9:15*). But shortly she shall put off her mourning. Christ will wipe the tears of blood off the cheeks of his spouse: 'the Lord God will wipe away tears from off all faces' (*Isa. 25:8*).

Christ will comfort his spouse for as much time as she has been afflicted. He will solace her with his love; he will take away the cup of trembling and give her the cup of consolation. And now she shall forget all her sorrows, being called into the banqueting house of heaven and having the banner of Christ's love displayed over her.

Use 5: Let me press several duties upon those who have this marriage union with Christ:

1. Make use of this relationship in two cases
(i) When the law brings in its indictments against you. The law says, 'Here there are so many debts to be paid', and it demands satisfaction. Acknowledge the debt, but turn it all over to your Husband, Christ. It is a maxim in law that the suit must not go against the wife, as long as the husband is living. Tell Satan when he accuses you, 'It is true that the debt is mine, but go to my Husband, Christ; he will discharge it.' If we took this course, we might relieve ourselves of much trouble. By faith we turn over the debt to our Husband. Believers are not in a state of widowhood but of marriage. Satan will never go to Christ – he knows that justice is satisfied and the debt book cancelled – but he comes to us for the debt so that he may perplex us. We should send him to Christ and then all lawsuits would cease. This is a believer's triumph. When he is guilty in himself, he is worthy in Christ. When he is spotted in himself, he is pure in his Head.

(ii) In the case of desertion. Christ may (for reasons best known to himself) step aside for a time: 'my beloved had withdrawn himself' (*Song 5:6*). Do not say, therefore, that Christ has gone for good. It is a fruit of jealousy in a wife, when her husband has left her a while, to think that he has gone from her for good. Every time Christ removes himself out of sight, it is wrong for us to say (like Zion), 'The Lord hath forsaken me' (*Isa. 49:14*). This is jealousy, and it is a wrong done to the love of Christ and the sweetness of this marriage relationship. Christ may forsake his spouse in regard of comfort, but he will not forsake her in regard of union. A husband may be a thousand miles distant from his

[249]

wife, but he is still a husband. Christ may leave his spouse, but the marriage knot still holds.

2. Love your Husband, Christ (Song 2:5). Love him though he is reproached and persecuted. A wife loves her husband when in prison. To inflame your love towards Christ, consider:

(i) Nothing else is fit for you to love. If Christ is your Husband, it is not fit to have other lovers who would make Christ grow jealous.

(ii) He is worthy of your love. He is of unparalleled beauty: 'altogether lovely' (*Song 5:16*).

(iii) How fervent Christ's love is towards you! He loves you in your worst condition, he loves you in affliction. The goldsmith loves his gold in the furnace. He loves you notwithstanding your fears and blemishes. The saints' infirmities cannot wholly remove Christ's love from them (*Jer. 3:1*). Oh then, how the spouse should be endeared in her love to Christ! This will be the excellence of heaven. Our love will then be like the sun in its full strength.

3. Rejoice in your Husband, Christ. Has Christ honoured you by taking you into the marriage relationship and making you one with himself? This calls for joy. By virtue of the union, believers are sharers with Christ in his riches. It was a custom among the Romans, when the wife was brought home, for her to receive the keys of her husband's house, intimating that the treasure and custody of the house was now committed to her. When Christ brings his bride home to those glorious mansions which he has gone ahead to prepare for her (*John 14:2*), he will hand over the keys of his treasure to her, and she shall be as rich as heaven can make her. And shall not the spouse rejoice and sing aloud upon her bed (*Psa. 149:5*)? Christians, let the times be never so sad, you may rejoice in your spiritual espousals

(*Hab. 3:17,18*). Let me tell you, it is a sin not to rejoice. You disparage your Husband, Christ. When a wife is always sighing and weeping, what will others say? 'This woman has a bad husband.' Is this the fruit of Christ's love to you, to reflect dishonour upon him? A melancholy spouse saddens Christ's heart. I do not deny that Christians should grieve for sins of daily occurrence, but to be always weeping (as if they mourned without hope) is dishonourable to the marriage relationship. 'Rejoice in the Lord always' (*Phil. 4:4*). Rejoicing brings credit to your husband. Christ loves a cheerful bride, and indeed the very purpose of God's making us sad is to make us rejoice. We sow in tears, so that we may reap in joy. The excessive sadness and contrition of the godly will make others afraid to embrace Christ. They will begin to question whether there is that satisfactory joy in religion which is claimed. Oh, you saints of God, do not forget consolation; let others see that you do not repent of your choice. It is joy that puts liveliness and activity into a Christian: 'the joy of the Lord is your strength' (*Neh. 8:10*). The soul is swiftest in duty when it is carried on the wings of joy.

4. Adorn this marriage relationship, so that you may be a crown to your husband

(i) Wear a veil. We read of the spouse's veil (*Song 5:7*). This veil is humility.

(ii) Put on your jewels. These are the graces which for their lustre are compared to rows of pearl and chains of gold (*Song 1:10*). These precious jewels distinguish Christ's bride from strangers.

(iii) Behave as becomes Christ's spouse:

(a) In chastity. Be chaste in your judgments; do not defile yourselves with error. Error adulterates the mind (*I. Tim. 6:5*). It is one of Satan's artifices, first to defile the judgment, then the conscience.

[251]

(b) In sanctity. It is not for Christ's spouse to behave like harlots. A naked breast and a wanton tongue do not become a saint. Christ's bride must shine forth in gospel purity, so that she may make her husband fall in love with her. A woman was asked what dowry she brought her husband. She answered that she had no dowry, but she promised to keep herself chaste. So though we can bring Christ no dowry, yet he expects us to keep ourselves pure, not spotting the breasts of our virginity by contagious and scandalous sins.

SOME OTHER TITLES BY
THOMAS WATSON
IN THE
PURITAN PAPERBACKS SERIES
BY
BANNER OF TRUTH

ALL THINGS FOR GOOD
Thomas Watson

Thomas Watson of St. Stephen's, Walbrook believed he faced two great difficulties in his pastoral ministry. The first was making the unbeliever sad, in the recognition of his need of God's grace. The second was making the believer joyful in response to God's grace. He believed the answer to the second difficulty could be found in Paul's teaching in Romans 8.28: God works all things together for good for his people.

First published in 1663 (under the title, *A Divine Cordial*), the year after Watson and some two thousand other ministers were ejected from the Church of England and exposed to hardship and suffering, *All Things For Good* contains the rich exposition of a man who lived when only faith in God's Word could lead him to such confidence.

Watson's exposition is always simple, illuminating and rich in practical application. He explains that both the best and the worst experiences work for the good of God's people. He carefully analyses what it means to be someone who 'loves God' and is 'called according to his purpose'. *All Things For Good* provides the biblical answer to the contemporary question: 'Why do bad things happen to good people?'

ISBN 978 0 85151 478 9
128pp.   Paperback

THE DOCTRINE OF REPENTANCE

Thomas Watson

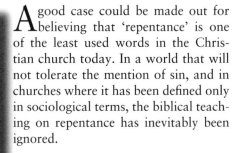

A good case could be made out for believing that 'repentance' is one of the least used words in the Christian church today. In a world that will not tolerate the mention of sin, and in churches where it has been defined only in sociological terms, the biblical teaching on repentance has inevitably been ignored.

Knowing what repentance is, and actually repenting are essential to true Christianity. Jesus Christ himself said that if we do not repent, we will perish! It is vital, therefore, to read and study what Scripture has to say about this theme.

Few better guides have existed in this or any other area of spiritual experience than Thomas Watson. He was a master of both Scripture and the human heart, and wrote with a simplicity and directness that keep his work fresh and powerful for the twenty-first century.

Watson was one of the leading spiritual guides of his day, and the author of *A Body of Divinity, The Ten Commandments, The Lord's Prayer* and *The Beatitudes*, also published by the Trust.

ISBN 978 0 85151 521 2
128pp.   Paperback

THE GREAT GAIN OF GODLINESS
Thomas Watson

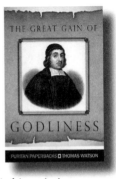

C. H. Spurgeon had a well-stocked library of around 12,000 volumes. However, one rare book was not to be found amongst that valuable collection: *Thomas Watson on Malachi 3:16-18*. With a note of sadness in his voice, Spurgeon said to his College students: 'This [volume] would be a great find if we could come at it, for Watson is one of the clearest and liveliest of Puritan authors. We fear we shall never see this commentary, for we have tried to obtain it, and tried in vain.'

In this reset and lightly edited edition you can now read the book that was on Spurgeon's 'wish-list'! *The Great Gain of Godliness* is Watson's exposition of Malachi 3:16-18. In it he aims 'to encourage solid piety and confute the atheists of the world, who imagine there is no gain in godliness.' This book has all the hallmarks of Thomas Watson's other writings: a combination of rich spirituality, nourishing doctrine, and sane practical wisdom coupled with fascinating illustrations and a very pleasant style.

ISBN 978 0 85151 938 8
176pp. Paperback

For more information about our publications, or to order, please visit our website.

THE BANNER OF TRUTH TRUST

3 Murrayfield Road,
Edinburgh EH12 6EL
UK

P O Box 621, Carlisle,
PA 17013,
USA

www.banneroftruth.co.uk